D0467352

The CAPITALIST COMEBACK

The CAPITALIST COMEBACK

The Trump Boom
and the Left's Plot to Stop It

ANDREW F. PUZDER

NEW YORK NASHVILLE

Center Street
Hachette Book Group
1290 Avenue of the Americas, New York, NY 10104
centerstreet.com
twitter.com/centerstreet

First Edition: April 2018

Center Street is a division of Hachette Book Group, Inc. The Center Street name and logo are trademarks of Hachette Book Group, Inc.

The publisher is not responsible for websites (or their content) that are not owned by the publisher.

The Hachette Speakers Bureau provides a wide range of authors for speaking events. To find out more, go to www.HachetteSpeakersBureau.com or call (866) 376-6591.

Library of Congress Cataloging-in-Publication Data has been applied for.

ISBNs: 978-1-4789-7543-4 (hardcover), 978-1-4789-7542-7 (ebook)

Printed in the United States of America

LSC-C

10 9 8 7 6 5 4 3 2 1

Dedicated to the memory of a true
American entrepreneur and a friend,

Carl N. Karcher
1917–2008

"The American Dream is alive and well in this country of ours. I know. I lived it."

Contents

INTRODUCTION

"A lie gets halfway around the world before the truth has a chance to get its pants on."

ATTRIBUTED TO WINSTON CHURCHILL

February 15, 2017

The vice president was calling.

I looked down at my phone's display as the call came through and hesitated a moment before answering. This, I knew, could very well mean the end of a short but already arduous journey. It could also mean that journey was about to take a brand-new turn. The final answer was waiting for me on the other end of the line.

Just over two months before, Donald J. Trump, then president-elect of the United States, had asked me to serve as the twenty-seventh secretary of labor. He had a definite plan in mind in appointing me. For the first time since Ronald Reagan assembled his initial cabinet, an incoming president had chosen someone who had been both a laborer and a successful business executive to head the department that looks out for American workers.

I was very pleased at the prospect of serving. As someone who began as a worker—who worked his way through school while raising a family—I knew what it was like to live paycheck to paycheck, juggling bills and sometimes coming up short at the end of the month. As a business executive, I knew how government regulations designed to help workers can often have the perverse effect of hurting them, because they raise the cost of employment and make it harder, in the real world of business competition, for companies to hire new employees.

I had been writing and speaking about those issues for years, which is why I was nominated. I really believed I could reform the Labor Department so that America could have both strong worker protections and a robust and growing job market, where wages and benefits go up because companies need and want employees and must compete against one another for labor.

Of course, I knew that such ideas were anathema to many on the Left, particularly the current group of Progressive politicians who had gained ascendency in the Democratic Party in recent years. I knew they would fight my nomination, and given the divisiveness of politics in America today, I knew that the fight wouldn't be pretty.

I was certainly right about that.

The Left's attack campaign, designed to defame and disparage, began almost immediately. The intent was to discourage supporters and encourage opponents. And, of course, truth was the casualty.

For a little over two months, labor unions and other left-wing groups threw every charge they could at me. The personal charges were one thing; I was a trial lawyer for many years and I have a pretty thick skin. But, I hated the impact on my family. They took personally the attacks on me, and they were not safe from old-fashioned scare tactics. Fight for $15 union shills showed up at our front door, held a rally near our home, and drove through our neighborhood with a billboard claiming I abused women. A threatening package containing white powder was sent to our home. Interestingly enough, the media chose *not* to report on that incident, though they reported the claims against me in minute detail.

All the while, I was focused on the whirlwind of activity that surrounds a cabinet nomination. I had no idea about the extent of the vetting process nominees undergo; it is intense, exhilarating, and good preparation for posts subject to regular congressional oversight.

I worked daily with the Trump transition team to prepare for confirmation hearings before the Senate Health, Education, Labor and Pensions Committee—known in Washington slang as the HELP Committee. I was meeting with the individual senators on the committee as well as their top staffers, giving them a sense of my positions and getting to feel them out before I formally appeared in front of them.

And I was getting ready for the job, thinking about potential nominees for the sub-Cabinet posts, and planning how to implement the Labor Department's piece of the president's agenda for job creation.

But by early February, the attack campaign reached such a fever pitch, and the attacks leveled against me were such a constant presence in the mainstream media, that some Republican senators were beginning to get nervous.

Betsy DeVos, the secretary of education, had only just barely been confirmed, and the press was gleefully reporting that the new Trump administration was incapable of putting together a functioning cabinet. Senators were swamped with emails and phone calls in opposition to the DeVos confirmation as well as left-wing attacks at town hall meetings. If the barrage kept up, my own party could sink my nomination before I even got the chance to make my case in a hearing.

Vice President Mike Pence had been working with Majority Leader Mitch McConnell to count the votes and see where I stood. The vice president and I trusted each other and knew we could count on each other to be straight and to the point, even if we weren't saying what the other wanted to hear.

Now, the vice president was calling with the results of his final conversation with McConnell. His words would determine whether I continued to gear up to face the HELP Committee hearing or began to pack my bags for home.

I pressed "Accept."

"Hello, Mr. Vice President."

I first met Donald Trump in May 2016 at the home of Tom Barrack, one of Trump's longtime friends and major supporters who later served as chairman of his Presidential Inaugural Committee. Since the previous December, I had been having informal discussions on economic policy with members of Trump's economic policy team. I also had similar discussions with staffers from the Jeb Bush, Ted Cruz, Carly Fiorina, Marco Rubio, and Scott Walker campaigns. I knew personally and had spoken and met with many of the front-running candidates.

Though I have been a conservative since the 1980s (I voted for George McGovern on my first trip to the ballot box), I am not, by nature, a "political" person. I had some involvement in the political process and often shared my views on economic policy, but by and large, the business of politics never appealed to me. I preferred the business of business.

My particular business was restaurants (quick service specifically). I was a lawyer by training, and I fell into the fast-food world in the mid-1980s, when I met Carl N. Karcher. Karcher had grown a small Los Angeles hot-dog stand into the successful Carl's Jr. restaurant chain and was the head of its parent company, CKE Restaurants. In 1991, I became Karcher's personal attorney and moved to California. In 1997, I became CKE's executive vice president and general counsel.

I stayed with the company through its highs and lows for the next twenty years, becoming CEO in 2000. With a lot of hard work, we took CKE from near bankruptcy to become a fast-food powerhouse, with 3,800 locations in the United States and 40 foreign countries that generated, together with our franchises, over $4 billion in annual revenues and employed over 75,000 people in the US alone.

I have never felt shy about sharing my views on economic policy; perhaps that's because I saw firsthand, from different perspectives, the real impact of government policy on working Americans. I believe it is important for political leaders to hear from those of us who personally know the importance of good jobs to working families, and who also know how government regulations can discourage companies from creating jobs by making it against their economic interests. I'd always been happy to support qualified candidates for office who understood that. But as for myself, I always felt more comfortable in the courtroom or the boardroom than in the political arena.

Perhaps that was part of what drew me to Donald Trump. He was decidedly not a typical politician. One of the things that struck me when I met him for the first time was how similar his mannerisms and personality were, in that small setting, to what I had seen on television.

His remarks were unscripted, freewheeling, and honest, a refreshing change from the prepackaged, poll-tested language of most politicians. He may have been a bit more understated in that setting, but Trump's essence was unmistakable. When I shook his hand and spoke to him face-to-face for the first time, he was, above all, genuine. With Donald Trump, what you saw was what you got.

A few months later, in mid-July, I happened to be seated across the table from Trump at another dinner, this time at the home of Dr. Carla Sands, a real-estate investor in Los Angeles. I had been advising the Trump campaign, and as it happened, the *Wall Street Journal* was preparing to run a joint op-ed from myself and fellow Trump economic adviser Stephen Moore in the following morning's paper.

We argued that Trump's economic plan was vastly superior to Hillary Clinton's, explaining, "Although we disagree with him on some issues, we have both signed on as economic advisers to Mr. Trump because we are confident in the direction he would take the country." Specifically, we praised his pledge to repeal Obamacare and his plan to enact the most sweeping tax cut since 1981.

I mentioned the upcoming op-ed to Mr. Trump—I even pulled up the text on my phone and slid it across the table to him. We were unable to discuss economic policy in detail that evening, but he was obviously pleased to see the op-ed and clearly something got his attention. I would be seeing a lot more of Mr. Trump in the near future.

Shortly after that dinner, on July 19, my son and I watched from a suite overlooking the floor as Trump was formally nominated at the Republican National Convention in Cleveland. The contained chaos of the general election campaign followed, capped by Trump's stunning win on November 8 despite nearly all pollsters and pundits predicting a runaway Clinton victory.

I was certainly pleased that we were going to have someone with sound economic ideas in the White House to clear away the rubble of the Obama years. However, I had to turn my mind to more immediate matters. Just a week after the election, I was due to speak at the Restaurant Finance & Development Conference, which kicked off on November 14 in Las Vegas.

Radio and TV host Hugh Hewitt was also speaking at that conference and, totally unbeknownst to me, had decided to aggressively promote me in his remarks as a candidate to be the next secretary of labor. I may never know whether this was coincidence or not, but in the midst of that conference, I got a call from Vice President-elect Mike Pence. I had known Pence since his days in Congress, and saved his number in my phone, so my dining companions were able to see "Mike Pence" show up on the display when the call came through. One of them leaned over and said, "You'd better take it."

Pence called to invite me to the Trump National Golf Club, Bedminster in New Jersey to meet with the team about joining the administration. He specifically mentioned the idea of my heading up the Small Business Administration. I agreed to meet, and a few days later, on November 19, I found myself in a room with Pence, Reince Priebus, Steve Bannon, and Donald Trump.

I had entered with some general ideas about how to run the Small Business Administration, but the president-elect raised the possibility of my becoming secretary of labor.

Without any hesitation, I told him I was interested. Here was a chance to help craft policies that would get America back on track toward real economic growth and more people employed at good-paying jobs. Trump asked what my plan would be, and I told him that it boiled down to two simple ideas. First, I wanted to protect American workers by creating more jobs to increase their wages and benefits. Secondly—to accomplish the first goal—I wanted to reform any regulation that hampered economic growth, while at the same time implementing every policy I could that would *increase* growth. Trump took it in and told me that was exactly what he was looking for.

The meeting ended on a good note, but the president-elect was noncommittal, and Priebus was cautious. That was to be expected; staffing a new administration is a delicate business, like putting a jigsaw puzzle together, each piece having to fit in with the overall picture. But I felt that after the interview I was on the short list for secretary of labor.

The president-elect and I shook hands before the assembled media. As I walked away, one reporter shouted, "What did he offer you, Andy?" I responded truthfully, "I'd be happy to do anything I could to help the president succeed."

After the meeting at Bedminster, the waiting game began. I knew there were other people under consideration for secretary of labor, including at least one serving member of Congress. While I thought the meeting with Trump and his senior advisers had gone well, I knew it was possible they could choose someone else for the job and that I might end up at the Small Business Administration after all—or potentially somewhere else altogether. I did believe, from the amount of interest that the president-elect and his team had expressed, that I would end up somewhere.

I was ready for that. In January, I had informed the Executive Committee at our company that, at age sixty-five and after fifteen years as CEO, I was ready to pass the leadership baton when they found a replacement. In recent years, my interest in public affairs and my desire to give back to the country that had given me so much had grown. They were months into the search for a replacement when I met with the president-elect.

Wherever I wound up, I was determined to support President Trump and make the most of this chance to bring real free-market ideas back to Washington and to actually help American workers instead of leaving them at the mercy of government intervention. I went to work, studying up on policy materials and outlining policy recommendations, much as I'd done during the campaign.

Finally, the summons came from Trump Tower in Manhattan, the headquarters of the presidential transition. When I arrived for my meeting on December 8, all I was told was that President-elect Trump wanted to speak with me. When I was shown into Trump's office, I found the same cast of characters from the Bedminster meeting (except the vice president), only in a different setting. There, once again, were Steve Bannon and Reince Priebus, and of course, behind the desk piled high with papers, Donald Trump himself.

"Andy, I'm going to give you the job," he said, getting straight to the point as usual.

I gave the only reply I could think of. "Thank you, Mr. President, but just so we're clear, which job?" As far as I knew, I was in the running for at least two different positions.

"Secretary of Labor," Trump responded immediately. "You had it from our first meeting."

I left Trump Tower excited. Now it was time for the real work to begin. For the rest of December and into the New Year, I was coordinating with lawyers and others on the transition team to make sure all my financial disclosure and ethics forms were in order. Contrary to later press coverage, all my filings with the Office of Government Ethics were turned in by January 3, 2017—among the earliest of any of the new cabinet nominees. Meanwhile, I was back at the books, reading policy papers, studies, and economic forecasts and working to fine-tune my own position statements.

In the end, I decided on a succinct four-point plan to help turn the Department of Labor from an advocate for bigger government and an abettor of Big Labor into a force that put the American worker first. As has become obvious since his election as Chairman of the Democratic Party, the prior secretary of labor, Thomas Perez, was a Progressive and a strongly (very strongly) partisan big-government Democrat. There was going to be a lot of work getting the Department of Labor refocused on helping create jobs and increasing wages and benefits rather than growing government and supporting Big Labor.

To begin with, I wanted to zoom in on one of the most vulnerable sectors of the American workforce by increasing opportunities for employment among minority communities and in large cities. Tens of millions of Americans who could work and who *wanted* to work were stuck, unable to find jobs, and that spawned negative ripple effects across entire communities.

I hoped to increase efforts to help people in these high-risk areas find good-paying jobs that would double as investments in their communities. There was a lot of government red tape preventing that from happening, and it was past time for it to go. Our immigration policies also needed a closer look. It seemed counterproductive to allow low-skilled workers to immigrate in large numbers when there were millions of citizens who could work receiving unemployment.

My second priority was also aimed at increasing employment by expanding opportunities for education and training. It was a tragedy that hundreds of thousands of good-paying, skilled-labor jobs remained open in America simply because potential workers lacked the necessary training.

I felt we could easily address this problem by working more with the private sector on worker training programs to match workers with the jobs that actually exist. I also hoped we could work together on vocational and technical training programs, like apprenticeships or internships for unemployed or underemployed Americans. I wanted the Department of Labor to have a constructive role, working with the private sector to accomplish this goal.

My third priority reflected my own experience. I got married and had a family at a young age. I had three children by the time I graduated from law school at age twenty-eight. I felt that workplace policies should better reflect the needs of young families and that there was a role for government to push in that direction.

I wanted to implement the president's desire for paid family leave, and I believed that if it was done with sensitivity toward the realities of business—and particularly if the rest of our economic agenda resulted in a healthy labor market—it would be possible to enact paid family leave in a way that did not discourage hiring and job creation.

For years, I had been preaching that America could have both strong worker protections and a strong labor market. The family leave issue was a chance to put that theme to work and create a model for similar reforms in the future.

My final priority, which would have helped the entire department run more smoothly to accomplish the first three, was to start swinging the axe in the overgrown forest that government regulation of the private sector has become.

It was essential for Washington to understand that while regulation is necessary and can be quite beneficial, it can be devastating to the job market unless it's done in a way that is sensitive to how businesses really think and react.

Regulations undermine job creation far more than most Americans know, and far more than taxation. Like most Americans, I'm not a fan of taxes. I believe it is always better for Americans to keep more of what they earn. But, when done properly and with the intent of raising revenue rather than punishing success or redistributing income, taxes do at least have the benefit of generating revenue for the government. Regulations, on the other hand, usually *lower* revenue because they stunt economic growth. So, unless a regulation delivers real progress toward some social goal, it is a net loss for everyone.

I believed that regulatory reform held the promise of spurring economic growth, increasing government revenue, and improving the job market, all while making worker protections more effective. I was looking forward to making that point, especially to left-leaning senators and members of Congress.

Armed with this plan, I went forward to the next challenge: going to Washington for meetings with the senators on the HELP Committee over the course of January and early February.

Senate Majority Leader Mitch McConnell and Senator Lamar Alexander from Tennessee, the HELP Chairman, were extremely welcoming and helpful from the very beginning. All my meetings with the Republican committee members went well. There was not a hint of awkwardness. In fact, one of the most enjoyable was my session with Senator Susan Collins from Maine, which was to prove somewhat confusing considering future events.

Many of my meetings with Democratic senators were constructive as well considering none of them expected to be sitting across from a Republican cabinet nominee.

It was clear to me after meeting with the Democratic HELP members that these senators were still somewhat in shock after the November election. They clearly had bought into the popular notion that demographics had changed, Republicans could not win the presidency, and Hillary Clinton had the election locked up. I got the sense that in their minds, Democrats were destined to hold the White House for decades. And yet, there I was, a Republican nominee for secretary of labor, sitting across from them. I was a messenger from reality in a suit and tie.

Despite this, I got along with many of the Democrats with whom I met. Senator Christopher Murphy from Connecticut asked particularly thoughtful questions, and I thought we established a good rapport. My meeting with Senator Tim Kaine from Virginia was especially cordial, which surprised me considering he had just been defeated as Clinton's running mate. But he and

I got along so well that I genuinely felt, in a less fractious political climate, he would have voted for me. My meeting with Senator Michael Bennet from Colorado was similarly upbeat. Indeed, none of the Democrats, though they may have pointed out their ideological differences, expressed any doubts about my eventual confirmation.

Perhaps the most pleasant surprise was my sit-down with Senator Bernie Sanders from Vermont. I had geared up for this one, expecting him to waste no time tearing into a CEO who had been fool enough to cross his office threshold. In reality, Senator Sanders acknowledged our differences (he is an admitted Socialist after all) but seemed open to discussing common ground, and of that we had more than I expected.

Indeed, in my own notes I quoted a floor speech of his from 2013 in which he said that rising numbers of Americans with little education and little to no job skills were "creating a permanent underclass" and that "the best anti-poverty program is a paycheck." I agreed, and I hoped to address this with more education and job training, if confirmed.

Additionally, while we both recognized that free trade could benefit everyone, we agreed that it was important to negotiate better trade deals with an eye toward protecting the working class from the pain those deals can bring.

Meeting with Senator Al Franken from Minnesota proved to be a strange experience. It was almost as if I met with two different people. At the outset, he seemed to make it a point to be as obnoxious as possible. I wasn't even treated to the legendary wit that made him so famous on late-night TV. He just seemed to be in a foul mood.

When I mentioned my interest in additional vocational training and apprenticeship programs, his reaction, to my surprise, was to take offense. "I introduced a bill on that in 2013," he informed me, haughtily demanding, "How could you come in here without knowing that?" I apologized for the oversight but added that now I knew of his interest in that area and I hoped we could work together on these initiatives under the Trump administration. To that, he was noncommittal.

Midway through our meeting Senator Franken was called out of the room. When he returned, his demeanor had done a 180-degree turn. He was more jovial and interested, and the second half of our meeting went much better than the first. I don't know what caused the change in demeanor, but whatever happened certainly gave me a break!

Perhaps he decided that since we already agreed on at least one key issue, maybe it was time to stop being so hostile. Senators often use a carrot-and-stick approach to these interviews. Franken may have thought he had used the stick enough and needed to inject a little carrot into the interview. I mentioned that his fellow Saturday Night Live alumnus Dennis Miller and I were friends, and the mood lightened considerably. I was sure the senator would vote against me, but I thought we might actually be able to work together.

Sadly, Senator Elizabeth Warren from Massachusetts offered little in the way of surprises.

Senator Warren seemed to have made up her mind about what I believed, and nothing I said could have swayed her. She expressed concern with what she assumed was my opposition to increasing the minimum wage, an opposition fabricated by the left-wing press and subsequently repeated in her book despite our meeting. I had to explain to her that I had never opposed raising the minimum wage. In fact, I thought it should be raised, but I was opposed to raising it to the point where it would kill entry-level jobs.

Met with indignant skepticism, I told her that she could

confirm this by speaking with anyone at the National Restaurant Association or the International Franchise Association as I had been trying to convince both organizations to get behind such a minimum wage increase for the past two years. I told her our differences on the issue were not on whether it should be raised but rather how much.

Taken aback, she then claimed there was no evidence that substantial minimum wage increases would kill American jobs. That's simply untrue. Among other things, I referred her to a Congressional Budget Office report from 2014 where the CBO stated that increasing the minimum wage to $10.10 "would reduce total employment by about 500,000 workers."[1] She argued that this was just an average and that the CBO had actually given a range of possible outcomes that acknowledged the impact could be a "very slight reduction."

I was intimately familiar with that report, and I knew she was cherry-picking data from the most favorable scenario among the many it discussed. I pointed out that the upper end of that range was the loss of one million jobs and that, as I had stated, the CBO's projection was a loss of some five hundred thousand jobs. I explained that I felt it was safest, when forging policy, to consider the CBO's actual estimate, but she refused to accept that.

Perhaps Senator Warren's display of hostility was for the benefit of the two staffers who accompanied the senator and who had apparently been instructed to sit behind her with stony glares on their faces and glower unspeaking throughout the whole meeting. I made it a secondary objective to get at least one of them to crack, and by keeping the mood light, I did manage to get one to smile by the end.

At the same time as I was making my case to the senators one by one, the media was full of stories in which my opponents launched smear after smear against me, personally and professionally. They brought up the undocumented housekeeper my family had employed years ago. I thought that incident should have weighed in my favor, because once I realized her immigration status, I discharged her and then offered to help her document her status with the authorities. In other words, over five years before I had any thought of serving in public life, when it would have been easy for me to ignore the unlawful status of a worker in my home, I acted when that status came to light.

The negative media coverage continued to grow. In mid-January, Senate Minority Leader Schumer made it clear that I was "one of the Democrats' biggest targets in the confirmation hearings."[2] The media heard him and continued to rehash allegations of spousal abuse that my ex-wife had made during our divorce almost thirty years ago.

The irony is that my former wife, Lisa, and I have a great relationship. Shortly after our divorce became final, Lisa acknowledged that the charges she had made were wholly untrue. She stated that she had made them at the behest of her lawyer, who thought they would give her an advantage in the divorce and who had a personal political vendetta against me. She repeated this in discussions with reporters and HELP Committee staff who called to speak with her.

She wrote a lengthy and very heartfelt letter to the HELP Committee, saying in part, "First, let me be clear. Andy is not and was not violent or abusive. He is a good, loving, kind man and a deeply committed and loving father. He is, as my own father noted years ago, the 'salt of the earth.'" The *Washington Examiner* published the letter.[3] The left-leaning media basically ignored it or attempted to discredit it while repeating the thirty-year-old allegations, stating something to the effect that she "later recanted."

Unable to find any actual evidence of abuse (since there was none) or anyone who could say there was abuse (this was always a he said–she said situation and he and she had been saying there was no abuse for almost thirty years), the media reached out to people who had never met either Lisa or me. After repeating the now "recanted" allegations, they were willing to say they "believed" there was abuse. Alternatively, they would quote Lisa's former attorney, who could have faced serious ethical or legal consequences had he not claimed to believe there was abuse. No one ever even attempted to interview my attorney, my adult children, or my wife of thirty years.

In her letter to the HELP Committee, Lisa stated that she later came to realize her attorney had "encouraged" her "to file abuse charges" because he "was more interested in hurting Andy because of a political vendetta than in representing [her] best interests." The "political vendetta" Lisa referred to grew from my involvement in the pro-life movement in St. Louis in the 1980s. As part of that work, I had co-authored a law review article proposing pro-life legislation, which Missouri adopted in 1986 as part of a larger bill. A St. Louis–area abortion clinic challenged the law, and it was in the courts at the time of our divorce. While Lisa supported my position on this issue, she had hired an attorney whose wife worked at the clinic challenging the law. Lisa admitted essentially the same thing to me in a 1991 letter after I had moved to California.

The attacks worked. In 1989, when the Supreme Court upheld the legislation I had proposed, the media went after me based on the abuse allegations, giving me an image consistent with their narrative on pro-lifers. It was the first time I was attacked by the left-leaning media for my beliefs. It certainly wouldn't be the last.

Perhaps the clearest example of media bias on the false and long-recanted abuse allegations came after it was announced that I had withdrawn my nomination for secretary of labor. A *Politico* reporter unabashedly tweeted that *Politico*'s newsroom (which had regularly repeated the abuse allegations) broke out in applause.

The whole incident wounded Lisa deeply; it reopened a difficult time in her life and mine. She called me regularly during the confirmation process, apologizing in tears. I was and am grateful to her for her integrity and courage in stating and restating the truth despite the frustration and embarrassment she suffered.

One thing I learned during the nomination process was that, whatever the attitude of the nominee toward the charges against him, families take them personally.

My family was outraged when a group tied to the Service Employees International Union sent protestors to our front door in Franklin, Tennessee, held a rally in our hometown, and drove a billboard through our neighborhood that accused me of abusing women.

The obvious intent of these tactics was to intimidate me directly or through my family rather than to persuade any senator to vote against me. There are no senators living in Franklin, Tennessee.

I also deeply regretted and resented the distorted attacks on our company's excellent record on protecting employee rights. This attack harmed not only me but the hardworking, decent, and committed workers and executives at our company.

For the record, none of the charges of employee abuse against me and the company I ran were true. They were not just distorted; they were false.

Our company has an outstanding record of compliance with the law and of concern for its employees. In fact, that's part of our business model. We want the best employees—the kind of people who care about their jobs and their customers—and we know we must treat our employees well to get and keep the best ones.

Diana Furchtgott-Roth, a former chief economist of the Department of Labor, looked at our record and wrote in *Investor's Business Daily*: "The attacks on Puzder are politically motivated and are not grounded in fact. If you want to support a law-abiding company, go eat at Hardee's or Carl's Jr., CKE's chains of fast-food restaurants."[4]

And, while I have a lot of faults, violence toward women isn't one of them.

The most serious incident came in January, when a package addressed to my wife—not even to me—was found to contain mysterious white powder, a paper doll with a noose around its neck, and a pink piece of paper with "TRUMP" scrawled on it. I quarantined the package in the garage and called emergency services. Before long, our neighborhood was invaded by fire engines and firemen in HAZMAT suits, along with an FBI counterterrorism team. Fortunately, nobody was hurt. Strangely, even the local media apparently never saw fit to report on that incident.

The next morning, I told my wife that I was concerned about putting her and our family through this. I hated to do it, but in fairness, I thought I should offer to withdraw as nominee. Incensed, she shot back, "So, you'll just let the bad guys win?"

While my family held up under the abuse, I can't say the same about the senators. By early February, a cloud had begun to form over my nomination proceedings. The team helping me work through the transition had been getting reports that some Republicans on the HELP Committee were getting nervous. If only three committed to voting against me, that would be enough to sink my nomination.

Part of the problem was that my hearing had been repeatedly delayed as we waited weeks for the Office of Government Ethics to respond to the filings I had made on January 3. I kept hearing that the head of the OGE was an Obama administration appointee and that the delay may have been intentional as, unlike with Betsy DeVos's hearing, the Democrats on the HELP committee refused to allow my hearing to proceed until we had the OGE's response. The longer it took to schedule my hearing, the more time and effort Big Labor and the Democrats could focus on me and the false media narrative they had created.

Majority Leader McConnell was kind enough to go before the Senate Republican Caucus and make the case for my confirmation personally. Senator Alexander reportedly told the assembled Senators that I was "Mitch's favorite of all the Trump Cabinet nominees...and that includes Elaine." It got a big laugh from everyone, including Senator McConnell, given the tongue-in-cheek reference to McConnell's wife, Elaine Chao, a stellar secretary of labor under President George W. Bush and Trump's nominee for Secretary of Transportation.

Vice President Pence assured me that he would come to the Hill to break a tie if I could get fifty votes, as he had with Secretary DeVos. I told the vice president that I wasn't one to tilt at windmills. If it didn't look like I could get fifty votes, I saw no reason to put the administration through the ordeal of a hearing and the risk of losing a vote in the Senate.

Pence said he and President Trump understood and would support whatever decision I made. Before I made my final decision, he asked if he could check with McConnell one more time on the latest vote count. If it looked like we could get fifty, I was anxious to go ahead with the hearing.

On February 15, he called back with the final word.

"Hello, Mr. Vice President."

The news was not good. It looked as though three Republicans from the HELP Committee had defected: Susan Collins from Maine, Lisa Murkowski from Alaska, and Johnny Isakson from Georgia. If that happened, other senators would be disinclined to take the political risk of supporting a nominee who wasn't going to be confirmed. McConnell told Pence that we just didn't have the votes.

I informed the vice president that I was withdrawing my name from nomination. He expressed regret but said he understood.

If my losing a confirmation vote would not have hurt the president, I would not have withdrawn until after the hearing, despite the odds. During the nomination process, I had to keep under wraps. I couldn't defend myself; that's the protocol for nominees. I would have enjoyed the chance to go at it with my critics, to get at the heart of the real reasons I wanted to be secretary of labor, and the real reasons they fought against me.

I've decided to do that now, in this book.

The economy has, technically, been in a recovery since June 2009. Most Americans don't know that because the "recovery" felt a lot like a recession prior to President Trump taking office. Our annual gross domestic product grew at an anemic 2.1 percent from the end of the recession through the end of the Obama presidency, far below the rate of recovery in every other post–World War II recession, resulting in too few jobs, stagnating wages, and closing paths to the middle class.

It was all so unnecessary.

Eight years ago, a reduction in regulatory costs could well have generated real economic growth. Growth not only puts cash in consumers' pockets, it increases returns for start-ups and expanding businesses, which drives further economic growth and the demand for labor, increasing both wages and benefits. Small businesses becoming big businesses drive job growth, open paths to the middle class, and reduce income inequality. The eight years of the Obama administration prove that Progressive economic policies that expand government do the opposite.

Even without an absolute reduction in the number of regulations, American workers could have experienced meaningful job and wage growth had the Obama administration respected the free market's role in producing wealth and tailored its regulatory agenda in a way that minimized the negative effects on job and wage growth. But because of its blindness and, let's face it, hostility to the benefits of capitalism, the Obama administration caused American workers to suffer through the feeblest economic recovery since the Great Depression.

This was a sad state of affairs for the greatest economic system the world has ever seen. But one of the greatest things about capitalism is that it's resilient.

It is the only system in history that incentivizes individuals to create the wealth necessary to meaningfully lift people out of poverty, if only the government will allow it to work its wonders—to create opportunity and foster innovation, rather than succumbing to the Progressive notion that a small group of elites, however they're chosen, can create our futures for us.

So why are those in today's Left, the Progressives who suppose themselves protectors of the workers and helpers of the weak, so unwilling to recognize the benefits that free markets offer and their potential to create the wealth that both the private and public sectors need to assist the vulnerable? Why foster government dependence rather than personal independence?

As I said above, I began my adult life as a Democrat, and over the years, I've gotten to know and appreciate many people who are prominent on the Left. Many are smart and accomplished people. What is it about their ideology, or the power structures they depend upon, that causes them, in public anyway, to proclaim so many silly things about their own economic system?

What causes them to be so willfully blind to the benefits of capitalism, and even to attack with unrelenting hostility those who try to explain those benefits?

On February 28, I watched from my couch as President Trump gave his first address to a joint session of Congress, what is called, in every year besides a president's first, a State of the Union address. It was a good speech, and at times a great one. The president understands the importance of economic growth and especially the importance of jobs—good jobs, that can support a family and give people a sense of independence, fulfillment, and hope.

He was successful in his own business career, as I was. He knows, as I do, that business and labor need each other and that the government is wrong to treat them as adversaries. He is attacked for his beliefs every day by the same Progressive forces that attacked me, and far more than I was attacked. He's not going to let the critics shut him up, and neither will I. The barrage of smears against me was a desperate move by a political power structure that is still reeling after President Trump's shocking victory. But, as the unrelenting attacks against President Trump demonstrate, it was far from their last move.

We now have a US president who understands the importance and benefits of America's free-market system. The Progressive ideology rejects the idea of the American Dream and routinely attacks people like me, and him, who have lived it, vilifying America and its economic system. President Trump wants to make the idea of success great again, for everyone.

Having a president who understands the benefits of free-market capitalism and its potential to create economic prosperity is a terminal threat to the Progressive Left's ideology and power. If their reaction to his presidency seems desperate, bordering on hysterical, that's because it is.

This book will seek to expose that ideology and the forces behind it, to show how their creeping influence has been tilting this country, bit by bit, away from the virtues of freedom and the potential for every human being to make his or her way in the world. These very virtues turned thirteen backwoods colonies into the world's largest economy and created a phenomenon the entire world now knows as the American Dream.

The stakes are too high for me to stay silent. President Trump has a real shot at turning this country around (as he says, "Making America Great Again"), but he's going to need help. Consider this book a "Most Wanted" list of the institutions standing in the way of freedom and prosperity and a guide to help America reach its full potential—from a guy who's learned a thing or two about how to get that done and about the people who would prefer to prevent it.

The CAPITALIST COMEBACK

CHAPTER ONE

Making America Great Again: Year One

"From now on, America will be empowered by our aspirations, not burdened by our fears; inspired by the future, not bound by the failures of the past; and guided by our vision, not blinded by our doubts."

PRESIDENT DONALD J. TRUMP

As with all of life, a presidency is made up of moments. The most significant are moments of truth, when the results of a president's actions and influence can break through the partisan rhetoric designed to obscure positive accomplishments. No president can have a perfect year. We elect human beings, not gods. Nonetheless, President Trump's first year in office was filled with moments of truth that benefitted all Americans and will be remembered. His positive effects on the economy have been remarkable.

President Trump's election immediately ignited long-dormant business optimism. His administration's rapid regulatory rollback drove economic growth at a pace few expected. Led by President Trump, Republicans looked to pick up that pace with tax cuts that encouraged business investment, reduced the tax burden for working- and middle-class families, and eliminated the perverse incentives that drive our businesses, jobs, and dollars to other nations. As a result, the economy is surging as businesses grow, job opportunities increase, and government shrinks.

With the attention of Democrats and the media focused on scandals that the president's opponents fabricate (or pay others to fabricate), while parsing his every offhand remark or tweet in search of a word or phrase that might support their "never Trump" narrative, these moments often failed to get the coverage they deserved.

Literally from the day he was elected, business confidence soared like a coiled spring let loose from its restraints. The National Federation of Independent Businesses' Small Business Optimism Index "blasted off the day after the 2016 election and remained in the stratosphere for all of 2017."[5] By the year's end, the NFIB Index reached the highest monthly average in its history, exceeding the record year of 2004.

According to NFIB Chief Economist Bill Dunkelberg, "[w]e've been doing this research for nearly half a century, longer than anyone else, and I've never seen anything like 2017. The 2016 election was like a dam breaking. Small business owners were waiting for better policies from Washington, suddenly they got them, and the engine of the economy roared back to life."[6]

The NFIB Index wasn't the only record-setting survey. In November 2017, the Conference Board Consumer Confidence Index rose to a seventeen-year high.[7] The National Association of Manufacturers' Outlook Index also hit the highest annual average in its history.[8]

The stock market was similarly enthusiastic. On election night, the BBC interviewed me and asked what I thought about stock market futures dropping 700 points when it became obvious that President Trump would be our next president. *New York Times* opinion writer and Progressive economist Paul Krugman was predicting that the stock market would never recover.[9]

I told them that, in the morning, I'd be a buyer. I never got the chance.

The next day, the Dow Jones Industrial Average surged up 250 points.[10] It hit record highs more than seventy times in President Trump's first year, the highest number ever recorded for a single year.[11] On average, the stock market hit a new record high every fourth trading day. The DOW rose 5,000 points in 2017, the largest annual points gain in its 121-year history.[12]

By the end of the year, optimism among professional investors was at 66.7 percent in the highly regarded Investors Intelligence Survey, reported as "the highest reading since April 1986."[13] According to the year-end CNBC All-American Economic Survey, "for the first time in at least 11 years, more than half of respondents to the survey rated the economy as good or excellent, while a near record 41 percent expected the economy to improve in the next year." As one pollster for the survey stated, "We're not measuring a marginal change in the economy, we're measuring a different economy."[14]

Much of the initial enthusiasm was based on the anticipation that President Trump would reverse President Obama's antibusiness policies by aggressively reducing government regulations and cutting taxes. That optimism sustained itself throughout 2017 because he delivered.

President Trump took a machete to the Obama era's rules and regulations that have been choking American businesses like parasitic vines. In fact, an analysis by the Competitive Enterprise Institute (CEI), a libertarian think tank, found that during his first nine months, Trump was deregulating the economy at a pace greater than any other president.[15]

According to the CEI, Trump reduced the Federal Register's page count by an impressive 32 percent compared to President Obama at the same time in the prior year. This put him on course to beat President Reagan's record of a "one-third reduction in Federal Register pages following Jimmy Carter's then-record Federal Register." But that reduction took Reagan years to accomplish. Trump had been in office nine months. The CEI concluded that "by this metric, Trump [was] moving much faster," already making him the "least-regulatory president since Reagan." He will surpass Reagan to become the most anti-regulation president we've ever had.

This will make perfect sense if you were paying attention during the campaign. Candidate Trump said he would "cancel every needless job-killing regulation and put a moratorium on new regulations until our economy gets back on its feet."[16] He pledged to change the rules so that "for every new federal regulation, two existing regulations must be eliminated."[17] He told an audience in Detroit, Michigan, that he would "remove bureaucrats who only know how to kill jobs [and] replace them with experts who know how to create jobs."[18]

He hit the ground running once in office, designating regulatory task forces to identify antibusiness regulations we could do without.[19] All new proposed regulations would have to be approved by a Trump-appointed official.[20] After just ten days in the White House, a new Trump executive order set a policy of getting rid of two regulations for every new one created.[21]

Clearly, these early decisive actions worked.

By the summer, 860 Obama administration regulations were either suspended or gone for good.[22] This was part of the process for removing what the administration called "that slow cancer that can come from regulatory burdens that we put on our people."[23]

In September, the president told a group of manufacturers, "We have taken unprecedented steps to remove job-killing regulations that sap the energy, creativity and dynamism from our country. We are cutting regulations at a pace that has never even been thought of before."[24]

At a December 14, 2017 press briefing, Trump's chief regulatory officer, Neomi Rao, announced that for the 2017 fiscal year (which ended in September), the Trump administration eliminated not just two but twenty-two regulations for each new regulation that was issued.[25] This resulted in a net reduction in regulatory costs of $8.1 billion.

She also stated that the administration was "on track to continue to be better than three for one" in 2018 with "448 deregulatory actions and 131 regulatory actions" on the agenda. The administration projects that those reductions will result in about $10 billion worth of additional cost savings.

If you wonder whether all of this really mattered, ask someone who owns a business. Or just look at the impact on gross domestic product (GDP), which measures the value of all goods and services produced in a period (generally quarterly or annually) and is the most commonly used measure of economic performance.

The key to meaningful GDP growth is business investment. During President Obama's tenure, the regulatory state expanded, taxes increased, and investment declined, hobbling growth.[26] Obama's annual GDP growth rate never hit 3 percent in any calendar year (the first president since Hoover who failed to do so).[27] Growth averaged a meager 2.1 percent following the end of the recession, when it should have surged.[28] According to an analysis from the Congressional Research Service, the ten post–World War II recoveries averaged GDP growth of 4.3 percent, about double Obama's average.[29] For 2016, Obama's final year in office, GDP growth slowed to an anemic 1.5 percent.

This dismal performance led to predictions of prolonged economic stagnation. In March 2017, Obama administration economist Jason Furman forecast ten years of GDP growth, "around 2 percent a year."[30] In May, his fellow Obama alumnus Larry Summers said that expecting the Trump administration to deliver 3 percent GDP was like believing "in tooth fairies and ludicrous supply-side economics."[31]

Of course, they were wrong.

Under the Trump administration, regulations went down and business optimism went up, along with investment and GDP growth.[32] During the first two full quarters in which Trump held office, the second and third quarters of 2017, the economy grew 3.1 and 3.2 percent respectively.[33] The initial estimate for the fourth quarter was 2.6 percent, making the average for the Trump administration's first three full quarters 3 percent.[34] The White House further estimated that if not for the damage from the two massive hurricanes that hit the country, third quarter GDP growth would have hit 3.9 percent, which would have made the average for the first three quarters 3.2 percent.[35]

The benefits of this growth are already apparent in the employment numbers. The economy added nearly two million new jobs in 2017.[36] Manufacturing, a sector on which Trump has focused, added nearly 200,000 jobs after losing jobs in 2016. As a sign that growth is indeed picking up, construction added 210,000 jobs.

By December 2017, the unemployment rate fell to 4.1 percent, the lowest rate in nearly seventeen years.[37] At 6.8 percent, the unemployment rate for black Americans, was at its lowest level since that data has been collected.[38] At 4.9 percent, Hispanic unemployment was close to its historic low.

Perhaps not surprisingly, according to a January 2018 Gallup poll, "Americans' optimism about finding a quality job averaged 56% in 2017, the highest annual average in the 17 years of Gallup polling this metric and a sharp increase from 42% in 2016."[39] With job openings historically high at around six million since June 2017, their optimism is justified.[40]

This was all before December 22, 2017, when President Trump signed into law the historic tax cuts Republicans in Congress had enacted without a single Democrat's vote. The president had been fighting for that tax reduction for months. These cuts gave much needed relief to American employers and employees. The business tax cuts encourage investment by allowing businesses to keep more of their profits, to bring funds they're holding overseas back to the United States without an excessive penalty, and to write off the totality of their investments in things like new plants and equipment.

It worked immediately.

Within a month, over 250 companies had announced plans to either increase employee compensation or invest in growth (or both).[41] Those initial investments will undoubtedly exceed half a trillion dollars. AT&T will invest $1 billion in 2018.[42] J. P. Morgan is spending $20 billion to raise wages, open more offices, and create more positions.[43] Comcast NBC Universal announced that it would spend $50 billion over the next five years, investing in infrastructure.[44] Apple declared it would be contributing over $350 billion in the next five years.[45] CNBC economic commentator Jim Cramer called Apple's investment plan alone "a modern day Marshall Plan."[46] That, of course, refers to America's plan to rebuild Europe after World War II (an investment of about $13 billion or $140 billion in current dollar value).[47]

None of this should have been a surprise to anyone who understands America's economic system. Capitalist economies are dynamic by nature. As this book will show, capitalism is the only economic system that benefits *all* the people. It allows everyone to maximize the earning potential of their greatest gifts. As consumers, it empowers everyone to control what is produced and offered. It channels the self-interest of every man and woman outward to the benefit of all.

American capitalism is still far and away the single greatest example of the economic benefits of freedom in the world, or in the history of the world. Only oppressive government policies—like the tax and regulatory state unleashed during the Obama years—can prevent American capitalism from creating jobs, raising wages, and increasing the living standard of the American people.

So *of course* the Republican tax bill is causing job growth and increasing wages. Anyone who has ever had any real experience in business knew that it would. When companies make profits and have a positive economic outlook that signals growth ahead, what will they do? Invest those profits back into their company, creating more jobs and expanding opportunity. More opportunity means competition for employees, and that makes companies raise wages, resulting in a better deal for workers.

In other words, Republicans led by President Trump focused their tax reform efforts on exactly the right goal: economic growth that benefits everyone. Not that long ago, this made sense to Democrats as well. As President Kennedy once described it, economic growth is that "rising tide" that "lifts all boats," a far cry from the class warfare rhetoric coming from his party today.[48]

Many unforeseen factors can influence whether GDP will continue to grow at an accelerated pace. However, from an economic perspective, at the end of year one, President Trump is unquestionably keeping his promise to "Make America Great Again." After seven and a half years of anemic growth, the economy is surging, and all Americans are benefitting.

So, why the frantic opposition to President Trump's agenda? Why does the whole Progressive world—Democrat politicians, the left-wing media, union leaders, and icons of the entertainment industry—resist so hysterically economic policies that are clearly moving the country in the right direction? To answer that, it's important to understand what President Trump is defending, who his opponents really are, and what they deem to be at risk.

In reality, it isn't the failure of President Trump's economic policies that Progressives fear. It's their success. The rest of this book explains why.

CHAPTER TWO

America: Land of the Self-Made

"The most effective way to destroy people is to deny and obliterate their own understanding of their history."

ATTRIBUTED TO GEORGE ORWELL

American Exceptionalism

America was founded on a promise: No matter who you are or where you're from, you will have the opportunity to pursue your dreams, and keep the benefits of your success free from government oppression.

In a world ruled by absolute monarchs and their noble elite supporters, it was a promise no other nation had ever made. It was a promise that shook the existing power structure to its core and released an entrepreneurial energy that turned thirteen backwoods colonies into the world's largest and most prosperous economy in just over one hundred years.

This is the promise that made America an exceptional nation. While we have been less than perfect in keeping it, the ideals that gave birth to that promise keep Americans striving for perfection. Despite our shortcomings, American free-market capitalism has spread more wealth across broader demographics and lifted more people from the working class to the middle class (and beyond) than any economic system ever devised.

Many on the Left argue that free-market capitalism encourages greed and is a detriment to the common man and woman. They even attempt to mischaracterize the defense of capitalism as an argument that greed is good. But greed is not good, and capitalism is not based on greed. Capitalism takes self-motivation, the desire of all people to better their lives, and turns it into altruistic conduct designed to benefit others.

To succeed in a capitalist system, you have to please others enough to entice them into a voluntary exchange. It forces you to pay attention to the needs, wants, and even feelings of a broad cross section of people. It encourages a kind of empathy with regard to your potential customers.

To entice consumers to visit our restaurants as opposed to our competitors, I had to put myself in the shoes of people who might buy hamburgers and ask myself not what I thought and wanted, but what they thought and what they wanted. At CKE, we spent an enormous amount of time and effort trying to get into the consumers' heads so we could understand and meet their needs and expectations.

That wasn't unusual. Any businessperson will tell you that if you don't understand your customers, you will fail. If you do understand them and provide what they want, you will succeed. In a capitalist system, you succeed not by getting what you want but by providing others with what they want. Individuals in capitalist societies are constantly striving to satisfy the needs of others, resulting in tremendous economic growth and elevated standards of living across broad demographics.

The only way a business can survive without making its customers happy is if the government compels people to purchase the product that business offers; in other words, government elites, rather than consumers, direct the economy as in a socialist (or aristocratic) system.

In a socialist economy, people are unable to offer others what they want. You must compete with other individuals for what you need from a limited and regulated or rationed supply. The focus is on getting as much as you can from the government to the exclusion of others, who are competing with you for a limited quantity of whatever the government decides to offer, whether its people standing in bread lines or attempting to get medical care. There is no alternative source for goods or services.

To better your life in a socialist system (as in an aristocratic system), you must please those who have political power rather than potential customers. You might not get what you want even if you do please them, but you certainly won't get it if you don't. And since political leaders want to maintain or improve their position in the political system, your success under socialism is directly related to how useful you are to them in their greed for power. That's the nature of government, and it's as true in democratic systems as it is in autocratic ones. How long would your congressman or senator care what the voters think if they didn't need their votes?

Under socialism, you improve your life by addressing the needs of those in power—government elites—and striving to get what you can before someone else does. Under capitalism, you improve your life by satisfying the needs of others—consumers—and making sure they get what they need. In reality, it is capitalism that encourages altruistic behavior, produces vast economic benefits, and lifts standards of living across broad demographics (everyone benefits to differing degrees). Socialism encourages greed, diminishes economic growth, and lowers (equalizes) standards of living for all but the government elites.

Yet those on the Left seek to reempower a centralized government and its cronies to direct the course of our economy and our lives. Their ideology harkens back to a time when those with political connections succeeded while those without found frustration and despair under the yoke of government oppression.

Surely every individual should have the opportunity to reach his or her full potential free from unreasonable government restraints. History alone affirms the power of this simple idea to spread prosperity, improving all our lives. It was an independent, freedom-loving people who made America the most prosperous nation in history, not a nation of government-dependent serfs.

Resistance and Distortion from the Left

However, capitalism and its uniquely American promise diminish the narrative of dependence and victimhood Progressives use to justify the need for more government in our lives. Individuals who are independent and free to succeed are not victims. This is precisely why Progressives work so diligently to silence anyone willing to speak up in defense of our economic freedom. It is also why the Left must disparage those whose lives demonstrate the potential of individuals to thrive in a system where economic freedom is secured by limited government.

If those on the Left believed in this uniquely American promise, they would hold up the self-made Americans who have experienced unparalleled success as positive examples to show future generations what they are free to become with hard work and determination. They would also explain how throughout American history self-made men and women, free from government interference, forged ahead with innovative ideas and solutions that created jobs, wealth, and prosperity not only for themselves but for the entire nation. America's entrepreneurs and innovators, from Cornelius Vanderbilt and Henry Ford to Steve Jobs and

Elon Musk, continue to be the envy of the world. They improved their fortunes and, in the process, the lives of their fellow citizens and the human condition.

These people don't succeed because they are superhuman, perfect in every aspect of their life and character. Most of them are pretty much like the rest of us, a mix of good and bad. But they do have a few things in common: They are risk takers, hard workers, and passionate in the pursuit of their goals. Their passion and ability can pay off for the rest of us.

I was successful as the CEO of the Hardee's/Carl's Jr. restaurant chain. Tens of thousands of other people are employed by that company today. Some make very good livings, and many others will use their experience with the company to be successful elsewhere. Millions have done so for over seventy-five years.

None of us could have prospered as we have but for a young man with an eighth-grade education named Carl Karcher, who in 1941 decided to stake everything on a small hot-dog cart in South Central Los Angeles. With hard work and determination, he grew that business into a major restaurant company over the following decades.

Unlike the vast majority of people in the vast majority of countries in the history of the world, Americans live in a nation where people can do that. Had Carl not lived in a nation that respected his freedom to succeed, he would have died without realizing his potential and spreading the benefits of that potential to others.

To respect such accomplishments and those who have achieved them, we don't have to treat entrepreneurs as models of morality (although Carl was a deeply religious and patriotic family man). Free-market capitalism is neither a religion nor an ethical creed that purports to have the answers to how we should live. It's an economic system. While it encourages altruistic behavior, it cannot by itself create a society where people care about one another and treat one another as they should.

However, free-market capitalism does expand the range of freedom in occupational lives while encouraging people to satisfy the needs of others. In doing so, it empowers people to create the wealth that makes possible real charity for the helpless as well as opportunity and prosperity for those willing to take the risks and put in the effort. It encourages people to realize their full potential and spreads the benefits of their success to others in the form of jobs, wealth, and prosperity.

Unfortunately, the Left is feeding future generations a very different message, particularly at our major universities. A 2016 poll conducted by Harvard University, which surveyed young Americans aged 18 to 29, found that a majority—though a small one, at 51 percent—did not support the capitalist system. The *Washington Post* called this "an apparent rejection of the basic principles of the U.S. economy."[1]

At first, this might come as a shock, but keep in mind that the young Americans who responded to this poll have grown up in a world where Progressives openly vilify business leaders at every turn, aided by the increasingly Progressive media and their allies in the entertainment industry. If the Harvard poll is any indication, this strategy appears to be working.

But why? What reason could Progressives have for constantly working to demonize the self-made men and women who have done so much to improve our lives and grow our economy? What interests are served in attempting to shame a whole generation of Americans into rejecting free-market capitalism, the one system that assures them of the opportunity to succeed?

The answer lies in the Progressives' quest to centralize power in a group of political elites. Some choose to do so because they believe big government is ultimately a source for good as an agent to help the needy or equalize wealth. Others view government as the means to increase their own power. I've known a fair number of left-wing politicians who started in the first camp and ended up in the second.

But, whatever the motive and as certainly as night follows day, increasing the power of government decreases individual freedom. When we become more dependent on government, we become less dependent on ourselves. Progressives have seen citizens in other countries accept the grim realities of government-run economies, such as those in the former Soviet Union, Cuba, North Korea, or (the Progressives' recent favorite) Venezuela. They see the poverty, despair, and starvation that result from socialism, and yet, against all reason, they continue to see more government as the ultimate solution to virtually every problem. So, to complete their power play, Progressives must convince the American people to place their faith in big government despite the loss of freedom, the risk of tyranny, and the inevitable indignity and decay that come with it.

That means delegitimizing the free-market capitalist system and the people who prosper in it. It means obscuring the noble truth that made our country what it is: the promise that you can be born into any background, any geographic setting, or any social status and make your way in America. Even articulating this notion runs contrary to Progressive dogma. It presents a counternarrative that shows what can happen when a system rewards hard work and success and affirms that government's proper role is to facilitate rather than obstruct the path to success. Progressives have to discredit this narrative in order to sap the spirit of would-be entrepreneurs who strain against the yoke of government. In other words, they must silence or disparage the successful men and women of humble beginnings who proved the worth of freedom and opportunity.

Capitalism's Journey to America

To put this Progressive threat in context, it's important to understand the historical significance of the American promise. How did this experiment on the eastern edge of the North American continent end up changing the world? In this respect, it is tragic that many of our institutions of learning no longer require that students take a course in American history (which helps explain the results of the Harvard poll).

From its inception, the United States has been an experiment in classical free-market liberalism. That may sound like a mouthful, but it is simply an "ideology advocating private property, an unhampered market economy, the rule of law, constitutional guarantees of freedom of religion and of the press, and international peace based on free trade."[2]

In this respect, the Revolutionary War was both political and economic. Like the republican form of government the Founders established, America's capitalist system was radically different from the systems in any other contemporary nation. But, the Founders weren't quite flying blind; they had inspiration upon which to draw, notably the work of the Scottish economist Adam Smith.

For centuries prior to the eighteenth century, the landed aristocracy held economic power in Europe. To the extent there was economic growth, it principally benefitted this group of nobles, who maintained their status through inheritance. While they controlled the wealth and had significant influence on government, ultimate authority rested in the hands of an absolute monarch—a king or queen.

General concepts of freedom and liberty existed in limited forms, but they were intended to protect the nobles against, and limit the power of, absolute monarchs. For example, this was the goal of the English barons who, in 1215, pressured King John into signing the Magna Carta. Rather than freeing the common man, the Magna Carta guaranteed the nobility certain essential rights and freedoms. Those with political power maintained a level of freedom for themselves while they subjugated the majority of the population—by force, if necessary.

Force was an important factor in Old World economics. The chances were that members of the ruling aristocracy got there thanks to an ancestor being on the winning side of a conquest. When a leader won a war, he parceled out the land to his supporters to govern. They built their castles or took those of the defeated and ruled as feudal lords with little or no concern for the masses.

Land was the key to their wealth. In the long term, a mere title with no accompanying land was all but useless. The ruling aristocrats owned the land, and the land produced wealth for the aristocrats.

Economic options for the masses were limited. A relative few could achieve success with a trade, such as blacksmithing, or as artisans skilled at other crafts. Some joined military units in service to the local lord or king. A select group joined religious orders, where they could receive an education and a somewhat elevated standard of living in exchange for a life of service to the church. Opportunities as merchants were limited since wealth was concentrated in the ruling class. Aristocrats and wealthy merchants controlled trade. There simply weren't enough jobs for everyone. Most of the common people were forced to work their lord's land as serfs. The only other options were often to become a criminal or starve.

If this seems bleak and oppressive, that's because it was. The feudal economic system was simply incapable of consistently feeding everyone who depended on it, much less creating an environment where people could improve their lives or even imagine a better future for themselves or their children. With economic power based on conquest and inheritance rather than merit, the unrealized human potential of serfs and peasants died with them.

However, the eighteenth century witnessed the dawn of a new system with the potential to fundamentally reshape society. This was capitalism, the idea that trading goods and services in a free market controlled by private owners would generate more wealth for more people than a centralized state-run system. In his seminal 1776 work *An Inquiry into the Nature and Causes of the Wealth of Nations* (commonly referred to as *Wealth of Nations*), Adam Smith, one of the brightest stars of the Scottish Enlightenment, laid out the basis for free-market economics.

An important element of his theory was the division of labor. The idea was that a group of individuals can more efficiently accomplish a task when everyone involved is responsible for a clear part of the whole and was skilled in that particular part. As an example, Smith pointed to the manufacture of pins.

The process of pin making, Smith explains, works best when "it is divided into a number of branches," which are themselves "likewise peculiar trades."[3] For instance, "one man draws out the wire, another straights it, a third cuts it, a fourth points it, a fifth grinds it at the top for receiving the head," and so on through the packaging of the finished product.[4] This drastically increases the output of the pin factory and, by requiring a skilled pair of hands for so many different parts of the process, creates more jobs in the pin-making industry.

But this begs the question: What motivates people to manufacture pins or to show up for work at the pin factory every day? Adam Smith's answer was self-interest. In *Wealth of Nations*, he famously states, "It is not from the benevolence of the butcher, the brewer, or the baker that we expect our dinner, but from their regard to their own interest."[5] Under capitalism, their "own interest" is to improve their lives by satisfying the needs of their customers.

This self-interest, or motivation to improve your life, is the primary and most effective means for generating economic activity. This is not to say that people act only for selfish motives. A person may be motivated by any number of factors, including to support their family, to serve their community, or for the love of their craft. Doctors certainly expect to make a living from practicing medicine while improving the health of their community.

However, for Smith, the primary motive was the desire to better your circumstances. People start pin manufacturing businesses because they will make a profit, and people work in those businesses because they will earn an income to support themselves and their families. The key to Smith's approach is to both acknowledge that motive and harness it in order to improve the condition of others and to drive broad-based economic growth.

Individuals working to better themselves and their families improve economic conditions for others by providing goods and services that others find beneficial. The fact that these other individuals find the goods or services of benefit is what justifies a business's existence and keeps it alive. An individual's motive for providing goods or services may be to better their economic circumstances, but capitalism harnesses that motive to improve conditions for others as well.

To use Smith's example, we pay the butcher for our meat. The butcher in turn pays a tailor to buy a new suit who in turn pays a painter to fashion a new sign for his shop, all in concentric circles of job creation emanating out from each individual transaction. Billions upon billions of these transactions occur every day, moving and growing wealth while guiding the economy toward the preferences of the people making those purchasing decisions, in other words, toward what they believe will better their lives.

The result is an economy in which people attempt to better their circumstances by meeting the needs of society as a whole, guided by the combined economic decisions the members of that society make every day, rather than the decisions of a ruling elite.

Smith was careful to point out that most people do not go about their business conscious of the market forces around them. They usually keep their heads down, focused on increasing their own prosperity. An individual, says Smith, "neither intends to promote the public interest, nor knows how much he is promoting it." Rather, "he intends only his own gain, and he is in this, as in many other cases, led by an invisible hand to promote an end which was no part of his intention."[6]

That end, guided by Smith's famous "invisible hand," is the increased prosperity of society, brought about by a free people working to enhance their individual prosperity. This is the essence of the free-market capitalist system that the Founders put into practice and which—despite the Left's best efforts—is still humming along today.

If *Wealth of Nations* was the most significant economic document published in 1776, unquestionably the most significant political document was the United States Declaration of Independence.

In its opening, Thomas Jefferson famously asserts that government's purpose is to guarantee for the people "certain unalienable Rights, that among these are Life, Liberty and the pursuit of Happiness." The "pursuit of Happiness" is understood to include the pursuit of personal economic prosperity. Money may not buy happiness, but the Founders understood that it was certainly helpful in creating a thriving and prosperous society.

Later in the Declaration, Jefferson enumerated the reasons why King George III had failed in his duty to protect the "unalienable rights" of his American colonists. Included among the grievances were two charges that the king had politically exploited the colonists in ways that damaged their economic interests. Jefferson indicts the sovereign "for cutting off our Trade with all parts of the world" and "for imposing Taxes on us without our Consent."

The fact that both the Declaration of Independence and *Wealth of Nations* burst onto the world stage in 1776 may be one of the most provident—and profitable—coincidences in history. America's thirteen colonies rebelled against a ruling monarchical and aristocratic government because of political and economic oppression, fear of greater oppression, and the sense that Britain and her American colonies had become so different in their culture and beliefs that a separation was necessary. The British aristocratic caste system was simply unfit for the increasingly independent colonists. They sought a new system that would acknowledge and protect a free people's rights to "Life, Liberty and the pursuit of Happiness" as granted by "the Laws of Nature and of Nature's God."

Their first attempt at a unifying document was known as the Articles of Confederation, which Congress agreed to on November 15, 1777, and the states ratified on March 1, 1781. Fearing a strong central government, the Articles created a government so weak that it was unable to function effectively in many areas, including economic and financial affairs.

The central government lacked the power to enforce legislation it passed, and it had no president, executive agencies, or even a judiciary. To pay its obligations, Congress had no tax base and could only request money from the states. Its requests were generally ignored, leaving the legislature with insufficient money to run the government or to fulfill its obligations, including those to bondholders and soldiers. Both Congress and the states could regulate currency and issue money, resulting in an excess of currency, which drove down currency values and led to inflationary pressure on the Continental dollar.

Perhaps most importantly, the central government was unable to regulate interstate commerce, resulting in the states initiating their own tariffs, taxes, and disputes over navigational rights. Foreign countries were unwilling to negotiate trade agreements with the United States since the central government had no power to enforce them.

The weakness of the central government led to political unrest and economic instability, creating support among the states for a stronger central government and resulting in the Constitutional Convention of 1787.

Two years later, in 1789, these thirteen former colonies adopted a constitution establishing a republic with a centralized federal government of greater, although still limited, powers. The Constitution prohibited tariffs and taxes on interstate commerce and empowered the federal government to regulate commerce among the states and with foreign nations. The federal government could control the currency, fix standards of weights and measures, operate post offices, build roads, and establish both uniform bankruptcy laws and laws governing patents and copyrights. In effect, it formed a "common market" consisting of the thirteen former colonies (now states).

Shortly thereafter, Congress and the states added a bill of rights acknowledging certain essential individual freedoms upon which this limited government could not infringe. In addition to important personal freedoms, the Bill of Rights recognized essential economic freedoms including the right not to be deprived of property without due process of law, a prohibition on government taking private property for public use without just compensation, and the right to a jury trial in all civil cases involving more than twenty dollars.

The Constitution created a government with the power to facilitate free markets and to regulate attempts to make them less free. It encouraged innovation and risk taking by rewarding individuals for taking the risks required to make their endeavors successful without undue government meddling.

Adam Smith's *Wealth of Nations* clearly had an impact on the individuals who established this system. James Madison and Alexander Hamilton had read it. Hamilton relied on it in his *Report on Manufactures.* In 1790, shortly after the states ratified the new Constitution, Jefferson wrote in a letter to Thomas Mann Randolph that "in political economy I think Smith's *Wealth of Nations* the best book extant."[7]

Over the following several decades, free-market capitalism, combined with the rapid development of manufacturing technology during the Industrial Revolution, changed the world. The lives of ordinary people began to improve markedly as their economic influence increased.

Production of goods shifted from artisan work, affordable only by the wealthy, to factories that produced large quantities of affordable goods for the masses. Many people were able to find good employment in these factories, and thereby gain more individual purchasing power with their wages.

The Industrial Revolution—and the capitalist system that drove it—have received criticism for this shift toward mass production (remember Smith's hypothetical pin factory), but the important change was that the economy was now driven by mass production for *all* rather than limited production for the wealthy. The economy produced more goods and services, employed more people, and provided more people the access (and the purchasing power) to buy them.

As the American economy grew, the power of its consumer class also grew. Consumers—not a privileged class—were increasingly making decisions through their collective purchasing power that would direct economic benefits. Those decisions would guide the economy, determining whether one business succeeded and another failed. The balance of economic power flipped. Those who ran the economic engines became subject to the desires of that greatly expanded consumer class.

That balance is maintained to this day. When Henry Ford began mass-producing automobiles on his assembly lines, he wasn't making them for royalty. He made the Model T for the common man and woman. Steve Jobs didn't produce iPhones as a rarified gadget for aristocrats; he made them for the masses. Whether it's Richard Sears and the Sears Catalog in the late 1800s or Jeff Bezos and Amazon.com today, the idea isn't to provide easy access to goods for the wealthy; it is to provide access for everyone.

Rather than impoverished masses serving a ruling elite, that ruling class now found itself concerned with finding the best way to please the masses. The masses, in turn, benefitted from this newfound economic power. It is especially ironic then that Progressives, who claim to be fighting on behalf of the people, continually undermine the only system that puts real economic power in the hands of the people, in favor of a system that transfers that power to government elites.

More freedoms came along with the growth of the free market. As industry and commerce spread across the northeastern United States and free-market capitalism flourished, it became increasingly clear that human slavery had no place in this new economic order. In 1794, five years after the Constitution's ratification, Congress passed the Slave Trade Act, the first of several acts that would outlaw the slave trade in the United States. As the abolitionist movement grew, most of the northern states outlawed slavery in the years preceding the Civil War.

Unfortunately, the American South developed quite differently. As the cotton industry came to dominate the regional economy, the demand for slaves grew. In an economic system resembling the European feudal system, a privileged, almost aristocratic class owned the great plantations on which the Southern economy depended. It would take a brutal war and a constitutional amendment in 1865 to assure the end of slavery in the United States.

Nonetheless, over time, members of every class in the United States became patrons, buyers, and consumers who, in an economic form of democracy, voted with every dollar they spent. People were no longer restrained by the whims of an aristocratic hierarchy whose members felt entitled to rule based on military might or the accident of their birth, as had been the case in Europe for so many centuries.

This isn't to say that the upper economic class disappeared. Rather, the qualifications for entering that class changed. In America, it wasn't birth or political influence alone that could propel you into the upper class (although political influence is always a plus). You could now join the ranks of the wealthy by figuring out what consumers wanted and providing it to them more effectively and efficiently than your competition. Where you were from was no longer as important as where you were going.

By unleashing the power of the will to succeed, capitalism also encouraged innovation among all classes of society, with people from all walks of life devoting their energies to enterprise in their quest to come up with the next big thing. Adam Smith's invisible hand was lifting people from poverty to prosperity in ways the oppressive, centralized rule of monarchs never could.

The release of this dynamic entrepreneurial energy in the United States resulted in the most innovative society the world has ever seen. America's entrepreneurs created more wealth and spread it across broader demographics than any nation that ever existed. By the late 1800s, barely over a hundred years after America's founding, these former backwoods colonies became the world's largest economy, the most desired destination for immigrants from across the globe, and a living testament to the wisdom in Adam Smith's *Wealth of Nations.*

America's Self-Made Men and Women

At least part of the credit for America's stunning economic growth and prosperity goes to the self-made men and women who forged new businesses that met consumers' needs, increasing both their personal wealth and the prosperity of the nation as a whole. Cornelius Vanderbilt represents the first generation of America's homegrown success stories.

Vanderbilt was born in Staten Island, New York, in 1794. He was descended from the area's early Dutch settlers. His first ancestor in America, Jan Aertsen, arrived in what was then known as New Amsterdam in 1650. Aertsen was beyond poor. He was an indentured servant to a wealthy Dutch settler family, and he had to spend three years working for them before being freed to pursue his own path. According to Harvard professor Henry Louis Gates, Jr., Aertsen probably added "van der Bilt" to his name to signify that he was "from the town of Bilt" in Holland.[8]

Cornelius Vanderbilt's own father was a farmer who also ran a small ferryboat operation between Staten Island and Manhattan. Neither the farm nor the ferry was very profitable, so the family was poor. Vanderbilt left school early—he was only eleven years old—and dove headfirst into the family business.

In 1810, when he was just sixteen years old, Vanderbilt bought his own boat and became a ferryman. According to one account, he made the purchase with a loan from his parents, promising them a stake in his operation. At sixteen, Vanderbilt was a budding capitalist, and he was able to both repay their loan and provide them $1,000 as their share in his profits.[9]

Two years later, when the War of 1812 broke out, the military set up defensive positions all around New York City. Vanderbilt made a bundle transporting supplies for the soldiers as his ferry service grew significantly.

By 1818, Vanderbilt's business was humming along nicely, but he saw change on the horizon. The steamship was overtaking the sailboat as the seagoing transportation of the future, and Vanderbilt knew he had to adapt. But he couldn't break into the business on his own, so he partnered with Thomas Gibbons, another local ferryman.

For more than a decade, Vanderbilt worked with Gibbons and learned the steamship business inside and out; he earned serious money along the way. But just like his decision to leave his father's apprenticeship, Vanderbilt broke off from Gibbons in 1829, establishing his own steamship line along the Hudson River. By offering fast, comfortable transport at a fraction of the cost of his competitors, Vanderbilt soon grew to serve ports in Rhode Island and Connecticut, and by the 1840s, his line of one hundred steamships was the largest employer in the country.[10]

Some years later, he felt the winds of change once again. He had achieved considerable success carrying prospectors to California during the Gold Rush of 1849, helping transform California from a sparsely populated territory into the Golden State. But Vanderbilt could see that steamship transportation was going to have a hard time competing with an up-and-coming ground transport method: the railroad. He started buying up railroad lines and combining them under his control, reportedly earning $25 million in five years.[11]

While Vanderbilt made a fortune in transportation, his contribution to our prosperity as a nation is undeniable. His shipping and railroad endeavors created thousands of jobs and literally made America mobile, enabling billions of dollars in trade. His rails played a major role in forming the iron backbone of a burgeoning nation.

Vanderbilt's success also bred success for others. Historians Mike Wallace and Edwin Burrows remarked that a single railroad terminal Vanderbilt constructed in Manhattan brought in some two hundred additional businesses, attracting commerce to it like a "gigantic magnet."[12]

Business concerns did not stop him from coming to the aid of his country. In 1862, he lent his best steamship (named for himself) to the Union Navy at President Lincoln's request.[13]

In 1869, he stepped in to provide capital when Wall Street found itself on the brink of a crisis in the gold market. This, according to writer Martin Morse Wooster, "may well have saved the United States from a major financial crisis."[14]

His last major project was the building of Grand Central Station in New York City, a lasting memorial to his railroad interests.

When he died in 1877, his worth was about $100 million, or about one-ninth of the money circulating in the United States at the time.[15]

Could Cornelius's father, the poor farmer and ferry operator, ever have imagined his son soaring to such heights? Going even further back, what would his indentured-servant ancestor Jan Aertsen Van der Bilt have thought? Since Aertsen's arrival in America, as Professor Gates notes, "in about five generations, the Vanderbilts would go from having nothing to having everything."[16] The American system allowed Cornelius Vanderbilt to rise far above the circumstances of his birth and family background by working harder and smarter than his competitors.

While it was impressive that the Vanderbilts rose from indentured servitude to massive wealth over five generations, more impressive still was the ingenuity, drive, and meteoric success of another American who, some decades later, rose from far worse: Sarah Breedlove, who would become known to history—and to millions of cosmetics users—as Madam C. J. Walker.

In 1867, when Cornelius Vanderbilt was entering his last decade, a baby girl was born into circumstances about as far from Vanderbilt's opulent New York world as one could imagine. Sarah Breedlove was born in Delta, Louisiana, on a cotton plantation—the same plantation on which the owners had, until recently, enslaved her parents. Now they worked the land for pay, but their financial lot had barely improved. Sarah was the last of her parents' children, and the only one to be born free. She was to make the most of her freedom in ways few could have imagined.

Her early life was difficult. She only went to school for three months, spending most of her time, even as a child, working in the cotton fields. When she was only seven years old, her parents died, and the orphaned Breedlove went to live with her sister and brother-in-law. The brother-in-law was abusive, and Sarah could only stand seven years of his mistreatment before she married at the age of fourteen "to get a home of my own," as she put it.[17]

She and her husband had one child, a daughter, born when Breedlove was seventeen years old. Shortly thereafter, her husband died. She was now a single black female raising a child in an area with few economic opportunities. She had been working as a washerwoman, cook, or a servant for much of her life. There were many threats to an African American's safety in the deep South since white supremacist organizations had arisen in the area after the Civil War. Violence against African Americans was rampant, and the victims were left with little recourse. Like many Americans, she recognized the power of and felt the need for a fresh start.

She found that fresh start in St. Louis, Missouri, where she arrived in 1888 with her young daughter in tow. She had brothers living there, and she found a welcoming African American community. But for several years, she still was stuck doing laundry.

Though the work was steady, Breedlove, who entered into a short-lived second marriage in St. Louis, was still looking for more. In the early years of the twentieth century, she found a new opportunity with another African American woman named Annie Pope-Turnbo, who sold hair care products through her St. Louis–based company. Breedlove joined the company and started working in sales. Soon, in 1905, she was sent to Denver to expand Pope-Turnbo's operation.[18]

The following year marked a major shift in her personal and professional life: a man she met in St. Louis, C. J. Walker, joined her in Denver. They married, and she left Pope-Turnbo's company, going into business for herself.

After taking her new husband's name, she created a personal brand, Madam C. J. Walker, and began aggressively selling her "Wonderful Hair Grower." She was a genius at product promotion, according to Harvard's Dr. Henry Louis Gates, Jr., who notes that "in pumping her 'Wonderful Hair Grower' door-to-door, at churches and club gatherings, then through a mail-order catalog, Walker proved to be a marketing magician."

She also clearly understood her market, consisting mostly of African American women like herself. "She sold her customers more than mere hair products," Gates explains. "She offered them a lifestyle, a concept of total hygiene and beauty that in her mind would bolster them with pride for advancement."[19] In just a year's time, Walker, who had earned about $300 in a year of doing laundry, was making that much every month as an entrepreneur.[20]

Over the next few years, Madam C. J. Walker's business thrived and expanded. She recruited thousands of other African American women to join her sales force, setting up a marketing model that presaged the type still used by Mary Kay or Avon cosmetics today. And she took care of her workers. Dr. Gates points out that "at a time when unskilled white workers earned about $11 a week, Walker's agents were making $5 to $15 a day."[21] In 1910, she relocated operations to Indianapolis and set up her own manufacturing facility.[22]

She was also willing to share the secrets of her success with others. Intent on advancing African American society however she could, she donated generously to charitable causes.

When Booker T. Washington convened the Thirteenth Annual Convention of the National Negro Business League in 1912, Walker was not invited to speak—nor were any women—but she showed up anyway and, taking the stage, made an impromptu address to the crowd. "Surely you are not going to shut the door in my face," she proclaimed. "I am a woman who started in business seven years ago with only $1.50. . . . This year (up to the 19th day of this month . . .) I had taken in $18,000."[23] She was met with "prolonged applause."

The next year, the same group clearly learned their lesson and gave Walker a speaking slot. She advised the attendees that it "pays to be honest and straightforward in all your dealings" and especially reminded the black women in the audience to "not be afraid to take hold of a business endeavor and, by patient industry, close economy, determined effort, and close application to business, wring success out of a number of business opportunities that lie at their doors."[24] All good business advice for anyone, anytime, anywhere.

When Madam C. J. Walker (who had divorced her husband but kept the name that had become her brand) died in 1919, the *New York Times* reported that "estimates of Mrs. Walker's fortune had run up to $1,000,000."[25] She has been called "America's first black female millionaire—and the first woman of any race to become a self-made millionaire," but those precise details are difficult to pin down.[26] Another estimate says her personal net worth at the time of her death was about $600,000, though today that would be closer to $6 million.[27] We do know that when she died, Walker presided over a business empire with today's equivalent of $3 million in annual revenues.

By any measure, Madam C. J. Walker's rise from impoverished beginnings one generation removed from slavery to become a successful entrepreneur shows the openness and universality of the American capitalist system. Walker sought to build a better life for herself and her daughter, and she made the most of the opportunities that allowed her to achieve that. She learned a business working for someone else, then went into the same business for herself, created jobs for others, and found even greater personal success. She cultivated a strategy and team to support her goals and died a prosperous cosmetology tycoon.

The stories of Cornelius Vanderbilt and Madam C. J. Walker should inspire every American. They show that no matter where you come from, in America anyone can make it.

Some would cynically scoff at that idea, or say that the game has changed, that we're not a meritocracy anymore, or that the system is rigged. I simply don't believe that. I know our system works because it worked for me, and before that, for my family.

The story of the Puzder family certainly is not as dramatic as those of Vanderbilt or Walker, but it nonetheless reflects the American tradition of building prosperity over generations. I offer it not by way of comparison but as a personal, if less impressive, example of the opportunities our nation still affords those willing to work hard and take risks.

My grandfather grew up in the years before World War I in what is now Slovakia, at that time a far-flung corner of the Austro-Hungarian Empire. While in the United States the Vanderbilts were prospering and Madam C. J. Walker's company was dominating its industry, the capitalist revolution had largely ignored his part of the world.

In his homeland, economic patterns that had defined so much of Europe for so long had managed to endure into the twentieth century. Ruling from the Hapsburgs Emperors' dynastic capital in Vienna, aristocrats still held all government power and controlled most of the wealth. The economy was firmly in the aristocracy's hands. The desires of the commoners—the class to which my grandfather was born—were ignored if not disdained.

For families like his, the opportunity to improve your life was virtually nonexistent. His future was all but preordained. Assuming he survived World War I, he would live as a peasant, lucky to eke out a living as a serf beholden to a landed aristocrat. But, by the early 1900s, there was a nation where even a peasant from Slovakia could have a chance at a better future. As a teenager, he left his home and headed to America.

He came with two simple dreams: to own a home of his own and to see that his children received the education he never had. These may seem like small dreams today, but they were huge dreams at the time. By the end of his life, he had fulfilled them both. He owned his own home in Cleveland, Ohio, and both of his children were attending school.

One of those children, my father, saw combat in Europe during World War II before returning home to become a Ford car salesman and raise a family of his own. He worked hard at it and provided well for his family. The five of us lived in a little ranch house outside of Cleveland. We were a typical working-class family. We were not rich by any stretch of the imagination, but we were not doing too badly considering we were just one generation removed from serfdom in the Old World.

It was through my father's job that I was inspired to work even harder and go even farther. Around 1960, when I was about ten years old, I rode with him to deliver a car to a very wealthy customer. This gentleman, named Mr. Humphrey, lived in a suburb on the east side of Cleveland called Hunting Valley, which was, and still is, one of the wealthiest areas in the United States. We only lived a few miles away, but I was about to learn that we lived in another world.

We pulled through the ornate iron gate, and I immediately saw a big, beautiful house that dwarfed the little ranch house where my family lived. I was in awe but surprised when my father didn't slow down and simply drove past. When I asked why he didn't stop, he said, "That's the guest house."

We continued up the drive, past another impressive building that turned out to be the stables. Mr. Humphrey's horses appeared to have more living space than my family.

Finally, we pulled up to the main house, which was stunning not only in grandeur but also in sheer size. It was unlike anything I'd ever seen. We walked up to the main entrance. I'm not sure what I was expecting—a butler in a tuxedo?—but Mr. Humphrey, who knew and liked my father, came to the door himself. He took the keys to the new Ford, thanked my father, and handed over the keys to the car he was trading in.

As we walked over to the car, I took a last look around the estate. I was still dumbfounded. Where had all this wealth come from? So, I asked my father what Mr. Humphrey did. "He's a lawyer," my father replied, "and he runs a business."

I can still remember thinking, "A lawyer? I could be a

lawyer." Although I was admittedly unsure what exactly a lawyer was, I had a feeling it was something attainable. If Mr. Humphrey was a lawyer, maybe I could become one. So naturally, my next question to my father was, "What's a lawyer?"

Looking back on my first direct experience with real wealth, I can still remember what I felt, but I've also come to appreciate the importance of what I *didn't* feel. My first reaction wasn't to resent Mr. Humphrey or deride him as part of an evil one percent. I didn't feel like we deserved some of his money just because his guests—and indeed, his horses—had a nicer place to live than I did. That thought never even occurred to me.

On the contrary, rather than thinking Mr. Humphrey had taken something from me, I wanted to know what I needed to do to *get* something for myself. I felt like I could do it. Luckily, I lived in a nation where I could. I didn't know it, but the invisible hand had just given me its first nudge.

There has never been another nation in the history of the world where a kid from a working-class family could even have the slimmest chance of reaching those heights. I knew I wanted to become a lawyer and I knew I would have to work hard to get there. The road was neither glamorous nor easily traveled. But, unlike the world where my grandfather grew up, there was a road.

The first job where I earned a paycheck was at Baskin-Robbins, scooping ice cream for about $1 per hour, the minimum wage at the time. While I never expected to support myself or a family with that entry-level job, I learned a lot that would benefit me throughout my career, such as the importance of showing up on time, working as part of a team, how to best serve customers, and the importance to a business of managing costs and inventory.

One of the proudest days of my professional career was the day the franchisee who owned that business called me into her office and handed me a key. She gave me a raise of 10¢ an hour and told me I was now the assistant manager. I could open and close the ice cream shop when I worked those shifts.

When I opened that door the next morning, I felt like I owned the place. My guess is that, within about half an hour, it was the cleanest Baskin-Robbins in America. Although, in retrospect, it was a small achievement, at the time I felt a level of accomplishment and self-respect that's hard to describe unless you've been there. It's the kind of self-respect that keeps you working, in school, off the streets, and out of trouble.

I went on to work my way through college and law school while supporting my young family without financial help from my family or the government. I worked at whatever jobs I could find. Among other things, I painted houses, cut lawns, played in bands, managed a music studio, and even busted up concrete with a jackhammer in the St. Louis summer heat.

All the while, I knew there were no artificial barriers to my dreams of a better future as a lawyer. I never imagined that legal work would lead me into the restaurant business, where I was able to carve out a successful career as a CEO at an international corporation. Because of the opportunities open to me as an American, like Mr. Humphrey and inspired by his success, I actually became a lawyer who ran a business.

But this is much bigger than me, and it goes back long before me. If not for the opportunities of our free-market economy, my grandfather might not have made the journey to the United States, leaving his home and family behind. He could have stayed home, which would mean that I would have ended up a bald and toothless farmer sitting on a porch in Slovakia. Instead, I was able to become a CEO and was even nominated by the President of the United States to serve in his cabinet. My grandfather would never have imagined that in a million years.

Despite what some in the media and on the Left might want you to believe, many CEOs rose from humble economic backgrounds. Many have stories like mine. They come from families of hard workers and are certainly hard workers themselves. Many exemplify the fact that America is a historically unique nation with an economic system that promises everyone the opportunity to realize their dreams, achieve their goals, and earn their success unrestrained by a ruling government elite.

Preserving that system also requires political leaders who understand its value. For most of America's history, there have been such political leaders, often due to their humble upbringings. The founders of both the Democratic and the Republican parties serve as good examples.

Andrew Jackson was the first US president to come from outside the ranks of the planter elite or urban gentry. Jackson's origins were so obscure that his exact birthplace, somewhere in the border region between North and South Carolina, is still a matter of controversy.[28] He taught himself the law and went on to success in the military, business, and politics becoming the seventh US president.

An imperfect but determined man, Jackson founded the Democratic Party, fought to preserve the Union, and is to this day associated with "Jacksonian Democracy"—the transition to greater democracy, a transfer of power to the common voter, and opposition to any signs of aristocracy.

In 1833, President Jackson appointed a young man named Abraham Lincoln as postmaster of the town of New Salem, Illinois. Lincoln was just twenty-four years old, and like Jackson, taught himself the law despite having little in the way of formal education. He grew up working on the family farm, splitting rails and reading in his spare time. In fact, his postmaster position paid so little that he continued to split rails and do odd jobs just to earn enough to get by.[29]

The previous year, Lincoln had lost a race for the Illinois state legislature. The following year, he ran again and won, launching a political career that would lead to one of the greatest presidencies in our nation's history. To this day, the Republican Party is known as "The Party of Lincoln."

Leaders who came from the backwoods like Jackson and Lincoln grew up with the frontier ethos that respected self-made success stories and understood the mind-set that built this country. The United States has since had many presidents, such as Calvin Coolidge, Harry Truman, and Ronald Reagan, who rose from humble beginnings and exhibited an understanding of the promise that has made America a great nation.

Unfortunately, Americans have lost sight of that promise in recent years. President Barack Obama certainly deserves credit for rising from his own difficult background as the son of a single mother, yet he was fortunate enough to receive an elite private education and has spent nearly his entire adult life in politics or academia.

Is it any wonder, then, that a president with little experience in the entrepreneurial American capitalist system—and even a suspicion of that system gained from an education in leftist ideas—campaigned first on a promise to "spread the wealth around" and then later told business owners "you didn't build that"? Furthermore, is it any wonder that he presided over this nation's worst average yearly GDP growth since World War II?[30]

Donald Trump did not come from the sort of hardscrabble upbringing that produced leaders like Jackson and Lincoln, but the story of how he got where he is certainly has parallels with some of the other successful Americans we've met in this chapter.

His grandfather was the first in his family to make his way to America. Friedrich Trump arrived in New York from Germany in 1885, the son of a widowed mother. Trump's only training was as a barber.[31] His first job was cutting hair, as he'd done in Germany, and like Madam C. J. Walker's brothers had in St. Louis.

He sought his fortune out west, opening restaurants in mining camps to serve prospectors looking for riches. It was a rough-and-tumble atmosphere, and these establishments were hardly temples of virtue, but they made Friedrich Trump good money. By the time he died, he had settled back in New York City and left $500,000 to his son, Fred.[32]

Fred Trump, of course, made his name in New York real estate and passed on the business to his son Donald, an inheritance he turned into a global economic powerhouse before winning the US presidency on a populist platform.

Jackson, Vanderbilt, Lincoln, Walker, and Trump all attest to the reality that, in America, where you're going is far more important than where you're from. If you're willing to put in the work, you will have the opportunity to make a better life for yourself, and an even *better* one for the next generation. That's the essence of our system, a system Adam Smith explained and the earliest citizens of our republic put into practice. My family and I have been blessed to be a part of this system.

Freedom and Opportunity at Risk

America was the first nation to offer millions of people—including immigrants reaching for a better life, the children of former slaves, and people from the humblest of beginnings—a realistic opportunity to make a better life for themselves and their families. There were barriers to success, there always are, but in America, opportunity was no longer solely dependent on membership in a class of elites. Success was determined not solely by your birth but rather by your desire to work harder, longer, or smarter than your competitor.

For nearly 250 years now, that attitude has informed the American way of life. But today, this may be changing. Those on the Left are working diligently to retake the power that capitalism seized from the government at our nation's founding. They would denigrate those who have succeeded and empower a ruling class of elites to guide our lives and redistribute our wealth.

Our liberties and freedoms are increasingly threatened. The Left's convictions that America is not exceptional, that individuals cannot succeed on their own, that success should be envied rather than emulated, or that wealth should be an object of shame rather than aspiration are gaining ascendancy. If these convictions legitimately rise in the national consciousness, we are at risk of destroying the American promise of opportunity free from government oppression that has kept America truly exceptional.

Once it's gone, it's not coming back.

CHAPTER THREE

The Great American Boom and the Progressives' War on Profit

> *"[T]he same revolutionary beliefs for which our forebears fought are still at issue around the globe—the belief that the rights of man come not from the generosity of the state but from the hand of God."*
>
> JOHN F. KENNEDY, *INAUGURAL ADDRESS*

A "Gilded Age" in the Aftermath of War

Ironically, the Progressive threat to America's capitalist system grew not from its failure but from a time during which the United States experienced the most sweeping improvement in the human condition the world has ever known. While Progressives would derogatorily label it "The Gilded Age," this period of unsurpassed growth and opportunity stands as a testament to capitalism's remarkable ability to generate widespread prosperity. This so-called "Gilded Age" is all the more remarkable because of the ruins from which it arose.

At the end of the American Civil War, the United States was at a crossroads. The war had torn the country apart and shaken its very foundation. A mere three generations after the former colonies ratified the Constitution, there was a very real question about whether the American system would survive. Could the concepts of God-given rights and limited government that the Founders so skillfully bound together in the Constitution survive the carnage on the fields of Shiloh, Antietam, and Gettysburg?

Abraham Lincoln understood what was at stake. In 1863, four and a half months after Union forces defeated the Confederacy at the Battle of Gettysburg, Lincoln delivered one of the most memorable speeches in our nation's history. He began with the iconic phrase "Four score and seven years ago," acknowledging the 1776 signing of the Declaration of Independence. He stressed the importance and vulnerability of our underlying ideals as a nation "conceived in liberty and dedicated to the proposition that all men are created equal," noting that the Civil War had tested "whether that nation or any nation so conceived and so dedicated can long endure."

Though the conflict was domestic in nature, Lincoln recognized the Civil War's implications for freedom worldwide. In the last sentence of this speech, he called on Americans to be "highly resolved" so "that government of the people, by the people, for the people, shall not perish from the earth." Had this American experiment in liberty and limited government perished from the earth so soon after its founding, Europe's aristocracies would have taken great comfort knowing their class-based system could endure now that the experiment in freedom and self-government across the sea had failed.

Of course, the American people would deprive them of that comfort.

Following the Civil War, Congress and the states ratified constitutional amendments abolishing slavery and empowering the federal government to protect essential civil rights from state infringement. This ended slavery in the South. It would take generations to remove the vestiges of that system, but there was now a legal foundation upon which all citizens could realize the American Revolution's potential.

Lincoln resolved to reintegrate the vanquished Confederate states and their citizens into the Union. The task, as he put it, was to "bind up the nation's wounds," guided by the principles of "malice toward none" and "charity for all." But the question remained: Even though the Union had survived, could the country recover?

As it turned out, the answer was an emphatic yes (and then some).

The Greatest Economic Surge in History

After the Civil War, the spirit of Adam Smith was unleashed on the nation his ideas helped inspire, and the American economy grew at an unprecedented rate.

The two decades following the Civil War—the 1870s and 1880s—were the most prosperous in our nation's entire history.[1] The combined wealth of all Americans amounted to $16 billion in 1860. By 1900, it shot up to $88 billion. By the outbreak of World War I, the United States was the world's richest nation, and Americans enjoyed the highest standard of living anywhere on the planet.[2]

Market forces operated at an almost fever pitch, performing their delicate dance with a precision and controlled frenzy that Smith himself could scarcely have imagined. According to Professor C. Bradley Thompson of Ashland University, "industrial and technological advances in the means of production that are the consequence of freedom, voluntary exchange and the entrepreneurial spirit" were responsible for this incredible economic growth and the resulting improvement in American's standard of living.[3] In other words, government stayed out of the way for the most part and allowed businesses to succeed, making life better for everyone.

In fact, rather than regulating growth, government had a positive role in facilitating it. In 1862, President Lincoln signed the Homestead Act, accelerating the settlement of lands in the West by granting 160 acres to adult heads of households, who would own the land after five years of continuously residing on and cultivating it.[4] But to settle those lands people had to get there and, to facilitate commerce, they had to get their goods to markets. Railroads were the solution to both problems.

Railroads, such as those financed by Cornelius Vanderbilt, spread across the country, enabling the passage of goods and people in numbers and at speeds few had ever anticipated. Government facilitated this growth. In 1862, Congress passed the Pacific Railway Act, which authorized the construction of a transcontinental railroad.[5] The first railroad joining the East and West Coasts was completed seven years later on May 10, 1869. Prior to 1871, there were approximately 45,000 miles of railroad track in the US. By 1900, there were an additional 170,000 miles and four more transcontinental railroads.[6]

With more people owning land and having access to ever-increasing markets, there was a real need for improved agricultural technology. In 1836, Congress passed the Patent Act, which created the federal Patent Office. The act eased the patent process and incentivized innovators, who could more readily benefit from new inventions.[7] The following year, the US Patent Office issued 436 patents. By 1900, that annual number grew to 24,656.[8]

The positive impact of technical innovation was tremendous. For example, in 1830, it took approximately 250 to 300 labor-hours to produce 100 bushels (five acres) of wheat. By 1890, the hours required declined to 40 to 50 labor-hours.[9]

More farmers were producing more crops and reaching broader markets thanks to federal land grants, improved rail transportation, and technological innovations. This allowed America's farmers to feed a burgeoning population that more than doubled from 31.5 million in 1860 to 76.2 million by 1900.[10]

Fewer people had to grow their own food, and with the robust expansion of America's manufacturing sector, massive numbers of people found employment in burgeoning industrial centers. In 1869, 1.8 million Americans were employed in factories. By 1909, that number had climbed to 6.3 million—4.5 million additional factory workers in just forty years.[11]

These rapid changes brought great improvements in the lives of ordinary Americans. Wages for unskilled laborers shot up 44 percent between the Civil War and World War I.[12] Per capita income more than doubled, jumping from $500 to $1,100 between 1860 and 1900.[13]

American dollars were also going further than ever before as inflation dropped in the Civil War's wake. Prices on consumer goods steadily decreased by about 1 percent each year until the 1890s.[14]

Americans were working hard, getting paid better for it, and stretching their dollars further. Furthermore, more efficient production methods combined with market and political pressure resulted in workers spending less time on the job. In 1850, Americans averaged 11.5 hours per day at work. By 1900, that was down to 9.8 hours, and in 1920, it dropped further to 8.5 hours, where it has basically held for most American workers ever since.[15]

Eager to take advantage of this rapidly rising tide of American prosperity, another great wave of immigrants came to the United States in the late nineteenth and early twentieth centuries. Tens of millions made the trip, mostly from Ireland and southern and eastern Europe. My own grandfather and two of his brothers were among the latter.

My grandfather's older brother Joe arrived in 1902, nine months after an anarchist had assassinated President William McKinley. Joe was eighteen years old. While my grandfather died before I was born, my great-uncle Joe lived to age ninety-one, passing away in 1975. I can still recall sitting in his farmhouse, listening to the Cleveland Indians on the radio, and hearing stories about his and his brothers' early years in America. How stunned they were by the energy, the abundance of consumer goods, food, and opportunity. You could almost hear the youthful optimism in his voice as he described the struggles he gladly faced and the life he was able to build.

All three brothers settled in Cleveland, Ohio, one of the largest cities in America and an emerging manufacturing center. They worked in factories or construction, earning livings unimaginable in their homeland. They earned enough to buy homes, also unimaginable in their homeland. (Uncle Joe eventually bought a forty-acre farm east of Cleveland near Chagrin Falls.) They raised families. Even as America's population grew, unskilled immigrants who spoke little or no English—like the members of my family—could earn an honest wage and go about the business of becoming Americans.[16]

In their efforts to undermine American free-market capitalism, Progressives would label this seemingly boundless era of prosperity as "the Gilded Age." From the moment Mark Twain introduced it as the title of a novel, that term has been laced with sarcasm. In the popular vision of the Gilded Age, a handful of super-rich "plutocrats" enjoyed a "gilded" existence they unjustly obtained thanks to the sweat and toil of the overworked and underpaid working class.

In this image, the overwhelming evidence that wages and standards of living rose dramatically—thanks, in great part, to the efforts of these entrepreneurs—has no place. It is inconsistent with the "class war" narrative that makes such a saleable story for Progressive politicians and institutions. My great-uncle Joe would have found that narrative unrecognizable.

To this day, so-called "respectable" news outlets regularly publish hand-wringing "think pieces" that peddle this false narrative, asking if America has entered "a new Gilded Age" fraught with income inequality. Given the benefits of an expanded economy for ordinary Americans in the original Gilded Age, one wonders whether a second one would really be so bad. So why was the "Gilded Age" seized upon as a sarcastic descriptor for a period in which Americans across the board saw their economic situation materially improve?

THE RISE OF THE PROGRESSIVES

For this, we can thank a group of academics and politicians whose response to America's unprecedented economic growth of the late nineteenth and early twentieth centuries was fear and resentment. They sprang into action with a flurry of reforms from around the 1880s until about 1920. They had different ideas but were united in their desire to expand government and restrain private enterprise.

This group was called the Progressives.

According to professors Ronald Pestritto of Hillsdale College and William Atto of the University of Dallas, Progressives felt the proper response to the massive economic and social changes going on around them was to "enlarge vastly the scope of national government."[17] Progressives believed they faced problems that "could not have been envisioned at the founding and for which the founders' limited, constitutional government was inadequate."[18] Their solution was to "progress, or to move beyond, the political principles of the American founding"—to reject the very principles that made our nation great.[19]

America's Progressives were not the first to respond to industrialization and economic growth with panicked attempts to expand government's reach and influence. The vanguard in this effort had already emerged: the socialists in Europe and the version of socialism distilled by Karl Marx, which he termed "communism." Communism's foundational text, *The Communist Manifesto,* appeared in 1848. It was a reaction to the first wave of industrialization that had swept Europe in the decades prior.

For Marx, "the modern bourgeois society that [had] sprouted from the ruins of feudal society [had] not done away with class antagonisms." Rather, it had "established new classes, new conditions of oppression, new forms of struggle in place of the old ones."[20] Marx defined the dreaded "bourgeoisie" as "the class of modern capitalists, owners of the means of social production and employers of wage labor."[21] Essentially, Marx felt that anyone who owned a business, the "bourgeois" capitalists, had become feudal lords themselves.

Of course, Marx believed that he had a solution: communism. "The theory of Communism," he declared, "may be summed up in the single phrase: Abolition of private property."[22] Instead, the state should own the "means of production," that is, all businesses and industries. This simple sounding solution would result in poverty, despair, tyranny, and death for the next 170 years.

While not every Progressive was a socialist or communist, there were always commonalities.

President Woodrow Wilson was one of America's earliest and most influential Progressives. His rejection of our nation's founding principles of individual liberty and economic freedom protected by limited government remain the Progressive's intellectual bulwark. A Progressive academic long before he entered politics, Wilson saw little daylight between socialism and democracy.

In his 1887 essay entitled *Socialism and Democracy,* Wilson argued that "in fundamental theory socialism and democracy are almost if not quite one and the same."[23] He claimed that the difference between them was "not an essential difference, but only a practical difference... a difference of organization and policy, not a difference of primary motive."[24]

Wilson believed Progressives could achieve socialist ends by democratic means through what he termed "state socialism." Wilson described the "thesis of the state socialist" as a recognition "that no line can be drawn between private and public affairs which the State may not cross at will; that omnipotence of legislation is the first postulate of all just political theory."[25]

Wilson's capitalization of "State" may have been a rhetorical flourish, but that hardly makes it any less ominous. Far more disturbing was his idea that government can meddle in any private affairs at will, and that legislation is omnipotent. This was a complete disavowal of our founding principles.

While the Founders viewed government as necessary to secure our liberty, they established a limited government with specifically enumerated powers because they also viewed government as a potential threat to liberty. As James Madison wrote, "If men were angels, no government would be necessary." Government is necessary because otherwise "the weaker individual is not secured against the violence of the stronger." According to Madison, the challenge lies in the fact that "you must first enable the government to control the governed; and in the next place oblige it to control itself" so as not to infringe on its citizen's God-given rights.[26]

An essential element of this view is the belief that God and natural law, not government, endow man's existence and grant him rights. The first sentence of the Declaration of Independence acknowledges its reliance on "the Laws of Nature and of Nature's God." Rather than creating liberty, government—a limited government—is necessary to secure our God-given rights.

The Progressives rejected this natural-law approach to human rights as more myth than reality, believing the state, rather than God, creates freedom. Because they viewed the state as supreme, they no longer regarded the freedom that energizes capitalism as something government was obliged to protect. Rather, Progressives viewed the private sector as a source of greed and oppression to be regulated and controlled.

This approach obviously flew in the face of both the ideals in the Declaration of Independence and the limited government with enumerated powers our Constitution created. Progressives required a new understanding of both the Declaration and the Constitution to empower the government, which the founding documents were specifically intended to limit. Wilson was ready and willing to offer them one.

According to Wilson, the Declaration of Independence "did not mention the questions of our day," rendering it "of no consequence to us."[27] He sought to discredit the Declaration's underlying assumptions, stating that "a great deal of nonsense has been talked about the inalienable rights of the individual, and a great deal that was mere vague sentiment and pleasing speculation has been put forward as fundamental principle."[28]

This is a far cry from Lincoln's belief that the Declaration's timeless principles resulted in a nation "conceived in liberty and dedicated to the proposition that all men are created equal." The Declaration's bold affirmation that individuals "are endowed by their Creator with certain unalienable Rights," including the rights to "Life, Liberty and the pursuit of Happiness," certainly seems like more than "vague sentiment and pleasing speculation." On the contrary, the Declaration "holds these truths to be self-evident." Jefferson could have written solely about the need to replace a despotic king with a just one (the issue of his day), leaving off the notion of inalienable rights, but he didn't.

So, if you think Wilson's views sound like a rejection of America's founding principles, you're right.

In fact, Wilson is credited with being "the first prominent thinker to argue that the founders' constitutional system was obsolete and needed to be radically altered."[29] He rejected the notion that "the ideal of government was for every man to be left alone and not interfered with, except when he interfered with somebody else; and that the best government was the government that did as little governing as possible."[30]

Rather, he believed "the law has to step in and create new conditions under which we may live." For Wilson, the constitutional protections that limited government power and secured both our individual liberty and economic freedom rendered the government unable to deal with contemporary problems.

Wilson opened his first major work *Congressional Government,* published in 1885, with an almost prideful questioning of the Constitution's relevance: "We are the first Americans to hear our own countrymen ask whether the Constitution is still adapted to serve the purposes for which it was intended; the first to entertain any serious doubts about the superiority of our own institutions as compared with the systems of Europe."[31]

Wilson was wondering whether the very systems European immigrants were fleeing by the millions might be superior to the American system to which they were flocking. Apparently, liberals looking to Europe with doubts about American exceptionalism is nothing new. I wish they could sit down and discuss the subject with my uncle Joe.

Wilson concludes *Congressional Government* by arguing that

the "constitution is not honored by blind worship." Rather, we should be "more open-eyed... to its defects." We should apply "with the unhesitating courage of conviction all thoroughly-tested or well-considered expedients necessary to make self-government among us a straightforward thing of simple method, simple, unstinted power, and clear responsibility." Wilson claimed this interpretation was nearer the "approach to the sound sense and practical genius of the great and honorable statesmen of 1787."[32]

Had Wilson more diligently studied those "great and honorable statesmen of 1787," he certainly would have known that a government of "simple, unstinted power" would have terrified most of them. After all, they had just fought a war against a monarch who exercised exactly that.

In his 1887 essay *The Study of Administration,* Wilson continued his attack on our founding principles, expressing his belief that government should be run not by elected officials who govern with the consent of the governed but by the administrators or the scientific experts in the government bureaucracy.

Wilson believed that, unlike the governments of certain European nations, Americans had been "more concerned to render government just and moderate than to make it facile, well-ordered, and effective."[33] Making government "just and moderate" may not sound like a criticism, but for Wilson it was. In Wilson's view, our government was "saddled with the habits of a long period of constitution-making" and failed to make the necessary changes to the administrative state due to "flaws in our constitution."[34]

Wilson argued that while one becomes a politician through popularity, "[t]he bulk of mankind is rigidly unphilosophical, and nowadays the bulk of mankind votes." On the other hand, one becomes an administrator based on intelligence and the selection of those able to stand "liberal tests as to technical knowledge."[35]

While politics expressed the people's will, the administration involved in executing the people's will should stay "outside the proper sphere of politics." Wilson viewed the administrator's expertise as the most effective way to achieve the ends upon which the populace agreed. He argued for granting bureaucrats the authority to regulate this process unhindered by popularly elected politicians who lacked the necessary expertise.

But, the creation of Wilson's regulatory behemoth required that Progressives overcome yet another fundamental constitutional principle: the separation of powers.

One of the US Constitution's founding principles is that a separation of powers between the three branches of government is necessary to avoid any branch of government accumulating too much power. It is essential to this concept that one branch of government cannot delegate its powers to another branch.

Nondelegation was of great import to the Founders. In Federalist Paper 47, James Madison stated, "The accumulation of all powers, legislative, executive, and judiciary, in the same hands, whether of one, a few, or many, and whether hereditary, self-appointed, or elective, may justly be pronounced the very definition of tyranny."[36]

Wilson viewed the separation of powers much as he viewed both the Declaration of Independence and the Constitution in general: outdated and outmoded impediments to achieving Progressive policy goals. Wilson said, "No living thing can have its organs offset against each other as checks, and live.... There can be no successful government without leadership or without the intimate, almost instinctive, coordination of the organs of life and action."[37]

Wilson favored a strong executive managing a centralized

administrative framework free from the constraints the separation of powers imposed. All but confirming the concern that a consolidation of power could well result in tyranny, Wilson stated, "Let [the president] once win the admiration and confidence of the country, and no other single force can withstand him, no combination of forces will easily overpower him"; the president's office "is anything he has the sagacity and force to make it."[38]

Wilson clearly anticipated Barack Obama, who would openly state, "We are not just going to be waiting for legislation in order to make sure that we're providing Americans the kind of help that [I believe] they need. I've got a pen, and I've got a phone. And I can use that pen to sign executive orders and take executive actions and administrative actions that move the ball forward."[39]

Obviously, this is neither the role the Founders envisioned for the president nor the one the Constitution provides. On the contrary, Thomas Jefferson wrote that the Constitution's role was "to bind down those whom we are obliged to trust with power."[40]

Wilson preferred a government with "unstinted power," able to regulate all aspects of our lives through "omnipotent legislation" as deemed appropriate and managed by a powerful president and intellectual elites who would make decisions for the people because they are better qualified to make those decisions than either the "rigidly unphilosophical" masses or elected representatives.

Wilson's Progressive America was not the nation the Founders envisioned. Nonetheless, his influence was evident well before Americans elected him as their twenty-eighth president in 1913. To understand the impact of Wilson's progressive ideology on our nation's future and to put his presidency in context, it is important to discuss Wilson's academic influence on the "muckrakers" and the Progressive policies of the twenty-sixth US president, Theodore Roosevelt.

THE MUCKRAKERS

The media has sustained the Progressives from the beginning. At the turn of the century, Progressive journalists who crusaded to stir up public anger against businesses, politicians, and other institutions were known as "muckrakers," after President Theodore Roosevelt compared them to "the man with the muck-rake," a character in John Bunyan's *Pilgrim's Progress*.

Perhaps the most famous of the muckrakers was the author Upton Sinclair. In 1902, a writer friend shared some socialist literature with Sinclair, an event that Sinclair described as "like the falling down of prison walls about my mind."[41] That same year, Sinclair officially joined the Socialist Party, and by 1903, he was openly admitting that the "deepest facet of my nature . . . is a fiery, savage hatred of Wealth, and of all that Wealth stands for."[42]

So when reading the rest of this section, keep in mind that Upton Sinclair, by his own admission, hated capitalism and those who prospered in it before he ever investigated anything about how it operated. Like many Progressives then and now, he knew what he believed before he began searching and found what he wanted to find.

Casting about for a way to channel his "savage hatred of wealth," Sinclair found a target in the Chicago meatpacking industry after the editor of the socialist magazine *Appeal to Reason* gave extensive coverage to a 1904 meatpacking workers' strike.[43]

In 1906, Sinclair published a shocking work on the meatpacking district called *The Jungle*. He used his considerable literary flair to describe the "square mile of abominations" that comprised the stockyards. He wrote of "tens of thousands of cattle crowded into pens whose wooden floors stank and steamed contagion" on their way to "huge blocks of dingy meat factories, whose labyrinthine passages defied a breath of fresh air to penetrate them," in which could be found "rivers of hot blood, and carloads of moist flesh, and rendering vats and soap caldrons, glue factories and fertilizer tanks, that smelt like the craters of hell."[44]

The villains in Sinclair's story were the meatpacking plants' capitalist owners. They were the barely-human predators in *The Jungle*, "the incarnation of blind and insensate Greed... devouring with a thousand mouths, trampling with a thousand hoofs." In their cold and merciless calculation, "a hundred human lives did not balance a penny of profit."[45]

Sinclair endeavored to convince readers that his novel shared "an exact and faithful picture of conditions as they exist in Packingtown." However, from the beginning, there were well-founded doubts about whether his writing was based in fact.[46]

In September 1906, Sinclair admitted in an interview in *Human Life* magazine that he had only visited meatpacking facilities three times and that a horrifying account of workers crushed into fertilizer came from "an uncouth story teller" he talked to in a bar.[47] Most of his major sources of information, according to historian Louise Carroll Wade, were more likely local socialist activists and journalists.[48]

Professor Wade found that the actual evidence from the time "exposes the many ways in which Sinclair loaded the dice to convince readers that packinghouse residents led heartbreaking lives in a capitalist jungle. In the process, he distorted the truth about the packers and their product and about immigrant workers and their community."[49]

Not everyone on the Left supported Sinclair. A fellow socialist, Ralph Chaplin, a labor activist who grew up in Chicago's meatpacking district and became a prominent member of the International Workers of the World, felt *The Jungle* was "a very inaccurate picture of the stockyards district which I knew so well."[50] Mary McDowell, a local charity worker who hosted Sinclair during his time in Packingtown, later said the final work "was filled with half-truths."[51]

But the truth was never Sinclair's concern. Another socialist activist working in the stockyards remembered Sinclair showing up and declaring, "I've come here to write the *Uncle Tom's Cabin* of the Labor Movement!"[52] He explained to readers of the ironically named socialist magazine *Appeal to Reason* that he wanted his tragic tale to show "the inevitable and demonstrable consequences of an economic system," specifically, capitalism.

"I believe in the Socialist movement," Sinclair said later, "otherwise I should never have written *The Jungle*."[53] In other words, Sinclair only lied because of the importance, in his mind, of the end goal.

The book certainly resonated with the public, but not in the way Sinclair had hoped. Readers were reviled by his descriptions of poor-quality meat, but he failed to ignite a socialist revolution. "I aimed for the public's heart," Sinclair reflected later, "and by accident I hit it in the stomach."[54]

THEODORE ROOSEVELT: THE FIRST PROGRESSIVE PRESIDENT

The Jungle played right into the hands of President Theodore Roosevelt. While Wilson's presidency would come after Roosevelt's, Wilson's ideas clearly influenced Roosevelt's policies.

Roosevelt took office in 1901 after the assassination of William McKinley. He remained in office until 1909. Ironically, at the beginning of his term, he acknowledged the prosperity capitalism had unleashed in the Gilded Age.

In his first address to Congress on December 1, 1901, in what sounds like a nod to Adam Smith, Roosevelt articulately and accurately stated that:

> *It is not true that as the rich have grown richer the poor have grown poorer. On the contrary, never before has the average man, the wage-worker, the farmer, the small trader, been so well off as in this country and at the present time. There have been abuses connected with the accumulation of wealth; yet it remains true that a fortune accumulated in legitimate business can be accumulated by the person specially benefited only on condition of conferring immense incidental benefits upon others. Successful enterprise, of the type which benefits all mankind, can only exist if the conditions are such as to offer great prizes as the rewards of success.*[55]

This was an excellent summary of the conditions existing in America when my great-uncle Joe arrived about six months later. It describes an America he would have recognized. It also presents a much different picture than Progressives would later paint.

However, in this same address, Roosevelt accepted the Wilsonian notion that the "old" American system was incapable of keeping up with the challenges of a more industrialized age. Roosevelt argued that industrialization and free-market capitalism in the Gilded Age had rendered the "old laws" of a limited government "no longer sufficient" to "regulate the accumulation and distribution of wealth." It was an argument Roosevelt would later use to justify his "trust busting" campaigns to break up large corporations.

Government regulation of "the accumulation and distribution of wealth" is a concept that appears nowhere in the Constitution's enumeration of government powers. In fact, it is antithetical to our founding principles. As noted earlier, the Constitution created a limited government with the power to facilitate free markets and regulate attempts to make them less free. Government has a role in preventing one business or group from dominating a sector, eliminating or substantially impeding competition. It also has the tools to do so.

But, to what lengths can or should government go in its efforts to level the economic playing field? Should the reformer's goal be to keep free markets free and enhance individual opportunity, keeping control of the economy in the hands of America's entrepreneurs and consumers? Or, should the reformer expand government powers beyond those enumerated in the Constitution, incrementally placing the economy in the hands of a political elite? The former goal creates continuing cycles of economic growth and opportunity. The latter creates a stagnant economy at best, poverty and despair at worst.

I have met and gotten to know many politicians in the last fifteen years. They are generally urbane and interesting people, and they are certainly skilled at getting elected, but they rarely understand capitalism in theory or business in practice. Rather, the inclination of those holding government power is to expand their power and use it to solve whatever problems they perceive. For those with the government hammer, every problem appears to be a private-sector nail. For an energetic president such as Roosevelt, the temptation to use the government hammer was irresistible.

While there were legitimate concerns about the size and influence of certain companies, for Roosevelt and other Progressives, "trust busting" became almost a religious calling. It was a function of the general antibusiness nature of their movement and a politically motivated tool to expand government power while disparaging the private sector and limiting its influence.

It was trust busting that first led Roosevelt to train his sights on the meatpacking industry. Alarmed at the prospect of some of the country's largest meatpacking firms merging and artificially increasing prices in the absence of competition, Roosevelt's Department of Justice prohibited this action by federal injunction in 1903.

That same year, the Roosevelt administration created the Department of Commerce and within it the Bureau of Corporations to further regulate American business. Wilson's enlightened bureaucrats now had a home. The Bureau jumped into the meatpacking fray, but apparently it was satisfied that the six meat companies they investigated made only "reasonable" profits of about 2 percent.[56]

Nonetheless, the meatpacking industry was now in Roosevelt's crosshairs. He next tried to target individual meatpacking executives, threatening them with federal charges, but the courts blocked these efforts.[57]

After Sinclair published *The Jungle* in 1906, Roosevelt realized he had a powerful new weapon.

Even Roosevelt knew Sinclair's work was untrustworthy. In July 1906, he remarked in a letter to another Progressive journalist, William Allen White, that Sinclair was "untruthful" and that "three-fourths of the things he said were absolute falsehoods." Nonetheless, he believed that Sinclair's work did some "service to us."[58]

This "service" was providing a pretext for going after the meatpacking companies, this time with the Department of Agriculture. Though federal authorities already conducted limited meatpacking plant inspections, Roosevelt sent additional teams to investigate, in one instance asking them specifically to follow up on charges made by Sinclair in *The Jungle*.

The investigators generally found a mixture of "good, fair and bad conditions, often within the same plant and sometimes in the same room" according to one review of the studies.[59] As for Sinclair's specific assertions, the report noted that the author "selected the worst possible condition that could be found in any establishment," not to mention that he "willfully closed his eyes to establishments where excellent conditions prevail."[60]

Having failed to get the indictment he wanted, Roosevelt sent a second team, hoping for a different result, but was again presented with a report detailing mostly clean and decent conditions. These last investigators appeared before Congress to share their findings and reported that they tried to verify Upton Sinclair's information "but found it impossible to do so."[61]

In those days, government officials still occasionally told the truth despite political pressure.

The falsity of Sinclair's claims hardly mattered. By this point, the frenzy surrounding *The Jungle* had whipped up public opinion strongly against the meatpacking companies. In the end, Congress passed a bill expanding federal regulation of the meatpackers, which the president was only too happy to sign.

The story of Upton Sinclair and *The Jungle* exemplifies a Progressive campaign to influence public opinion. A clever writer with socialist leanings crafts a narrative to demonize an industry. This, in turn, creates an opening for Progressive politicians to expand government power.

Progressives have repeatedly employed this tactic to expand government power and hobble the private sector, and they've had great success. President Obama's partisan passage and disingenuous defense of the Affordable Care Act is the best current example. Faced with the 2008–2009 recession, President Obama's then–Chief of Staff Rahm Emanuel perhaps best summarized the Progressive game plan at the time: "You never want a serious crisis to go to waste."[62]

After serving out the term begun by McKinley, Roosevelt won a landslide reelection victory in 1904. He promptly moved hard left, not only the meatpackers but also supporting big government regulatory policies that have made him a Progressive hero to this day.

In addition to meatpackers, the railroad, finance, and mining industries all found themselves in the Roosevelt administration's crosshairs as he increased government control over the economy through antitrust actions and increased regulation. He pushed through legislation that expanded the Interstate Commerce Commission's powers to set railroad rates and added the Department of Commerce with its Bureau of Corporations as new weapons in the government's regulatory arsenal, laying the foundation for the modern administrative state.

In 1907, near the end of Roosevelt's term, the economy faltered as Wall Street brokerage houses went bankrupt and both the respected Knickerbocker Trust in New York City and the Westinghouse Electric Company failed. In what became known as the Panic of 1907, the stock market plunged, and there was a run on the banks.

To restore economic order, financier and banker J. P. Morgan organized an effort with bankers and financial experts to direct monies from stronger institutions to weaker ones. Conditions improved, and the crisis passed.

Conservatives blamed Roosevelt's Progressive policies for the crisis, saying that the government should stop meddling in the economy. Not wanting "to let a serious crisis go to waste," Progressives argued that, to the contrary, this crisis demonstrated the need for government-directed reform of the banking industry. The Progressives prevailed.

Congress passed short-term legislation to alleviate the credit crunch and created a commission to study whether the government should play a greater role in managing the money supply.[63] As a result, in 1913, Congress passed the Owen-Glass Act, creating the Federal Reserve System. In that same year, Woodrow

Wilson, the academic who had sung the praises of "omnipotent legislation" well before Roosevelt became president, would become our second Progressive president and sign the Owen-Glass Act into law.

WILSON: THE PROGRESSIVE ACADEMIC TAKES POWER

In 1908, William Howard Taft won the presidency as Roosevelt's preferred successor. However, Taft was insufficiently Progressive for Roosevelt. When Taft ran for reelection in 1912, Roosevelt ran against him, starting his own Progressive "Bull Moose" party. Taft and Roosevelt split the Republican vote, handing the election to the Democratic candidate, Progressive academic and New Jersey governor Woodrow Wilson.

One can only imagine what went through Wilson's mind as he took the presidential oath of office, swearing to "preserve, protect and defend the Constitution of the United States," a document he held in low esteem.

In 1913, the United States experienced Wilson's inauguration and two of the most striking insertions of government into the lives of ordinary Americans to ever occur in the nation's history, both supported by his Progressive predecessor, Roosevelt. The first, as noted above, was the creation of the Federal Reserve System.

The second was the establishment of the federal income tax. They had to amend the Constitution to do it, but Progressives needed a source from which to pay for their ever-increasing government expansion. In this respect, the income tax was incredibly successful, enabling government to expand exponentially and spending to soar.

According to a 2015 report from Congress' Joint Economic Committee entitled *An Economic History of Federal Spending & Debt*, the Wilson years marked a "seismic shift in the role of government," producing a dynamic rise in federal spending. "From the nation's founding through 1920, total federal spending as a percentage of the economy (including the Civil War) averaged 2.80 percent; but since then (1921–2014), total federal spending has risen to an average of 17.27 percent."[64]

This growth in our government's power and influence was no coincidence. As noted above, Wilson was an influential advocate for the creation of what became the modern administrative state, with its labyrinth of federal agencies.

Clearly, the Roosevelt and Wilson presidencies set America on a path that undermined our founding principles, empowered government, and demonized the private sector. According to Professors Pestritto and Atto, the Roosevelt and Wilson administrations made government growth and the subjugation of the private sector to the administrative state a "new normal" in the United States. "Federal regulation of numerous aspects of public life" became commonplace.[65]

Immediately after the Wilson administration, Progressives faded from political prominence for a time. In some ways, their work was done. They had convinced the American public, and especially the business community, to accept government as a more prominent actor in their affairs. They even convinced the American people to hand over portions of their earnings to federal coffers.

To be sure, there was resistance to the Progressives' rejection of our founding principles. For example, on July 4, 1926, in his *Speech on the Occasion of the 150th Anniversary of the Declaration of Independence,* President Calvin Coolidge strongly rebuked Progressive disregard for the Declaration's timeless principles.

Coolidge acknowledged the Progressive argument that the Declaration was of "no consequence" because "the world has made a great deal of progress since 1776." However, he then convincingly rejected this notion, pointing out the timelessness of the Declaration's underlying principles. He stated, "If all men are created equal, that is final. If they are endowed with inalienable rights, that is final. If governments derive their just powers from the consent of the governed, that is final. No advance, no progress can be made beyond these propositions."[66]

Six years later, Progressives would take advantage of perhaps the greatest economic crisis in American history to once again seize the national agenda, further expanding government power.

ANOTHER PROGRESSIVE ROOSEVELT

During the 1932 presidential campaign, amid a terrible depression, the Democratic candidate, Franklin D. Roosevelt (FDR, a distant cousin of the first President Roosevelt), gave a major speech at the Commonwealth Club in San Francisco.

After steady economic growth throughout the 1920s, the 1929 stock market crash hurt nearly every sector of the American economy, resulting in millions of Americans losing their jobs and even the savings they thought were safe in banks.

FDR took this opportunity to paint the capitalist system as an economic dragon menacing the nation and government as the sword to slay it. Echoing both Theodore Roosevelt and Woodrow Wilson, he proclaimed that the Industrial Revolution had corrupted the American idea of individualism and made it obsolete and dangerous. According to FDR, at the turn of the century, those who saw things clearly "saw with fear the danger that opportunity would no longer be equal; that the growing corporation, like the feudal baron of old, might threaten the economic freedom of individuals to earn a living."[67]

Having set the Marxist undertones of his speech by comparing corporations to "the feudal baron of old," FDR pressed on. He stressed his lack of faith in the ability of America's entrepreneurs to grow the nation out of its economic crisis, saying, "A mere builder of more industrial plants, a creator of more railroad systems, and organizer of more corporations, is as likely to be a danger as a help."[68]

Nor was his solution to our nation's economic woes the "discovery or exploitation of natural resources" or "producing more goods." Rather than encouraging economic growth, FDR sought to create and empower a vast government bureaucracy to take charge of "administering resources," "reestablishing foreign markets," increasing "consumption," "adjusting production to consumption," and, most tellingly, "distributing wealth and products more equitably." According to FDR, "[t]he day of enlightened administration has come."

While this concept of "enlightened administration" harkens back to the eighteenth century's "enlightened despotism," from which the Founders had declared independence, at least FDR was upfront. He wanted an expansive administrative state to manage a stagnant economy rather than economic expansion driven by entrepreneurs and consumers. Not surprisingly, the government expanded, and the economy sank into an even greater depression in 1937.

Soon after his election, FDR launched his New Deal program that included the creation of some hundred new government offices, from the Federal Aviation Administration to the Tennessee Valley Authority to the Federal Arts Project. And yet, all FDR's offices and all his men couldn't get the depressed economy growing again. In fact, their punitive actions against American business kept the economy down, stifling any recovery and holding a vast swath of the American people in poverty.

According to historian Amity Shlaes, the centerpiece of the New Deal agencies—the National Recovery Administration—"mistook macroeconomic problems for micro problems—it sought to solve the monetary challenge through price setting." The result was policies "so stringent that they perversely hurt business. They frightened away capital, and they discouraged employers from hiring workers."[69]

But FDR didn't stop there. Shlaes notes that as his term in office continued, "business was terrified of the president." As a result, instead of expanding and letting market forces pull America out of the depression—as Adam Smith would have recommended—American businesses made the rational business decision "to wait Roosevelt out, hold on to their cash, and invest in future years" (much as they would later do under President Obama following the Great Recession).

Not to be outdone, FDR responded almost incomprehensibly with an "undistributed profits tax" calculated "to press the money out of them."[70] In Shlaes's analysis, this caused the country to dip into an even greater depression in 1937–1938.

This second depression, and FDR's failed attempt to pack the Supreme Court with justices of his choosing, finally led to the creation of the Conservative Coalition, a bipartisan group of Republicans and conservative Democrats opposed to FDR's Progressive power grab. In 1937, this group released a "Conservative Manifesto" that would frame the debate between conservatives and Progressives for decades to come.

The Manifesto's ten points primarily called for tax reductions, a balanced budget, a reduction in the size of government, recognition that "private investment and enterprise require a reasonable profit," maintenance of states' rights, and, finally, "[r]eliance upon the American form of government and the American system of enterprise."[71] It was about time.

This group of bipartisan senators was able to push back, in part, against FDR. Unfortunately, FDR was still the president, and slowing his Progressive agenda was insufficient to get the economy back on track. That took the surge in industrial production at the start of World War II.[72] While the members changed over time, the Coalition that opposed him would remain influential in Congress from 1937 to the mid-1980s.

In the 1930s, pro-growth economic policies could have gotten the economy back on track years earlier and without a war had economic growth been FDR's primary goal. As he admitted in his Commonwealth Club speech, it was not. Rather, he sought to use the Great Depression as a justification for expanding government, reigning in the business community and increasing reliance on government. He succeeded.

While FDR's New Deal failed to rescue the United States from the Great Depression (and actually caused a second more serious depression in 1937), FDR's government expansion proved pervasive and durable. Once again, a Progressive-minded president, who clearly saw himself as heir to the incremental "progress" of earlier Progressive politicians, took advantage of a crisis to impose even more government on Americans, changing our society forever.

But conservatism was also emerging as a more cohesive movement as the extent and dangers of the Progressive agenda became increasingly obvious. And it wasn't even strictly along party lines. The lead author of the "Conservative Manifesto" was a Democrat, Senator Josiah Bailey from North Carolina. Democrats like Bailey had realized what was now abundantly clear: The Progressives had declared open war on America's founding principles, a war that frames much of the political and economic debate in the nation to this day.

THE WAR ON PROFIT CONTINUES

Despite a debilitating civil war, the nation "conceived in liberty" did not "perish from the earth." It survived, it prospered, it surpassed all reasonable expectations, and continued to serve as a beacon of hope for immigrants from all over the world, such as my great-uncle Joe and his brothers. While those who led these efforts benefitted more than the general populace, everyone benefitted as the economic tide lifted all boats, both large and small.

Yet, rather than celebrating the incredible success of free-market capitalism, a group of would-be reformers set about to demean and demonize individual success and expand the power and scope of government. American businesses large and small became the enemy, targets of punishment at the coercive hand of government and its "enlightened administration."

Under Franklin Roosevelt, no business was too small to avoid feeling big government's oppressive hand. For example, in 1934, Jacob Maged, a Polish immigrant who came to America in search of a better life, ran a tailor shop in New Jersey. He was fined and jailed for charging too little to press a suit.[73] He had violated New Jersey's "tailors' code," enacted in conjunction with FDR's National Recovery Administration. The judge later released Maged early so he could give him "a little lecture on the importance of cooperation as opposed to individualism." Maged probably wondered if this was really the free nation for which he'd left Europe.

Make no mistake, this war on profit continues. With increased vigor and openness, Progressives and their allies are attempting to use America's business community as their foil to expand government well beyond its constitutionally enumerated limits, the very limits that shield Americans from tyranny.

President Obama continued and greatly contributed to the government expansion crusade. The Affordable Care Act (better known as ObamaCare) and the Dodd-Frank legislation are clear examples of continuing Progressive efforts to expand government's influence in our lives and overcome constitutional prohibitions on the growth of government power. Congress passed both laws in the Obama administration's early days, when Democrats held a controlling majority in the House and a filibuster-proof majority in the Senate.

Once Obama lost those legislative advantages, he resorted to Wilson's administrative state to accomplish his Progressive policy objectives. With Wilsonian use of executive branch power, Obama engaged in an unprecedented barrage of executive orders and regulations that restricted economic growth and hobbled American businesses. Much like Roosevelt's New Deal, Obama's legislative and regulatory initiatives extended the impact of the recession he inherited and hindered the subsequent recovery.

Due in no small part to this Progressive power grab, President Obama brought about the most significant decline in the power of the Democratic Party in modern times. Republicans took control of the House in 2010, merely two years into his administration. Democrats subsequently lost their Senate majority and then the presidency. All in all, the Democrats lost over one thousand state and federal elective offices during Obama's term.[74]

As promised, President Trump has succeeded in undoing much of the regulatory damage Obama and his Progressive predecessors have inflicted on the United States. As has already been noted, he is on pace to become the most anti-regulation president in American history. He could justifiably boast early in his term that his administration had "taken unprecedented steps to remove job-killing regulations that sap the energy, creativity and dynamism from our country. We are cutting regulations at a pace that has never even been thought of before."[75]

Is it any wonder that Progressives are in a panic and willing to make any unfounded or absurd allegation to stop President Trump's progress in dismantling their Wilson-inspired administrative state? Had I been confirmed, I would have done what I could to assist President Trump in his efforts to deregulate and reinvigorate the nation's economic growth. That was a major reason Progressive icons, such as Senators Elizabeth Warren and Bernie Sanders, so opposed my confirmation.

Progressives may be losing the battle to expand government under President Trump, but rest assured, they have a very long-term view when it comes to advancing their agenda. Their efforts to enlarge government power, reduce individual liberty, and subvert the influence of entrepreneurs, innovators, and business leaders will not end with President Trump's term in office. In their minds at least, they are winning their long-term campaign—progressively.

CHAPTER FOUR

The Ascent and Decline of the Labor Unions: The Progressives Find an Ally

"The issue is Socialism versus Capitalism."

EUGENE DEBS

UNION LEADER AND SOCIALIST ICON

Enter the Unions

To effectively execute their war on profit, Progressives have allied themselves with various special-interest groups over the decades. America's labor unions were the first and foremost among them. In many ways, it is a natural alliance since both movements arose around the same time and for similar reasons. At their core, both want to employ the power of collectivism to restrain the power of capitalism. This alliance has greatly benefitted the Progressives, who rely on the unions for financial support and votes as well as shock troops to assault those who resist Progressive polices. However, it has left the unions struggling for membership as their services have become less relevant to employees and their activities have become increasingly political.

Unions became a major force because of the changes brought

about by the Industrial Revolution in America. The labor market was evolving due to forces that disadvantaged employees.

Employers are always interested in attracting and retaining the most qualified employees, and they compete with similar businesses for such employees. Competition pressures employers to increase wages and benefits over time as good employees change jobs and seek better opportunities. This is particularly true in smaller businesses, where the employer-employee relationship is very personal.

But the standardized manufacturing processes and assembly lines of the Industrial Revolution simplified repetitive tasks, diminishing the importance of unique skills and making it easier to replace lesser-skilled workers.

While jobs and opportunities were plentiful, the tremendous influx of immigrants and migration from rural farming communities to the cities constantly replenished the supply of lesser-skilled workers. Employers could readily replace workers who complained about their working conditions or compensation. Individual workers had little negotiating power and conditions deteriorated in certain sectors, particularly manufacturing and mining. Reforms were needed.

These workers felt they could only improve their wages, benefits, hours of work, and working conditions if they joined together to demand change. What one worker was unable to accomplish because of limited negotiating power, a large number of workers could accomplish if unified to exert their collective power. To effectively deal with their employers, workers needed to organize and bargain collectively.

Enter the labor unions.

Membership in a union gave these laborers a sense that they had a voice in the workplace. Many were unskilled or illiterate people working in mass enterprises. While the free market for labor was benefitting them, perhaps more than they knew, they often felt powerless and at the mercy of their bosses. At their best, the unions gave workers a sense of investment in America's economic growth, a belief that they had a seat at the table and a feeling of empowerment. That sense of empowerment helped create a bond of social cohesion.

These workers were not wrong about the need for change. The early labor movement in the United States had some very credible achievements, including the standardization of decent working conditions and workplace safety across industries, the abolition of child labor, limits on hours worked without overtime pay, and the creation of workers' compensation and old-age insurance. For these early reforms, labor unions deserve a lot of credit. They made a positive difference for America's workers.

Yet, there were aspects of the labor movement that raised serious danger signals even in their early days. The movement's early association with violence and coercion, leadership's failure to understand how American capitalism benefits workers, and an overreliance on government have all empowered Progressives while driving a wedge between union leadership and American workers.

A History of Violence and Intimidation

From the beginning of the labor movement, strikes generally targeted American businesses. However, unions also used oppressive tactics to suppress dissent by workers (derisively called "scabs") who disagreed with their objectives or methods. Unions consistently attempted to demonize anyone who opposed them, whether on the labor or management side, and to force rather than persuade dissenters to capitulate.

One academic study noted that "the United States has had the bloodiest and most violent labor history of any industrial nation in the world." Professors Philip Taft and Philip Ross, writing in 1969, conservatively estimated that more than 700 Americans had been killed and many thousands more seriously wounded in union violence up to that point.[1]

Even those predisposed to support union goals acknowledged this problem early on in the labor movement. Henry George was a key figure early in the Progressive Movement and an author of the seminal Progressive text *Progress and Poverty.* In an 1898 open letter to Pope Leo XIII entitled "The Condition of Labor," George declared that "labor unions can do nothing to raise wages but by force."[2]

This force, according to George, could "be force applied passively, or force applied actively, or force held in reserve, but it must be force." He went on to emphasize that unions "*must* coerce or hold the power to coerce employers," but in addition, "they *must* coerce those among their own members disposed to straggle... to force other working-men either to join them or starve."[3]

George conceded that strong-arm practices are key to understanding how unions operate: "Those who would tell you of Trade Unions bent on raising wages by moral suasion alone, are like those who would tell you of tigers who live on oranges."[4]

Unions have continued to use violence in modern times. For example, in September 1993, during a United Mine Workers' strike, the Associated Press reported what many considered inflammatory remarks about potential strikebreakers by UMW president Richard Trumka: "I'm saying if you strike a match and you put your finger in it, you're likely to get burned," Trumka told the press. "That doesn't mean I'm threatening to burn you. That just means if you strike the match, and you put your finger in it, common sense will tell you it'll burn your finger." But,

Trumka's real point was that "when you inject scabs, a number of things happen. And a confrontation is one of the potentials that can happen. Do I want it to happen? Absolutely not. Do I think it can happen? Yes, I think it can happen."[5]

Two months earlier, during this same UMW strike, an environmental contractor named Eddie York headed to a mine site in West Virginia to perform maintenance unrelated to mining. A union member, Jerry Dale Lowe, apparently thought York was trying to cross the picket line and shot him in the head, killing him.[6] Eddie York got far worse than a burned finger.

Today, Richard Trumka is the president of the AFL-CIO and is one of the most powerful union bosses in the country.

Carl F. Horowitz of the National Legal and Policy Center has reported more disturbing examples of how unions deal with so-called "scabs." Eight nonjoining employees and four of their spouses sued the United Auto Workers (UAW) in the 1990s following two UAW strikes against Caterpillar, Inc. The employees and their wives alleged "extraordinary harm caused to them by the union's outrageous conduct."[7]

During the strikes, these workers received calls in which union supporters threatened "[l]ook out for your wife and son" and "[l]ook out for your house." Wives were told "[y]our husband could get shot" and "[y]our f**king husband better not cross that picket line if he knows what's good for him." One worker's daughter had a caller ask how she would "like to have [her] home burned down?"[8]

Rather than rejecting these tactics, the UAW local president said at a member meeting, "If you happen to recognize any of the people going across the line and it happens to be your neighbor, and you happen to catch him out at night with a baseball bat or a golf club and beat the hell out of him and put him in the hospital, that's alright, but no violence on the picket line." As Horowitz stated, "No doubt dissenting workers and their families were comforted by the prospect of a 'peaceful' picket line."[9]

While the labor movement's history is rife with violence, the real purpose was intimidation—suppressing dissent before it began. In most (but not all) cases, actual violence was unnecessary because the threat of it was always there and real. Perhaps it was in the background, but it was always there.

A Lack of Understanding or Appreciation for Capitalism

Another early danger signal was the inability of union leaders to understand or appreciate the virtues of America's free enterprise system. With few exceptions, union leaders historically and consistently have been unable to grasp how jobs are created, the complexities of managing a business, or the importance and legitimacy of profit. With their focus on collective action, it was difficult for many labor leaders to fathom the importance of entrepreneurs—America's self-made men and women—who take the risks necessary to start and grow businesses.

As a result, union leaders have always been in danger of slipping into a total "us versus them" mentality, of supporting the most primitive and counterproductive forms of socialism, and of failing to recognize any common interests between labor and management. This has hurt workers terribly in many industries and discredited the unions. However, it made union leaders ideal Progressive allies.

The labor movement's socialist roots date back to union leader and Socialist icon Eugene Debs.[10] Debs was instrumental in the founding of both the American Railway Union (1893) and the Industrial Workers of the World (1905). While in prison following a violent strike in 1894, Debs was given a copy of

Marx's *Das Kapital* and was said to have "read it slowly, eagerly, ravenously."[11]

He emerged from prison committed to socialism, writing in 1897 that "[t]he issue is socialism versus capitalism."[12] Although originally a Democrat, he ran for president five times between 1900 and 1920 as the candidate of the Socialist Party of America, becoming both a well-known labor leader and the best-known American Socialist.

Debs's influence and socialist ideology have remained a part of the American labor movement. The Eugene Debs Foundation "carries on informational and educational programs which aim to honor and promote the goals for which Debs struggled," in addition to maintaining Debs's home as a "shrine to labor."[13] According to the foundation's website, labor unions are among its "most active supporters."[14]

The Eugene Debs Foundation gives an annual award to honor Debs's memory and "to assist in keeping alive the spirit of progressivism, humanitarianism and social criticism epitomized by Debs."[15] In 1994, the foundation awarded the Eugene Debs Award to current AFL-CIO president Richard Trumka.[16]

In 2007, with surprising candor, Trumka admitted, "I got into the labor movement not because I wanted to negotiate wages. I got into the labor movement because I saw it as a vehicle to do massive social change to include lots of people."[17] In a 2011 interview with Bloomberg, Trumka discussed his support for the US becoming more like a European socialist nation, stating that he didn't object to conservatives calling him a socialist as "[b]eing called a socialist is a step up for me."[18]

The radical political stances of union leaders are part of the reason unions lose organizing elections at workplaces across America. Most employees may be cynical about their employers, but they don't think of them as evil, and they do understand that the economic health of the enterprise affects them. Employees certainly want better jobs, better wages, and better working conditions, but they don't want to be represented by Che Guevara.

The employees' instincts are right. At the end of the day, a growing economy creates the competition for employees that raises wages and increases benefits for union and nonunion workers alike. But the goal of America's labor unions has never been to generate broad-based economic growth, create jobs, or foster prosperity. Unions are and have always been narrow special-interest groups focused on forcing concessions from employers or convincing political leaders to regulate businesses without regard to the effects on growth. This narrow focus can produce results that are contrary to their own workers' best interests.

Clinton treasury secretary and Obama administration economist Larry Summers has acknowledged that unionization is a cause of long-term unemployment, stating, "High union wages that exceed the competitive market rate are likely to cause job losses in the unionized sector of the economy."[19]

"Job losses in the unionized sector of the economy" obviously are not in the best interest of union employees. Unions focus on getting a bigger piece of the pie in the short term, not on whether the pie is growing or shrinking. That misguided aim hurts all employees.

For example, the unions were almost wholly unhelpful in the efforts of American industries to adjust to economic changes underway in the 1960s and 1970s. Rather than helping American industries address competition from foreign manufacturers, the unions concentrated on increasing wages and government regulation of domestic businesses. They were, to some extent, successful but only in the short term.

Unions also certainly played a role in the demise of the US

garment industry and the decline of the once-dominant US steel and auto industries. The resulting jobs losses have benefitted no one.

In response to high domestic labor costs, businesses simply moved jobs to other countries. The impact on manufacturing jobs was substantial. The Census Bureau reported that an astounding sixty thousand US factories closed between 2000 and 2014.[20] Not surprisingly, as measured by the US Bureau of Labor Statistics, the number of people working in the US manufacturing sector also declined by over one-third, from its peak of 19.5 million in June 1979 to 12.4 million in June 2017.

In addition, the unions have failed completely to recognize the danger automation poses to the American jobs market. Machines are increasingly capable of performing tasks that are common in the manufacturing sector. The rest of the world is waking up to the potential of artificial intelligence in every domain of human activity. The unions act like it doesn't exist, criticize those who warn of the dangers, and continue to do everything they can do (or that they can persuade the government to do) to increase labor costs. Automation is, to some degree, inevitable. It will have the benefit of lowering prices for everyone, but the decline in employment opportunities will fall on the working class.

American workers need good-paying jobs. They increasingly recognize that economic growth—business growth—is the key to job creation and that our capitalist system is best able to generate that growth. They are also recognizing that the unions assume economic growth as a given, promote policies that hobble private-sector employers, and discourage investors, making all the trends that disadvantage workers worse.

In my career, I've been on both sides of this labor-management divide. I was a worker, and I know managers can be arbitrary and unreasonable—they're human. I know what it's like to feel like a cog in the wheel. At the same time, I never hated my employers, much less capitalism. I would not want to be represented by people who did. Many American workers today share my attitude; it's one reason why private-sector unions have experienced such a severe membership decline.

Overreliance on Government Diminishes Union Relevance

Overreliance on government action is another problem that arose early in the labor movement. Prior to the 1912 presidential election, the American Federation of Labor had avoided partisan politics, but Republicans had consistently rejected organized labor's agenda. So, in the 1912 election, the AFL, under the leadership of its president, Samuel Gompers, formally supported the Progressive Woodrow Wilson and the Democrats.

Labor historian Nick Salvatore observes that in backing Wilson, Gompers nudged the AFL "toward an actual partnership with the Democratic party," a partnership which has endured to this day.[21] Gompers summarized the unions' goals years before in a single sentence: "We do want more, and when it becomes more, we shall still want more."[22]

And so it began.

A high point of this partnership was the Progressive presidency of Franklin Roosevelt. In 1938, FDR signed the Fair Labor Standards Act (FLSA) into law, setting a federal minimum wage, establishing a forty-hour workweek, guaranteeing overtime pay for certain jobs, and prohibiting "oppressive child labor."[23] The FLSA put in place benefit standards and worker protections and placed the responsibility for advancing workers' interests with the government rather than the unions. While greatly advancing the Progressives' goal of expanding government's power over the private sector and codifying key union objectives, the FLSA also diminished the unions' role as the protector of workers' rights by transferring that responsibility to the federal government.

As a result, while during the first half of the last century unions achieved meaningful reforms, for the most part these reforms were all in place by the late 1940s, codified in federal statutes and no longer the subject of negotiation between employers and employees. The Occupational Safety and Health Administration, the Mine Health and Safety Administration, the Department of Labor's Wage and Hours Division, the Equal Employment Opportunity Commission, and the National Labor Relations Board, among others, are all federal agencies in place to protect workers.

Paradoxically, in many ways, the unions became victims of their own success. The fewer problems American workers face, the less they need unions. As Progressives have greatly expanded the government's role in protecting workers, the labor movement's relevance has diminished. By empowering Progressive politicians, the unions ceded much of their role to big government.

Samuel Gompers foresaw the potential threat to the unions. Interestingly, he foresaw it with respect to the minimum-wage issue, which continues to absorb union resources and attention today. Discussing a proposal for a federal minimum wage in 1912, Gompers stated that unions "want a minimum wage established, but we want it established by the solidarity of the working men themselves through the economic forces of their trade unions, rather than by any legal enactment." Gompers was very clear: "We must not, we cannot, depend upon legislative enactments to set wage standards." His reasoning was that once the unions "encourage such a system, it is equivalent to admitting our incompetency for self-government and our inability to seek better conditions."[24]

As we shall see, it was a warning union leaders were incapable of heeding.

Unions Struggle to Remain Relevant in the Private Sector

As previously noted, the changing labor market during the Industrial Revolution led to workers organizing to negotiate collectively through unions. Today's jobs market is much different than it was in the early 1900s or even the 1980s. In the current Technical Revolution, the fastest-growing jobs increasingly depend on individual training, education, skills, or creativity.

The reality is that the unions' whole model—collective bargaining—is of diminished value to twenty-first-century workers. Today's workers depend more heavily on their unique qualifications and individual performance for job security, increased wages, and promotions. They have less use for a collectively bargained one-size-fits-all union contract based on seniority.

According to the US Bureau of Labor Statistics (BLS), "eight of the 10 fastest growing jobs in the period 2000–2010 [were] computer-related."[25] The other two were in the medical field. For the period 2014–2024, manufacturing, mining, or other strongly unionized jobs didn't make the BLS's projection for the top twenty fastest-growing occupations.[26]

Given the changing labor market and with unions having ceded the responsibility for protecting workers' rights to various government agencies, workers are increasingly wondering whether union leaders even understand the issues they are facing. A 2016 Rasmussen survey found that "among voters who are now or have been a member of a labor union, only 25% think union leaders do a good job representing their membership" while 57 percent "say most organized labor leaders are out of touch with their members."[27]

As a clear indication of the disconnect between labor leaders and union members, the *Wall Street Journal* reported that in the run-up to the 2016 election, labor unions spent some $110 million to support Hillary Clinton and her fellow Democrats—an increase of nearly 40 percent from their spending in 2012 and almost twice as much as they spent in 2008.[28] But that election proved that union members' actual voting habits are changing.

Union leaders' support for Progressive Democrat Hillary Clinton was hardly surprising. With the diminishing value of collective bargaining, union leaders are increasingly reliant on government. If you are addicted to government coercion as the source of your success and proof of your effectiveness, you support the party that advocates expanding government power.

Prior to the 2016 election, AFL-CIO president Richard Trumka attempted to explain the strong union support of Hillary Clinton's candidacy. He acknowledged that Donald Trump "has successfully tapped into the anger and frustration out there among our members. But once we give them the facts, his house of cards starts to tumble down pretty quickly."[29] Unfortunately for Trumka, it didn't work out that way.

President Trump ran on a promise of economic growth and protection for America's working class. He committed to incentivize economic growth by reducing the tax burden on individuals and businesses, reducing government regulation, and increasing infrastructure spending with the intent of creating jobs. He promised to bring working-class jobs back to America by negotiating better trade deals. He also promised to reduce illegal immigration and the competition for jobs caused by illegal immigrants.

Not surprisingly, this message resonated with working-class Americans. Rather than tumbling his "house of cards" as Trumka declared, according to CNN's exit-poll figures, 42 percent of union households voted for Trump, helping propel him into the White House.[30] It was the best showing among union voters for a Republican presidential candidate since Ronald Reagan.

But these percentages include government as well as private-sector unions, each of which represent about 50 percent of union membership. According to a poll conducted by the Government Business Council and *Government Executive* magazine, released in January 2017, 62 percent of federal employees voted for Hillary Clinton while only 28 percent voted for President Trump.[31] Assuming only 28 percent of government union members voted for President Trump, 56 percent of the private-sector union members would have had to vote in his favor to offset the public-sector union member votes and get to a 42 percent total.

Working-class Americans—other than those with government jobs—understood that Trump was addressing their concerns and that Clinton was not. He campaigned on many issues where he agreed with official union positions, such as stronger enforcement of our immigration laws, better trade deals, spending on infrastructure, approval of the Keystone Pipeline, and reinvigorating the coal mining sector.

Other than infrastructure spending, Clinton was on the opposite side on each of those issues. Nonetheless, Trumka and the union bosses supported Clinton. But their members voted for Trump.

Private-Sector Employees Are Increasingly Rejecting Union Membership

Private-sector union membership has reached new lows. It was 35 percent in the 1950s, but by 2017, it had declined to 6.5 percent.[32]

In many sectors, unions have simply lost their appeal for working-class Americans. They have become irrelevant to the real concerns of the workplace; they focus too much on politics, and their politics don't represent the actual views of their members.

For example, in 2014, the United Auto Workers attempted to unionize workers in Volkswagen's Chattanooga, Tennessee, manufacturing plant. Volkswagen's management did not oppose the attempt. "This vote was essentially gift-wrapped for the union by Volkswagen," a Detroit-area labor lawyer told the *Wall Street Journal*.[33]

Nonetheless, the workers voted it down.[34] An assembly-line worker at the plant said, "If the union comes in, we'll have a divided work force. It will ruin what we have." A twenty-three-year-old who worked at the plant was more blunt: "I just don't trust them."[35]

In August 2017, the UAW attempted to unionize a Nissan plant in Mississippi. Workers at Nissan's plant in Smyrna, Tennessee, had previously rejected the UAW's attempts to unionize in both 1989 and 2001. The unions were hoping for a better result in Mississippi. They brought in Progressive senator Bernie Sanders and Democratic National Committee chair (the former secretary of labor) Tom Perez. They even called in actor Danny Glover for support.[36]

Senator Sanders wrote an op-ed in *The Guardian,* noting that the plant's employee base was "over 80% African American" and that union supporters were "connecting workers' rights with civil rights." Sanders wrote that businesses like Nissan have "obscene profits" as "a direct result of corporations' decades-long assault on workers and their unions." He ended by congratulating the union supporters for exposing "the system of racial and economic injustice that corporations like Nissan are perpetrating."[37]

None of it worked.

The workers at Nissan's Mississippi plant rejected the union by an overwhelming 62 percent to 38 percent margin.

One Nissan worker who voted against the union commented, "They know we didn't need it. They know we didn't need outside interference coming in our plant."[38] A forklift operator at the plant stated more simply, "With the UAW, all you've got to do is look at their history."[39]

Similarly, in February 2017, workers at Boeing's plant in South Carolina rejected an attempt by the International Association of Machinists and Aerospace Workers to unionize.[40] The vote rejecting the union was overwhelming, with 74 percent of the employees voting against the union. An Associated Press article described the vote as "a big victory for Southern politicians and business leaders who have lured manufacturing jobs to the region on the promise of keeping unions out."[41] Of course, that's the spin the press put on it. Most importantly, it was a victory for those workers.

It appears that many of today's workers prefer having a good-paying job with a healthy employer over having a union. This is particularly bad news for the UAW, whose then-president Bob King stated in 2011 that if it failed to organize transnational car companies, "I don't think there's a long-term future for the UAW, I really don't."[42]

The Union's Public Employee Base Is Also Shrinking

With private-sector union membership at historic lows and in decline, unions are increasingly looking to the public sector for support and dues. This trend got its start in 1962 when President John F. Kennedy issued Executive Order 10988, allowing workers in the public sector to collectively bargain.

Government workers jumped at the chance to unionize. By 2017, 34.4 percent of government workers were union members compared to 6.5 percent in the private sector.[43] That means about

1 in 3 public-sector employees belong to unions compared to 1 in 15 for the private sector. According to the BLS, while government employees make up only 15 percent of the workforce, they account for nearly 50 percent of union members.[44]

Not all Progressives believed allowing public employees to unionize was a good idea. Although a staunch labor ally, even FDR opposed collective bargaining for government employees, reasoning that the employer is the people. According to FDR, collective bargaining in the public sector faced "insurmountable limitations." The government or "the employer is the whole people who speak by means of laws enacted by their representatives in Congress." As such, it is "impossible for administrative officials to fully represent or bind the employer in mutual discussions with Government employee organizations."[45]

Allowing public employees to unionize is simply a recipe for corruption. To be effective, collective bargaining requires two parties who actually bargain. In the private sector, management represents the employer's interests and union leadership represents the employees. The owners (often public shareholders) select and employ management and are the ultimate beneficiaries of management's efforts. The union has little influence over whom the owners choose to represent their interests.

In the public sector, unions can have a significant influence over who represents the employer's (i.e., the public's) interests. In strong union states, union political influence can be the difference between electoral victory and defeat. This gives the unions a significant voice in determining who represents the public in negotiations for worker benefits, creating a conflict of interest for elected officials. Do they represent the public's interest or the interests of the union that got them elected?

Let's say, hypothetically, that the governor of a state with a powerful government employees' union is facing a reelection challenge. Union support, financially and at the ballot box, is critical to the governor's campaign. Let's also assume that the union is seeking an increase in retirement benefits for state employees.

The governor informs the union leader that the state budget is already stretched to the breaking point and lacks the resources to grant the increase. The union leader responds that since these are future retirement benefits, the financial impact will fall on some future governor. He also reminds the governor that he needs the union's financial support and members' votes in the upcoming election. In other words, the union can play a significant role in determining with whom it is negotiating. With Progressive pro-union politicians in place, the union controls both sides of the bargaining table and essentially negotiates with itself.

This obviously skews the bargaining process and creates a conflict for the governor, who must choose between granting the union's demands or potentially losing the election, along with his job and political clout. Some officeholders will, of course, choose to represent the public's best interests and cut a good deal. But many do not, which is why deeply Progressive states, despite high taxes, have huge shortfalls in both their public pension funds and their budgets.

By organizing and focusing on the public sector, the unions were guaranteed to emphasize their own worst tendencies. Government doesn't understand economics; neither do union leaders. Government doesn't like to adapt and change; neither do union leaders. Government tends, obviously, to be highly political; so do union leaders.

It was a bad marriage from the beginning, and it has disserved everyone. Eventually, this situation will even disserve public employees when they find that the lucrative pensions and benefits their unions got through political action will bankrupt their public employers, leaving them with fewer jobs and insecure retirements.

The Unions Compel Government Employee Union Membership

Unable to generate increased membership by demonstrating their relevance even to employees, the unions are looking to their Progressive political allies to use the hammer of government to compel unwilling workers to join.

Slightly more than half the states in the nation—twenty-eight—have right-to-work laws giving employees (including state government employees) the right to refrain from either becoming a member or financially supporting a union.[46] But there are still a number of other states that allow union agreements requiring that all employees either join the union or pay union dues or fees as a condition of employment.[47] Many of these states automatically deduct union dues and fees from public employees' paychecks, sending taxpayer monies directly to the unions.

Thankfully, that situation may soon be changing.

As this book goes to print, the Supreme Court is considering the case of *Janus v. American Federation of State, County, and Municipal Employees,* Council 31, which looks at whether requiring public-sector workers to pay money to unions even if they decline to join the union violates those employees' First Amendment rights.[48] According to AFSCME's own website, a decision in the plaintiff's favor "would make the entire public sector 'right-to-work' in one fell swoop."[49]

The *Janus* case follows the Supreme Court's 2016 decision in *Harris v. Quinn,* which came about when home health-care workers in Illinois objected to paying union fees even if they didn't join a union.[50] This case shows clearly how desperate even the public employee unions have become to increase membership and dues through compulsion rather than voluntary support.

State-run, Medicaid-funded home health-care provider programs, like that in use in Illinois, are usually a win-win situation for everyone. It keeps patients at home rather than in expensive institutions while preserving their dignity and self-sufficiency.

Government data, reported by Truven Health Analytics, shows that Medicaid cost totals for this program came to $45 billion in 2015,[51] while it cared for more than over 1.6 million people in 2014.[52] Naturally, the unions want to get their hooks in.

However, home health-care workers are not typical public employees. While the state pays the caregiver's salary, each individual patient is the actual employer rather than the state. Therefore, it becomes impossible for unions to collectively bargain with an employer for all caregivers over workplace issues. In addition, the employee is likely a close family member caring for someone at home, hardly a typical setting for a strike or walkout.

Nonetheless, eleven states classify these caregivers as government employees for collective bargaining purposes. Up until the Supreme Court's ruling in *Harris v. Quinn,* these states automatically took money for unions out of these caregivers' paychecks (funded by Medicare) whether they were union members or not.

In *Harris v. Quinn,* the Supreme Court shut down part of this arrangement. It held that these caregivers were, at most, partial government employees and that states violated their rights by forcing them to pay union fees. As the Court stated, "except perhaps in the rarest of circumstances, no person in this country may be compelled to subsidize speech by a third party that he or she does not wish to support."[53] That line, from Justice Samuel Alito's majority opinion, no doubt sent a chill down the backs of labor leaders and Progressives alike.

With *Harris v. Quinn* ending the practice of states forcing caregivers to pay union fees, monies intended for caregivers won't make their way to union hands.

The upcoming *Janus* case presents the Supreme Court with the broader issue of whether the First Amendment permits unions to compel any government employee to fund union activities. Following a decision in the *Janus* case, state government employees who decline to join a union may no longer be required to fund union activities as a condition of their employment. Unions will have to convince them to join.

Seeing the writing on the wall, public employees' unions across the nation are already preparing for the loss of thousands of members and millions of dollars in dues and fees.[54]

Perhaps it's time for the unions to ask themselves why, if what they are providing is of such great value to American workers, they can only maintain their membership through compulsion, intimidation, and subterfuge? Perhaps it's time to update their business model.

Union Membership Declines to Historic Lows

As union leadership has increasingly lost touch with its members' concerns, membership has steeply declined. According to the BLS, overall union membership (both public and private sector) stood at 10.7 percent in 2017.[55] That is the lowest percentage in over one hundred years.[56]

Given the new low in private-sector union membership, the *New York Times* reported in 2013 that "some labor specialists" have questioned "whether private sector unions were sinking toward irrelevance."[57] It's certainly a relevant question.

On the public-sector side, union membership has also declined from 38.7 percent in 1994 to 34.4 percent in 2017, the lowest level since the BLS began tracking the data in 1983.[58] It even declined during the union-friendly Obama presidency from 37.4 percent when he took office in 2009 to 34.4 percent when he left.

For unions, the trends are all bad. Wisconsin, Missouri, and Michigan—three states with long histories of labor membership and activity—have all passed right-to-work laws in recent years. That says something about the relevance of unions, both to workers and American politics.

The unions are in trouble.

The $15 Minimum Wage Ruse

The Service Employees International Union's Fight for $15 effort is a compelling example of the unions' desperate quest for relevance as well as their inability to understand how the economy works and their overreliance on government.

Remember that Samuel Gompers warned in 1912 that unions "must not, we cannot, depend upon legislative enactments to set wage standards" because it would be an admission of the unions' "incompetency for self-government and our inability to seek better conditions."[59] Despite this, the SEIU has been staking much of its reputation on an effort to increase the federal minimum wage to $15 per hour.

Decades in the restaurant industry have taught me that a federally mandated $15 minimum wage will kill jobs and reduce working hours—especially for the most vulnerable workers, the ones whom the Fight for $15 campaign claims it will help. It would lead to employers reducing the number of their employees, cutting hours for existing employees, and ultimately creating fewer entry-level jobs at restaurants and similar businesses. It is already hastening the advent of automation throughout the service industry. As for new businesses, although we can never measure the precise impact, fewer restaurants will open as increased labor costs also increase the risk of investing.

Here is an economic reality the unions have never understood.

To make a profit, a business must maximize revenue while minimizing cost. Labor is a cost. Balancing revenue and cost is the job of any good business owner or manager. When companies lose enough money for long enough, they go out of business, and everyone loses their job. It doesn't matter if your employees are well compensated if the company is bankrupt.

But when the government increases the cost of labor, and especially when it does so significantly and suddenly, business managers, regardless of their politics or their preferences, will seek to lower costs in some other way. Typically, the best way to do that, and often the only way to do it, is to reduce the number of employees and/or the hours they work.

Management must begin to look for some way to provide goods or services with fewer employees working fewer hours. Suddenly, it begins to make business sense to incur the costs of automating positions or to work managers more because the alternative is an increased expense the business is unable to bear.

This is not to say that all minimum-wage increases kill jobs. A rational minimum-wage increase, especially if it were predictable (giving businesses time to plan for it), could potentially provide employees with some extra cash without triggering costs high enough to compel the business to fundamentally change its labor practices.

Any such increase should also be adjusted to local conditions, which is why I believe the minimum wage is best dealt with at the state or municipal level. The problem with a national (i.e., federal) minimum wage is that a wage appropriate for New York, San Francisco, or Seattle will be too high for Birmingham, Fresno, or

Cleveland. A federal minimum wage must be at a level the most economically distressed areas can bear or it will further damage the areas most in need of help.

Since 2014, I have encouraged the National Restaurant Association and the International Franchise Association to support a rational minimum wage increase at the federal level but to stop short of the point at which such an increase would kill the jobs American youth so desperately need.

Even Senator Bernie Sanders understands the importance of these jobs. Addressing the importance of entry-level jobs for young Americans threatened by foreign workers, Sanders stated, "The best anti-poverty program is a paycheck. Well, let's give the young people of this country a paycheck. Let's put them to work. Let's give them at least the entry-level jobs they need in order to earn some income today, but even more importantly, let's allow them to gain the job skills they need so they know what an honest day's work is about and can move up the economic ladder and get better jobs in the future."[60]

On this issue, the democratic socialist and I happen to agree.

Almost anyone who has worked an entry-level job can attest to its importance. As was the case with my experience at Baskin-Robbins, it's the kind of experience that can keep a person working hard, off the streets and in school, but only if you can get that first job.

However, these entry level positions are precisely the jobs dramatic minimum-wage increases kill.

Progressive politicians and journalists often claim that large minimum-wage increases have no impact on employment. How they can believe that is beyond me. It's one of those claims that lack any connection to reality. Both common sense and the better research definitively shows that a $15 minimum wage would be a job killer.

In 2014, the nonpartisan CBO issued a report stating that increasing the minimum wage merely to $10.10 an hour "would reduce total employment by about 500,000 workers."[61]

In December 2015, the Federal Reserve Bank of San Francisco issued a paper examining the current research on the impact of smaller minimum-wage increases—the very research upon which the Progressive politicians and journalists rely—and found that the most credible research showed minimum-wage increases resulting in "some job losses" for these workers at levels well below $15 and "with possibly larger adverse effects than earlier research suggested."[62]

Two very affluent West Coast cities, San Francisco and Seattle, have already passed legislation taking their minimum wage to $13 per hour currently and to $15 per hour in the near future. An April 2017 report from researchers at Harvard Business School and Mathematica Policy Research showed that for every dollar San Francisco's minimum wage increased, there was a 14 percent increase in the likelihood of median-rated restaurants going out of business. As the minimum wage continues to increase to $15, the cumulative impact on closures, and the associated job losses, will obviously be far greater.[63]

In Seattle, a report by researchers at the University of Washington, published by the National Bureau of Economic Research, looked at the impact on low-wage workers of increasing Seattle's minimum wage from $11 to $13 per hour in 2016. The study found that hours worked fell 9 percent, costing low-wage employees $125 a month on average.[64]

In August 2017, the National Bureau of Economic Research released a paper entitled "People Versus Machines: The Impact of Minimum Wages on Automatable Jobs." Economists David Neumark of UC Irvine and Grace Lordan of the London School of

Economics found that "increasing the minimum wage decreases significantly the share of automatable employment held by low-skilled workers, and increases the likelihood that low-skilled workers in automatable jobs become unemployed."[65] The paper concludes that the effects "are larger for the oldest and youngest workers, for females and for blacks."[66]

Obviously, the CBO, the San Francisco Fed, the Harvard Business School, the University of Washington, the National Bureau of Economic Research, and the London School of Economics are not bastions of conservative economic thought. Nonetheless, they all released research confirming that a minimum-wage increase to $15 per hour would harm the low-wage workers the unions claim they are trying to help.

In a saner time, even the *New York Times* editorial board had to admit that minimum-wage increases are an economic error. In a 1987 editorial entitled "The Right Minimum Wage: $0.00," the editorial board called increasing the minimum wage "fundamentally flawed," noting that "there's a virtual consensus among economists that the minimum wage is an idea whose time has passed. Raising the minimum wage by a substantial amount would price working poor people out of the job market."[67]

What reality of economics or business has changed to make that conclusion wrong today?

The tax cuts the Republican Congress passed (without any hint of bipartisan help from Democrats) in December 2017 demonstrate very clearly one such economic—and capitalist—reality: government getting out of the way raises wages far more effectively than government compulsion.

Progressives hated the tax cuts. Minority Leader Nancy Pelosi warned of "Armageddon."[68] Senator Bernie Sanders called it "a disaster."[69] Senator Elizabeth Warren claimed Republicans were "just delivering one gut punch after another to hard working people."[70]

That "gut punch" came in the form of... well, bigger paychecks. President Trump signed the Republican's tax bill into law on December 22, 2017, and a number of major US employers immediately committed to investing billions in growth, paying special bonuses and raising wages:

- AT&T "plans to increase U.S. capital spending $1 billion and provide $1,000 special bonus to more than two hundred thousand U.S. employees."[71]
- Bank of America is "giving $1,000 bonuses tied to the tax-overhaul bill to more than half of its employees."[72]
- Boeing announced "an additional $300 million in investments."[73]
- Wells Fargo said they would "raise minimum hourly pay rate to $15, [and] target $400 million in 2018 philanthropic contributions."[74]
- Fifth Third Bancorp "announced plans... to raise its minimum hourly wage for all employees to $15 and distribute a one-time bonus of $1,000 for more than 13,500 employees."[75]
- Comcast NBC Universal will give out "special $1,000 bonuses to more than one hundred thousand... employees" and "spend well in excess of $50 billion over the next five years investing in infrastructure."[76]
- Sinclair Broadcasting "will be paying a $1,000 bonus to nearly nine thousand of its employees."[77]

You read that right: Wells Fargo and Fifth Third Bancorp increased their minimum wages—without government coercion—to $15 per hour.

Progressives dismissed these moves as publicity stunts calibrated to get on the White House's good side.[78] But Progressives view everything through the lens of government, which caused them to miss the broader economic significance of these announcements. To hire the best employees, businesses have to match the compensation their competitors are offering. Otherwise, they will lose the best employees to the competition. The tax cuts and earlier easing of regulations freed up money for companies to increase their employees' compensation. Add to that mix the anticipation of meaningful economic growth, and businesses acted quickly in order to compete for the best employees.

Within a week, another eight companies had announced base-wage increases to $15:

- Wisconsin-based Associated Bank[79]
- North Carolina–based BB&T Corporation[80]
- Pennsylvania-based PNC Financial Services Group[81]
- New Jersey–based OceanFirst Financial Corp.[82]
- Georgia-based Sun Trust Banks[83]
- Minnesota-based US Bank[84]
- the Bank of Hawaii[85]
- South Carolina–based Nephron Pharmaceuticals[86]

Within two weeks, Walmart, America's largest employer, announced that it was increasing its minimum hourly wage to $11, granting bonuses of up to $1,000, expanding maternity and parental leave, and providing $5,000 to employees who adopt a child, all due to the Republican's tax cuts.[87] In effect, this lifted the competitive base for low-wage workers to $11 per hour in one fell swoop.

While small businesses rarely make such announcements, many rapidly followed suit as they were competing with larger businesses for the best employees. Within a month, over 250 diverse businesses announced bonuses, pay raises, and new investments as a direct result of the Republican tax cuts.[88]

In all my years in business, I've never seen so many businesses in so many sectors of the economy spontaneously increase their wages. If that isn't evidence that tax cuts benefit workers, what is?

How did the unions react to these unprecedented benefits for American workers? On January 17, 2018, with a tone-deafness unprecedented even for a labor boss, AFL-CIO president Richard Trumka called it "a moral and economic abomination."[89] Rather than rational economic policy, Trumka saw a "worker-bashing tax cut designed to further enrich big corporations, concentrate wealth in the hands of the few and ship jobs overseas." He warned that workers were "ready to mobilize and organize in defense of our freedoms."[90]

On the same day as Trumka's comments, Apple joined the 250 other US businesses and announced that it would pay a $38 billion repatriation tax on its $250 billion in earnings held overseas, make a "direct contribution to the US economy" of "$350 billion over the next five years," open a new US campus, and create 20,000 jobs in the United States.[91] Apple also announced in a letter to its employees that it was "issuing a grant of $2,500 in restricted stock units" for each employee.[92]

The workers who received these bonuses and wage increases were surely surprised to hear from Trumka that they were "ready to mobilize and organize" to defend their freedoms. Freedom from increased wages and benefits probably wasn't something they were ready to mobilize and defend. Is it any wonder that so many private-sector union members ignored Trumka and voted for Trump?

Perhaps this kind of tone-deafness helps explains why the Fight for $15 protests seem to be running out of steam. The SEIU has to pay people to strike in support of the effort.[93] Since its inception in 2012, the SEIU has reportedly spent $90 million on the cause without much to show for it. Indeed, instead of increasing its membership, the SEIU has actually lost about twenty-one thousand dues-paying members since 2011.[94]

With the misguided Fight for $15 campaign, we see all the old negatives of the union movement coming to the surface: labor bosses using pressure instead of persuasion, relying on politics instead of challenging themselves to deliver relevant services to the people they represent, and a complete and willful ignorance of how the capitalist economy works—the very economy workers depend upon for their current jobs and their future prospects.

What the unions failed to achieve, capitalism—in the form of tax cuts—achieved immediately and organically. More workers are set to earn $15 per hour, and they don't have the unions to thank for it but rather President Trump and the Republican Congress.

Some Things Never Change, Even When They Should

Despite the decline in union relevance and membership, big labor seems determined to continue with the tactics that led to its current diminished state. I have personally experienced the effects.

As the CEO of a quick-service restaurant company willing to speak up on the issues impacting our workers, I have been in the unions' crosshairs for years. I was an early advocate for the workers who would lose their jobs—or the potential for a job—due to increasing the minimum wage to $15 and the danger of dramatic minimum-wage increases accelerating the move to automation.

As a result, even prior to my nomination for secretary of labor, Fight for $15 protestors demonstrated at our corporate offices and at our restaurants. The impact was minimal. Sales were unaffected, and we were aware of a single protestor who actually worked at one of our restaurants.

Not surprisingly, the protest activity increased dramatically following my nomination. The tactics they employed were disturbingly consistent with those unions have employed for decades.

Fight for $15 and the SEIU held protests nationwide at our restaurants and waged a social media campaign based on claims about our company that were, at best, misleading and, at worst, patently false.[95] Initially, there was little impact on either the nomination process or our restaurant sales (Hardee's sales for that January actually improved).

To step up pressure, two leftist groups organized a protest in my hometown of Franklin, Tennessee.[96] One of the groups was "Middle Tennessee Jobs With Justice." Not surprisingly, this organization gives its mailing address as the SEIU's Nashville office.[97] There is also a national "Jobs With Justice" organization. Its website lists AFL-CIO president Trumka and SEIU president Mary Kay Henry as members of its Board of Directors.[98] To bring it all full circle, in 2017, Jobs With Justice was given an award by the Eugene Debs Foundation, the same award that Trumka won in 1994.[99]

They drove a truck pulling a billboard through our neighborhood claiming that I abused women. About fifty of them held a protest in the town square about a quarter mile from our home. A dozen or so came to our home one Saturday afternoon. When I refused to engage with them (and barely managed to convince my wife not to do so), they left an envelope on our front porch that turned out to be filled with cards asking me to withdraw my nomination.

We opened this envelope carefully, as it was a disturbing reminder of the day a week or so before when we found an envelope on our front porch addressed to my wife containing white powder, a pink piece of paper with "Trump" scrawled on it, and a paper doll with a noose around its neck. (The FBI is currently investigating that incident.) The *Washington Free Beacon* reported later that "the SEIU did not respond to a request seeking comment about whether the union condemned such behavior."[100]

None of these actions were designed to influence the vote of any senator. There are no senators living in Franklin, Tennessee. They were legacy tactics of the unions at their worst. Demonize the enemy. Coerce him into silence.

As a former laborer from a working-class family and a former restaurant company CEO, I had a unique and personal perspective on the historical weaknesses of the unions and how those weaknesses have grown to dominate the movement. I knew how they were hurting the very workers they purport to help; that's why I was prepared, if necessary, to fight the unions on behalf of those workers. I was also prepared to work with the unions to advance the interests of those workers.

The fact that I was not confirmed changes neither the overall trend lines nor the implications of those trends for the unions. The world has grown beyond the unions' control; they have to change or perish. They must rediscover a relevance to the average employee in the average workplace and undertake to convince those employees of their importance. They have to understand the realities of economics and adapt their goals to be consistent with those realities.

Otherwise, private- and public-sector employees will continue to reject them, they will continue to be more and more vestigial as the real economy chugs on, and the unions' influence will continue to diminish, even within the Democratic Party. Union members understand this better than their leadership, as their support for President Trump demonstrated.

CHAPTER FIVE

Education: Reading, Writing, and Redistribution

"One believes things because one has been conditioned to believe them."

ALDOUS HUXLEY, *BRAVE NEW WORLD*

Since the Soviet Union collapsed in 1991 and America became the world's only superpower, free-market capitalism has significantly reduced poverty and suffering while creating opportunity worldwide. The implosion of the Soviet Union's socialist economy resulted in better standards of living for millions of Eastern Europeans. China's transition from unabashed socialism to at least a partially free market and India's move to a more open economy significantly reduced poverty in the world's two most populous nations.

In 2013, the *Economist* estimated that *one billion* people had been removed from the ranks of extreme poverty over the previous twenty years because of American-style free-market capitalism.[1]

The World Bank also reported that the number of people living in extreme poverty worldwide "has decreased dramatically in the past three decades, from half the citizens in the developing world in 1981 to 21 percent in 2010, despite a 59 percent increase in the developing world population."[2]

The Index of Economic Freedom, published by the Heritage Foundation and the *Wall Street Journal*, has examined rising economic freedom and declining extreme poverty across the globe for over twenty years. According to the Index's 2018 edition, "by opening the gates of prosperity to ever more people around the world, economic freedom has made the world a profoundly better place." In fact, thanks to increasing economic freedom, "by a great many measures, the past two decades have been the most prosperous in the history of humankind."[3]

There has been an "explosion of economic liberty" resulting in "a massive worldwide reduction in poverty, disease, and hunger." Not surprisingly, increasing economic freedom has also produced "massive improvements in global indicators of income and quality of life." These improvements have resulted in "a paradigm shift in the debate about how societies should be structured"; a debate that "has largely been won by capitalism."[4]

The Index concludes that the "ideals of economic freedom are strongly associated with healthier societies, cleaner environments, greater per capita wealth, human development, democracy, and poverty elimination."[5] Economic freedom's impact on poverty elimination has been particularly compelling. "[A]s the global economy has moved toward greater economic freedom, world GDP has nearly doubled," lifting "hundreds of millions of people out of poverty" and cutting "the global poverty rate by two-thirds."[6]

As these numbers indicate, the world desperately needs economic growth to offset increasing populations and to reduce both poverty and starvation. Free markets have provided that economic growth, and all signs indicate their strong capacity to continue to do so.

These numbers paint a picture that would make sense to most rational people, but there are some who seem unable to understand it, or at least refuse to recognize it. Ironically, these are usually the same people who claim to be obsessed with science, data, and empirical thought. These, of course, would be the members of the academic community who still cling to an irrational fear of capitalism.

This fear is increasingly infecting the students these academics teach. Perhaps that's why, almost a year after Donald Trump was elected, 45 percent of millennials answered a poll saying they would rather live in a socialist country than a capitalist one.[7] The Young Democratic Socialists of America, energized by Bernie Sanders's campaign, saw campus chapters jump from just twelve in 2016 to nearly fifty by October 2017, prompting Vice News to remark, "Seizing the means of production is so hot right now."[8]

But these idealistic students have a hard time describing what socialism actually means, as the Campus Reform website found when they put that question to students in Washington, DC. The answer they got was usually a variation of "I don't know." But whatever socialism was, these kids sure liked it! One called it "getting rid of that wealth gap in the United States," while another declared, "I think people throw that word around to try and scare you, but if helping people is socialism, then I'm for it."[9]

Where could these kids be getting such a rosy, benevolent view of socialism? From their teachers, who just really, really wanted it to work.

The Socialist Miracle That Wasn't

For the Progressive Left, the collapse of the Soviet Union and the ascendance of capitalism was a disaster. It put the lie to claims of a socialist workers' paradise. For over a century, many on the Left had invested their credibility in a utopian vision of socialism as the cure for capitalism's supposed ills. They truly believed that a vanguard of smart and particularly virtuous people—themselves, of course—could achieve that vision.

How they labored in support of that utopian vision! They took over institutions, developed and refined different versions of Marxism, and indoctrinated as many people as they could in what was, for them, more of a religion than an economic theory. They gave themselves awards and honorifics while exhorting their ranks to greater efforts, devoting their lives to advancing the "revolution" they were certain would come to the United States. Think about the effort people with high IQs expended writing books and articles, organizing workers and activists, establishing careers and reputations, all in support of what turned out to be utter nonsense.

It's impossible to overstate the impact on the Progressive Left of the crucial years from 1981 to 1991. Those years stand witness to the collapse of the socialist vision and the reinvigoration of capitalism in both the United States and Great Britain. The Progressives were wrong about everything, completely and comprehensively wrong, and it was now so obvious that even herculean efforts at doublethink could no longer hide it.

The masses in Russia were far worse off after decades of socialism. Socialist societies proved to be less equal, not more. A privileged elite ruled over impoverished masses that experienced equality only in deprivation. Rather than banishing greed, socialism made it worse. The vanguard of socialist leaders was not more enlightened; in fact, they were more murderous, repressive, and corrupt than any leaders the world had ever seen. And so, the Russian people finally rejected socialism. History had rendered its verdict. The evidence was spelled out in the archives of the Soviet state itself.

The supremacy of capitalism became clear, and the necessity of maintaining that system was nothing less than essential to world stability. Without the incentive of personal success, without profits, the world's economies would revert to the poverty—the oppression, the hunger, and the disease that ran rampant in socialist nations, such as the USSR and Red China. They run rampant today in the socialist nations of Cuba, Venezuela, and North Korea (ranked 178, 179, and 180 respectively out of 180 nations on the 2018 Index of Economic Freedom).[10]

These destitute socialist nations stand as the last vestiges of a vision that—it can't be repeated enough—its Progressive proponents actually thought represented the imperative and irreversible direction of history.

Venezuela in particular stands as a post–Cold War example of the complete bankruptcy of the Progressives' socialist ideology. President Trump perhaps said it best in his September 2017 speech before the United Nations:

> *The problem in Venezuela is not that socialism has been poorly implemented, but that socialism has been faithfully implemented. From the Soviet Union to Cuba to Venezuela, wherever true socialism or Communism has been adopted, it has delivered anguish and devastation and failure. Those who preach the tenets of these discredited ideologies only contribute to the continued suffering of the people who live under these cruel systems.*[11]

The verdict of the twentieth century was that while you may be able to build a functioning society on delusion for a time, you cannot sustain one based on the socialist delusion. Strong societies, of whatever stripe, require a functioning, innovative economy, and socialism produces dysfunction. The future may belong to authoritarianism, or sharia Islam, or (hopefully) revitalized capitalism and democracy, but it will not belong to the economic fantasies of the American and European Progressive Left.

So, what remains for the Left?

They have been unable to reconstruct a new utopian vision. They can neither defend nor escape their own beliefs; they can only continue to beat a horse that experience killed thirty years ago. To be sure, as I discuss below, socialism survives on college campuses, but it survives only and ironically because the wealth created by advanced free-market systems gives the West the luxury of subsidizing these networks of people who have learned little, contribute little, and are increasingly viewed with annoyance and contempt by everybody outside the Progressive bubbles in which they operate.

Yet, they do continue to dominate the higher academy, indoctrinating young, impressionable people in their failed ideology. Few besides the young would fall for it. As a result, students emerge from our institutions of higher learning monumentally ignorant and so insecure in their ignorance that they need "safe spaces" because reality is so threatening to them. Many of them are unprepared not just for the real economy but for real life, having been comprehensively taught nonsense about both.

The Return of the Academic Left

When the Soviet Union fell in 1991, it seemed like the century-long struggle against communism had finally ended. A decade of economic prosperity and growth during Ronald Reagan's presidency, coupled with the fall of communism in Eastern Europe, had signaled the triumph of capitalism. Contrary to former Soviet Premier Nikita Khrushchev's predictions, in a direct clash, capitalist free markets had buried socialist central planning. People joked that the only place where anyone still believed in a centrally planned economy was Harvard's political science department.

But, for a time, even in university faculty lounges, communism and central planning were in disrepute. At the end of the Cold War, few left-wing professors were willing to publicly admit any connection to communism or Marxism. A law professor at the University of Michigan Law School told the *New York Times* in 1989, "For a long time it was fashionable to be a Marxist. Now it's getting unfashionable again, and many are retreating."[12]

Marxists were so scarce on campus that a historian at the Massachusetts Institute of Technology quipped, "A Marxist revolutionary is hard to find."[13] Even in the detached world of academia, it seemed like the era of big government, centralized planning, and redistribution was finally over.

However, as memory of the Soviet Union's failure dims or is rationalized away, there has been a resurgence of support in the academic community for socialist central planning. In fact, it has returned with a vengeance.

Left-wing professors now dominate higher education in America, especially at the nation's most prestigious schools. A 2016 study of professors at forty of America's highest-ranked colleges and universities found that on average there are 11.5 Democrat professors for every 1 Republican.[14] The higher-ranked have the most bias. Yale University has 16 Democrats for every Republican.[15] Cornell and Columbia University are tied with 30 Democratic professors for each Republican. Republicans at Brown University are the most outnumbered, with 60 Democrats for each Republican professor.[16]

It wasn't always so biased. According to extensive surveys by UCLA's Higher Education Research Institute (HERI), the number of professors who identify as "liberal" or "far left" grew from 42 percent in 1990, just before the fall of the USSR, to more than 60 percent by 2014, as noted in the chart that follows.[17]

The Heterodox Academy is "a politically diverse group of

social scientists, natural scientists, humanists, and other scholars" concerned about the "loss or lack of 'viewpoint diversity'" in their academic disciplines and universities. As they explain, "When nearly everyone in a field shares the same political orientation, certain ideas become orthodoxy, dissent is discouraged, and errors can go unchallenged."[18]

According to Heterodox, in the fifteen years between 1995 and 2010, American universities "went from leaning left to being almost entirely on the left." Explaining the chart below, based on the HERI data, Heterodox says that "the 12% in the [Far Right/ Conservative] line for 2014 is mostly made up of professors in schools of engineering and other professional schools; *the percent conservative for the major humanities and social science departments is closer to 5%*" (emphasis mine).

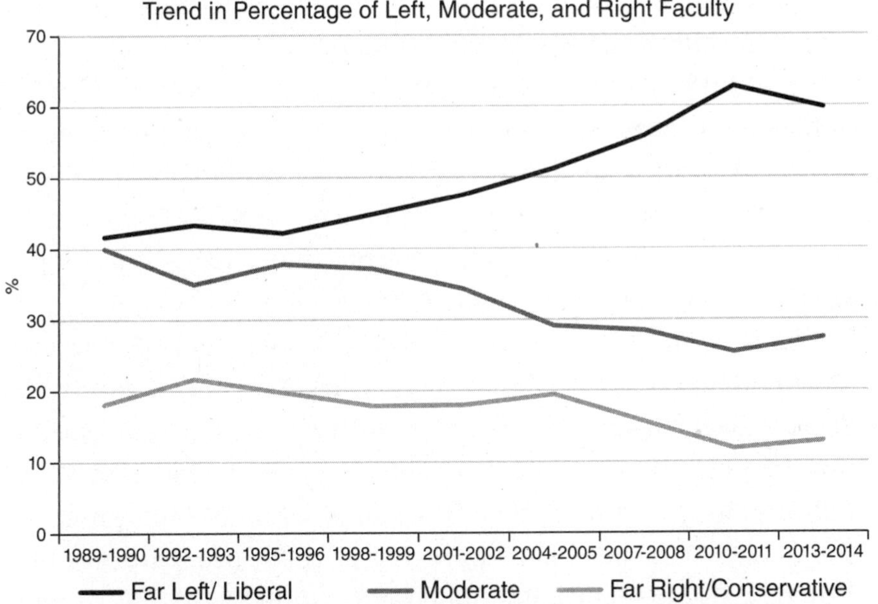

Data from Higher Education Research Institute, based on a survey of college faculty conducted every other year since 1989. Plotted by Sam Abrams.

Many of those liberal and Far Left humanities and social science professors are especially hostile to capitalism. A poll of social science professors in 2006 found that 24 percent are self-described radicals, 21 percent are activists, and 18 percent are Marxists—and those were the professors willing to admit it.[19] The Marxists are especially prominent in college sociology departments (where more than one out every four professors self-identify as Marxists) and liberal arts schools (where Marxists make up about one out of eight professors).[20]

Erik Olin Wright is a good example of the problem. A professor of sociology at the University of Wisconsin–Madison, he is a radical, an activist, and a Marxist.[21] Detailed descriptions of his course offerings show that he offers multiple courses on Marxist theory. His website features the draft manuscript of a book titled *How to Be an Anti-capitalist for the 21st Century.*[22] On the first page of the manuscript, he ruminates about how "the hallmark of capitalism is poverty in the midst of plenty," which he also notes is "not the only thing wrong with capitalism."[23]

In a 2015 article for the socialist magazine *Jacobin,* Wright outlined the need for "anti-capitalist forces to amass enough power to destroy capitalism."[24] He suggested that capitalism is most vulnerable after major financial collapses and anti-capitalists have four options to confront the system: "smashing" it, "taming" it, "escaping" it, or "eroding" it.

He's also an outspoken activist who has participated in large-scale political protests. When Wisconsin's Republican governor, Scott Walker, signed his anti-union/pro-economic growth legislation into law, Wright signed a public letter that condemned the reforms along with more than three hundred of his fellow professors.[25] In 2011, he personally participated in the occupation of the Wisconsin State Capitol Building to protest this legislation, where he sang the pro-labor anthem "Solidarity Forever" with thousands of other protestors.[26–27]

You might think that Wright is just an academic type who spends his time writing papers that few people read. In large part, that's probably true. However, his radical views and commitment to political activism have paid dividends in the world of academic sociology. Wright was elevated to the presidency of the American Sociology Association in 2012.[28] His biography on the group's webpage identifies him as "one of the most prominent sociologists on the planet" whose writings have become "standard items on prelim reading lists."[29] The University of Wisconsin—a public school funded by taxpayers—pays him a six-figure salary to teach kids about how capitalism and wealth are evil systems worthy of destruction.[30]

He has many allies in academia.

Radical American anthropologist David Graeber is one of the fathers of the Occupy Wall Street movement and a professor who teaches class and social theory at the London School of Economics.[31] Graeber, who once taught at Yale, is an anarchist who also hates capitalism. According to *Rolling Stone,* he personally came up with Occupy Wall Street's central motto: "We are the 99 percent."[32]

Many anthropologists like Graeber have gained fame and fortune by disparaging business and capitalism. Anthropologist Karen Ho, a professor at the University of Minnesota, described what she believed was the rotten culture on Wall Street in her 2009 book *Liquidated: An Ethnography of Wall Street.* A review in Princeton University's alumni magazine compared Ho to Margaret Mead, the anthropologist who famously traveled to New Guinea to embed herself with cannibalistic tribes worthy of study. In Ho's case, she traveled to New York to embed herself with investment bankers worthy of study.[33] The comparison lacked only in subtlety.

Even some academic economists (who ought to know better) have abandoned free markets. Economics professor Kshama Sawant was elected to Seattle's City Council as a Socialist Alternative Party candidate. On her government-funded website, Sawant laments that "the current economic and political system has given working people recession, unemployment, underemployment, and homelessness," while also underplaying the fact that capitalism has made Seattle one of the world's most prosperous cities.[34]

The most famous liberal economist in America is *New York Times* columnist Paul Krugman. His career as an economics professor has included posts at multiple prestigious universities, including Yale, Princeton, Stanford, and MIT.[35] Krugman won a Nobel Prize in Economics for his work on international trade. He advocated a free-market, pro-trade position.[36]

Krugman supported the North American Free Trade Agreement in 1993. As recently as 2001, he was writing articles extolling the benefits of sweatshop labor and international free trade and decrying the opponents of free trade as "doing their best to make the poor even poorer."[37] He believed that free trade improved the lives of sweatshop workers in Southeast Asia even if the workers had to endure awful conditions.[38]

These days, he's famous for holding Progressive views on markets, normally in his column in the *New York Times.* There, he has been a champion of Obamacare, redistribution, and government regulation.[39]

When the United Kingdom voted to exit the European Union, Krugman wrote that removing EU regulations had no chance of creating economic growth: "Pay no attention to claims that Britain, freed from EU rules, could achieve spectacular growth via deregulation. You say to-mah-to, I say voodoo, and it's no better than the US version."[40]

Krugman is a consistent opponent of deregulation, supply-side economics, low taxes, and any other policy resembling Ronald Reagan's economic agenda. If a reform somehow shrinks government and limits the role it plays in the economy, Krugman is ready, pen in hand, to fight the reform.

Krugman is so left-wing that the naked partisanship in his columns can be overwhelming. He has variously accused Republicans of "destroying civilization" and being part of an "axis of evil."[41] He described a Republican attempt to repeal Obamacare as "the Worst Bill Ever," which they were only able to sell because they "lied nonstop."[42] He's written pieces on "understanding Republican cruelty."[43] He referred to Donald Trump's election victory as "the tainted election."[44] He's asked important questions like, "Who ate Republicans' Brains?" Krugman is about as partisan as they come.

Yet, some university economics programs are so extremely out of hand that even Krugman disapproves of the left-wing bias. The University of Massachusetts Amherst, for example, has a Far Left economics department that the *Boston Globe* has described as a home for students interested in a "good dose of Marxist and feminist economic theories."[45] Students taking economics courses there can choose between a dozen different classes that reference Karl Marx in the course descriptions, and options include "Marxian approaches to financial markets," "neo-Marxian theory," and even "instructionalist and feminist approaches to political economy with consideration of links to Marxian political economy."[46] Also offered are "Advanced Marxian Economics" and "History of the Marxian Theoretical Tradition."[47]

Unsurprisingly, tax-and-spend socialist Senator Bernie Sanders borrowed extensively from research performed by UMass

Amherst economists during his 2016 presidential campaign.[48] One professor there predicted that if Bernie Sanders were elected president, the economy would grow faster than 5 percent per year. Paul Krugman called on Sanders to distance himself from such "fantasy economics."[49]

The consequence of such hysteria is virulent anti-capitalist views shared by students and faculty members. They blame capitalism for a whole host of maladies that have nothing to do with free markets or economics.

In 2013, Brown students used capitalism as a pejorative when they met to "interrogate beauty as privilege and constructed by systems of white supremacy, ableism, capitalism, and heteronormativity."[50] The role that capitalism plays in all that was unclear (and unstated on the event's Facebook page), but capitalism seemed bad enough to put alongside white supremacy, so they included it.

In 2014, a student group at Cornell held an event centered on the claim that capitalism was responsible for "rape culture" and therefore must be destroyed.[51] Hundreds of students RSVP'd to the event.[52]

Ivy League history professors are a near-constant source of anti-capitalist mania on campus. In 2016, a history professor at Cornell with a specialization in African studies went on an anti-capitalist rant at a Black Lives Matter rally, in which he told a bunch of Ivy League students that "everybody here is a loser because of capitalism."[53] The line got huge applause from his audience.[54]

With professors like this, it is hardly surprising that Marx's *Communist Manifesto* is the fourth most commonly assigned book at American colleges, behind Plato's *Republic*, *The Elements of Style*, and a biology textbook.[55]

In the rare case that a professor expresses a free-market position, students react in shock and protest. N. Gregory Mankiw, an economics professor at Harvard who served as chairman of the Council of Economic Advisors under President George W. Bush, was trying to teach a course in basic economics when seventy Harvard students staged a walkout in solidarity with the Occupy Wall Street movement.[56]

In a statement to the *Harvard Crimson,* the protesting students expressed concern over "the way that this [course's] bias affects students, the University, and our greater society."[57] Mankiw responded in a *New York Times* opinion piece, where he expressed "sadness at how poorly informed the Harvard protesters seemed to be."[58] Amusingly, the class they boycotted was about income inequality.

Again, against the backdrop of the last thirty years, it is not surprising that the Left is reacting this way. They have a century of ego invested in socialism. They cannot abandon socialism, nor can they defend it—not against the screaming lessons of recent history and not considering the ongoing failure in Venezuela, Cuba, and North Korea. So, they shout louder and louder, and more and more intolerantly, discrediting themselves and the institutions they control.

Progressives Indoctrination Disguised as Education

This unrelenting academic assault on capitalism is the culmination of decades of concerted effort by educational reformers. Education in America was radically revamped during the Progressive Era and, as with the early labor movement, there were some initial positive results.

More children received a basic education, in most cases up through high school, leading to greater opportunities for success.

But it was also around this time that certain "reformers" began to see education as both a way to provide children with the basic skills they need to succeed as adults and a way to stealthily inculcate social change—change that adhered to their particular ideology.

These Progressive reformers sought (and seek) to push socialism and central planning on students and young children. Much of this approach to education can be traced to education reformer and socialist John Dewey, whose writings were highly regarded in the former Soviet Union. A twentieth-century American philosopher most famous for being the "father" of modern education, Dewey was also known for his Progressive political theorizing, socialist beliefs, and his support of the Soviets.

His proposed educational reforms transformed America's educational system (as well as the Soviet Union's). What exactly did he believe in? Dewey made it clear in an 1897 essay titled *My Pedagogic Creed*. He wrote, "I believe that education is the fundamental method of social progress and reform."[59] He argued that legislative attempts at social change were "transitory and futile," and the only way to truly transform America was through teaching young children what to think.[60] He fundamentally believed that "education is a regulation of the process of coming to share in the social consciousness; and that the adjustment of individual activity on the basis of this social consciousness is the only sure method of social reconstruction."[61]

Thus, Dewey gave birth to the era of socialist indoctrination in America's public education system.

Teachers' Unions: A Progressive Advocacy Powerhouse

Today, subtle and not-so-subtle attacks on capitalism, profit, and economic success occur at all levels of education. Even our youngest students get a daily dosage of anti-capitalist/pro-socialist thought in the classroom. It shouldn't come as a surprise considering who's doing the teaching. American teachers are in effect a left-wing interest group and make up a significant part of the Democratic voter coalition.

The nation's largest teacher's union, the National Education Association (NEA), made more than $20 million in political contributions in 2015 and 2016, with 90 percent of that amount going to Democrats or left-wing causes.[62] The NEA is firmly committed to progressive economic causes and wholly rejects market-oriented reforms. The issues page on the NEA website not so subtlety states that "privatization is another word for FIRED!"[63] The union believes universal health-care coverage is a "moral imperative" and that "education advocacy and social justice advocacy go hand in hand."[64–65]

But the NEA is moderate compared to the nation's second-largest teacher's union, the American Federation of Teachers (AFT). The AFT donated $12.4 million during the 2015 to 2016 political cycle, with 99.6 percent going to Democrats or liberal causes.[66] The AFT has called on teacher pension funds to divest from fossil-fuel industries because they think such investments are financing global warming.[67] The AFT passed a resolution to "take on Wall Street" and "too-big-to-fail banks."[68]

Income inequality is a major issue for the AFT, which claims that "a handful of hedge fund managers make more money per year than all the kindergarten teachers in America combined."[69] The AFT has committed to advancing anti-capitalist legislation that's totally unrelated to education. It's lobbied Congress to close the carried-interest tax loophole, to create a Wall Street "transaction tax" to finance (through redistribution) college loans and infrastructure projects, to break up the banks, and to end foreclosures during the school year.[70]

Of course, not all teachers support the unions or believe in what they advocate, but many do. When the Chicago Teachers Union voted to walkout on students to "shut down Chicago" in 2016, 96 percent of teachers voted to do it.[71] The strike, much like their walkout four years earlier in 2012, wasn't even about teacher salaries or education funding. It certainly was not about educating Chicago's youth.

The city of Chicago and the state of Illinois are deep blue, which is why Chicago's teachers are already among the highest paid in the United States.[72] In the words of *Jacobin* magazine, the strike aimed to advance "a broad social justice agenda."[73] Chicago Teachers Union president Karen Lewis told strikers, "This is about empowerment for people who have been disempowered for so long."[74]

Many "disempowered" people joined in on the strike. Fast-food workers demanding a $15 minimum wage walked off the job.[75] Students at the local universities showed up to help the effort. Leftists met at the Cook County jail to protest mass incarceration. The SEIU, airport workers, and various other unions joined the protest.[76]

It was unlike anything seen in the United States in decades. Vice News described it as "a lot like the type of strike that European or Latin American workers often engage in."[77] It was about capitalism, class warfare, and a whole host of other left-wing causes.

You can see it in the cast of protesters who, coming from basically every unionized (and even nonunionized) industry imaginable, had just one thing in common: they really hate capitalism. One gym teacher complained to the *Washington Post* that "[the Governor of Illinois] is a businessman, he wants this notch on his belt that he took down the Chicago Teachers Union."[78] The protestors saw him as an enemy because he represented business interests, which to them are simply evil.

Again, what is significant about these movements is the complete absence of a positive vision, which exploded with the collapse of socialism as a viable economic philosophy. All that is left for them is their anger toward capitalism and their fanatical, reactionary defense of the institutions they control against any kind of real reform.

The anti-capitalist enthusiasm earned the support of the World Worker's Party, a self-described "Marxist-Leninist party dedicated to organizing and fighting for a socialist revolution in the United States."[79] In a press release supporting the 2016 strike, it commented, "This strike promises to spread the power of solidarity like wildfire across this country. Not only are Chicago teachers fighting for working conditions and students' learning conditions, they are fighting for all of the demands that impact working-class and oppressed people."[80]

Again, there was no mention of the extensive evidence that, since the fall of communism, free-market capitalism has significantly reduced poverty and created opportunity worldwide. Reality simply doesn't fit the narrative.

Make no mistake, opposition to capitalism is rampant within the Chicago Teacher's Union. A few years before the strikes, a group of left-wing teachers formed the Caucus of Rank-and-File Educators (CORE) within the union, which essentially declared war on free-market reformers in the City of Chicago. Socialist magazines, elated with the union's leftward shift, celebrated the rise of CORE as the reassertion of traditional left-wing union activism.[81] *Jacobin* magazine described it as part of an effort to "take on the right flank of the Democratic Party and free market reformers."[82]

The union refused to form an alliance with Chicago's Democratic mayor, former Barack Obama adviser Rahm Emanuel, because he was deemed too right-wing. They also rejected efforts to team up with nonpartisan, nonprofit foundations that sought to institute market-based reforms that might improve Chicago's costly, and failing, public school system.[83]

In 2012, Chicago Teachers Union president Karen Lewis, who also led CORE, refused to greet Vice President Joe Biden at a Chicago rally because he was deemed insufficiently left-wing. CORE members donned red union shirts instead of Obama-Biden campaign T-shirts at an event because the administration was pushing for mild market-based school reforms.[84]

And how are these revolutionaries doing in what the public believes is their actual mission—education? Six years after CORE formed, barely one in four Chicago public-school students can read at grade level.[85] Just 25 percent of fourth graders in Chicago public schools are proficient or better in math, and only 27 percent are proficient or better in reading.[86]

In one press release, Chicago public schools omitted the actual numbers on proficiency and described the test results as a success story, but only because a 75 percent illiteracy rate isn't the worst they've ever done.[87] About a quarter of Chicago public-school students don't graduate from high school, and only 8 percent get their bachelor's degrees within ten years of beginning high school.[88–89]

None of these facts and figures apparently weighed on the minds of the 96 percent of teachers who voted to walk out of the classroom in support of "social justice." Sadly, both the 2012 and 2016 walkouts took place during the school year. That means that while teachers marched to shut Chicago down, 330,000 Chicago public-school students were locked out of their classrooms.[90]

These days an entire infrastructure exists for left-wing teachers to indoctrinate students in their delusions. More than a dozen national or regional organizations exist to provide guidance and lesson plans to high-school and middle-school teachers interested in teaching students about social justice.

There's the Association of Raza Educators, which plans to "establish a Raza educator-led social movement that will fight for the liberation of our people."[91] There's the Boston Teacher Activist Group and the national Education for Liberation Network, which helps teach people about the "injustices" their communities face.[92] There are so many groups that they have trouble coming up with new names, leading to the coexistence of the San Francisco–based Teachers 4 Social Justice and the Chicago-based Teachers for Social Justice.[93–94]

There is, of course, an element of self-interest in all of this. These unionized teachers are government employees. Though in the long run they are driving Illinois into bankruptcy, in the short run they benefit from big government, high taxes, and increased government spending. Like any other class of government worker, market-based reforms threaten their jobs. As a group, these employees have failed at their mission, that much is undeniable, and the free market wouldn't tolerate failure.

Tenure for Teachers vs. Performance for Students

The term *public school* itself is a euphemism for *government school*. That's the root of the system's bias: America's public-school system doesn't function like a business and therefore lacks the incentives to produce improved outcomes for students.

There are three major inefficiencies that make the public-school system different from more efficient private-sector firms:

(1) public schools have *captive consumers (students),* (2) school districts *reward poor teacher performance,* and (3) *teacher tenure* prevents bad teachers from being fired.

Captive consumers: In a normal marketplace, companies need to produce products that consumers want. Consumer choice fuels competition between private firms. Profit-seeking companies must adapt to the demands of the marketplace to stay in business.

When consumers can shop around for products they want, they have the power to determine what they end up buying. That places pressure on businesses to lower prices and improve quality. The system rewards the company that produces the best product at the lowest cost. That's the beauty of the free-market system. It doesn't eliminate self-interest; that is impossible. It puts the self-interest of business—the desire to make a profit—at the service of the customer.

Public schools don't have to compete for their clients. They have captive customers. Students who are unable to afford private school are forced to attend a local public school, which is often dictated by their address rather than their preference.

In education, middle-class, working-class, and low-income students (the students often most in need of a quality education) rarely have many options. Admission to alternative schools, like charter schools or schools for talented students, often depends on luck-based lotteries or passing admission tests.

When incentives fail to serve students' interests, students' interests simply don't get served. That's how you end up with unions staging walkouts during the school year, hurting the very students they're supposed to be helping. If private-sector workers simply refused to come to work in order to go downtown and cause chaos, they could very well lose their jobs once the frenzy subsided.

Letting down customers the way the Chicago teachers let down their already-disadvantaged students would be unacceptable at any reputable business. But the district's administrators know they will have students no matter how irresponsible or repugnant their teachers are.

For seventeen years, I ran a restaurant company that produced high-quality food at affordable prices. We had great franchisees who knew their business and great employees who cared about their work. I give them all the credit. But if our customers had been captive—if they had not had choices about where they bought their hamburgers—the ethic of our company would have broken down over time. We would have served our customers about as well as the Chicago public schools serve theirs.

Rewarding poor performance: In market-based industries, companies retain talent by rewarding good employees with benefits and higher pay. Compensation and salaries are based on supply and demand. Sometimes companies give ownership stakes to employees or compensate them for performance through profit sharing, annual bonuses, or commissions. Private-sector compensation is generally tied to the quality of the employee's performance.

Not so for teachers, who normally get paid based on the length of their employment rather than the quality of their teaching. They are rewarded for time spent rather than time well spent.

For example, New York City bases salary increases for public-school teachers on formulas rather than student achievement.[95] Schedules for teacher pay are available online and are directly tied to the teacher's educational attainment and time served rather than teacher quality.[96] Pay increases depend on keeping your teaching job for as long as possible rather than actually delivering results. A good teacher with ten years of experience will get paid less than a bad, activist teacher with twenty years of experience. That's just how the system works.

When the Chicago Teachers Union walked out of classrooms, one of their grievances was a proposal that would have introduced performance-based pay to public schools. The union actively opposed paying good teachers more, arguing that there was no evidence to support the notion that good employees are attracted to higher pay and that "merit pay practices undermine the goal of educational equity."[97] The union actually took the position that increasing teachers' compensation based on performance would create educational inequity.

No evidence supports the notion that good employees are attracted to higher pay? Seriously? Private-sector employers attract talent through performance-based pay all the time and with great success. If an incentive-based system didn't work, businesses wouldn't use it. The simple logic of performance-based compensation is that it incentivizes people to perform. If more people have an incentive to perform, more people will perform.

Maybe—or even surely—one of the reasons Chicago's students perform so poorly on English and math tests is because their teachers lack the incentives to actually teach them anything. Rather, they have incentives to stage walkouts in solidarity with "oppressed peoples." If the protesting teachers' own pay depended on the academic success of their students, canceling classes to protest would seem less important.

Teacher Tenure: This is perhaps the most destructive incentive-destroying policy at play in America's public schools. Tenure awards teachers and professors who stay through a probationary period with a contract guaranteeing them employment (absent "just cause," for termination, such as severe misconduct). Even with evidence of incompetence, the difficulty of successfully navigating the administrative process makes it all but impossible to fire tenured teachers in our nation's largest public-school systems. Simply, it's how the system protects incompetent teachers.

Underperforming employees at private-sector firms always face the risk of having their compensation reduced or being fired for poor performance. If an average private-sector employee stopped showing up to work, their employer would discipline or fire them. If the average private-sector employee engaged in gross negligence or sexually assaulted customers, their employer would fire them immediately. Not so for our public-school teachers.

Tenure is highly unusual in any industry, including in government, and originally existed to protect the academic freedom of controversial university professors who risked getting fired for holding provocative viewpoints. Over time, teachers' unions negotiated tenure benefits for primary and secondary public-school teachers.

But, what kind of controversial viewpoints does a third-grade music teacher have that require protections for academic freedom? Think about the incentives at play: When employees know they won't be held to account for poor performance, why would they ever improve?

In many cases, they don't, and tenured public-school teachers collect paychecks even after appalling behavior. The costs of firing a tenured teacher can reach hundreds of thousands of dollars, and the process often takes years.

In Paterson, New Jersey, a tenured second-grade teacher routinely urinated into plastic water bottles in front of his class and forced students to carry the bottles to the bathroom for disposal.[98] It took two years of lawsuits before the district was able to fire him, and he remained on paid leave the entire time.[99]

School districts must pay the fired teacher's salary while they're on leave, while also covering legal fees and the costs of a substitute to actually teach the course. An orchestra teacher in

Ann Arbor, Michigan, was fired for pursuing a romantic relationship with a student but collected paychecks for two years after his firing as he made legal appeals in court.[100] One school board in New Jersey spent $350,000 to fire a teacher who forced his elementary-school students to give him back rubs.[101]

Sometimes districts find a less expensive workaround, like when one Illinois district paid a science teacher $60,000 to resign after seven female students accused him of harassment.[102]

It's so difficult to fire a teacher in New York City that the city's school system famously set up "rubber rooms" to serve as holding pens for teachers who can't be trusted near students.[103] It was easier (and cheaper) to pay them to do nothing than to fire them. New York City's Department of Education spends $25 million a year on teachers who are removed from the classroom for misconduct or incompetence.[104] This hardly seems like a wise use of taxpayer dollars.

These teachers are not bugs in the system. They are features of it. Their cases demonstrate how difficult it would be to terminate or even penalize a teacher for something as mundane as incompetence, but incompetence damages student potential, particularly for the disadvantaged.

In 2014, eight high-school students sued California, arguing that the state's teacher tenure, seniority, and dismissal laws put "economically disadvantaged students, students of color, and English learners" at risk. Initially, they won. In *Vergara v. California,* a Los Angeles judge struck down these laws, holding that they unconstitutionally trapped disadvantaged students in underperforming schools and made it all but impossible to terminate underperforming teachers.[105]

The court described California's defense of these laws as an argument that the state has "a compelling interest" in separating students from competent teachers and in retaining incompetent ones. The effect of these laws on poor and minority students "shocks the conscience." In a state that is all but controlled by powerful teachers' unions, it was a very encouraging decision for underprivileged Californians. It also generated a panic among teachers' unions nationally.

The teachers' unions appealed the decision, contending that it eliminated job security for teachers. Admittedly, for incompetent teachers, it did.

Nonetheless, in a victory for state and national teachers' unions and their Progressive allies, the California Court of Appeals reversed the decision.[106] Incompetent teachers across the nation breathed a sigh of relief.

It certainly isn't difficult to understand how teachers who personally benefit from tenure policies, longevity-based pay, and guaranteed customers from a captive clientele might object to free-market reforms that impose performance requirements. When teachers benefit from the inefficiencies of a centrally planned, government-funded education system, they will eventually realize that market-based education reforms, like vouchers and privatization, are not good for them no matter how good they may be for their students.

Of course, not all teachers hate capitalism nor are all teachers happy paying union dues to organizations that are still flailing the dead horse of socialism. However, too many teachers support or remain silent about the outrages and abuses of their unions and the damage it causes to children.

On one level, that is understandable. It's in their short-term economic interest to go along with the unions. But that raises another irony: The unions attack capitalism because it supposedly places self-interest ahead of the good of others, when they and many of their members are doing exactly the same thing.

The Progressive Curriculum

Even well-intentioned public-school teachers can have little choice but to teach anti-capitalist viewpoints. A prominent high school textbook for Advanced Placement Economics—used to teach the best of the best American students—was written by Progressive advocate Paul Krugman.

This work makes the patently absurd claim that Reagan-era supply-side economics is "generally dismissed by economic researchers" due to "lack of evidence."[107] Apparently, the declines in inflation and unemployment accompanied by increases in gross domestic product and family income during the Reagan years are insufficient evidence, but if that's the book the school provides, that is what the teacher teaches.

One common high school history textbook is *A People's History of the United States* by Howard Zinn, an anti-American Marxist.[108] The book is a 729-page anti-American screed that treats American government and capitalism as evil oppressors of various marginalized groups.[109] Zinn calls for "radical change" that would take the "levers of power" away from "the giant corporations, the military, and their politician collaborators."[110] He says America needs "to reconstruct the economy for both efficiency and justice," which should lead to "an equal and ample distribution of goods."[111]

Eventually, he gets to his real point, saying that "certain basic things would be abundant enough to be taken out of the money system and be available—free—to everyone: food, housing, health care, education, transportation."[112] From each according to his ability, to each according to his need, as the old communist slogan goes.

A People's History is not some fringe book that nobody's reading. Rather, it's one of the most popular books on American history in print today. Since it was published in 1980, the book has sold more than two million copies and, nearly three decades later, remains in the Top 100 best-selling history books on Amazon.[113–114]

The *Zinn Education Project,* formed in 2008 to help teachers develop lessons informed by Zinn's Far Left ideology, has wide-reaching influence and includes teaching materials like "Rethinking Mathematics: Teaching Social Justice by the Numbers."[115]

In short, Zinn's malarkey gets passed off to millions of kids as history.

When parents of minority students in the Ann Arbor, Michigan, public schools complained that classes on American history were "alienating" their children, the superintendent of schools suggested that they start using *A People's History* as the standard textbook, to which the chair of the district's social studies department replied, "Oh, we're already using that."[116]

I have a suggestion to offer state legislators around the country, something that would genuinely help fewer students feel "alienated" from our unique American system. They should learn what it can do for them. States should require students to take, and pass, a seminar on capitalism as a condition of graduating from high school. Yes, the public-school establishment will scream about interference, but no one outside the bubble need or should listen to them. The lies of socialism have been debunked by both scholarship and experience; it's time for our representatives to insist that young people have real exposure to the truth about capitalism and basic economics.

A Progressive Education's Impact on Beliefs

Clearly, some intervention is needed because so many years of indoctrination has kept socialist ideology alive among a section of young people. A 2016 YouGov poll found that 43 percent of Americans ages 18 to 29 had a "favorable" view of socialism, compared to just 26 percent who had an unfavorable view. They were the only age group that had a more positive than negative impression of socialism.

The majority of millennial Democrats and Clinton voters say they support socialism over capitalism. One-third of millennials overall, regardless of political party, support socialism as an economic system. Many millennials have no conception of the costs of central planning or communism's disastrous record in the twentieth century or of capitalism's amazingly positive impact in reducing poverty worldwide since the fall of the Soviet Union.

A 2016 poll commissioned by the Victims of Communism Memorial Foundation showed that one-third of millennials believed that George W. Bush killed more people than Joseph Stalin, while 75 percent of millennials underestimated the number of people killed under communism. Admittedly, given the appalling extent of the slaughter under these communist leaders—Stalin in the Soviet Union killed as many as 60 million and Mao Zedong in China killed some 65 million—it is an easy number to underestimate.[117–118]

But I suspect this support for socialism among a minority of young people is very shallow. The more profound effect of this indoctrination has been the ignorance among young people about capitalism—their own country's economic system. Nationwide testing in 2012 showed that fewer than half of America's twelfth graders were proficient in basic economics. The system is failing minority students in particular. Just 17 percent of African American students and 26 percent of Hispanic students are proficient in economics.

On topics like personal finance, it's even worse. In 2016, FINRA, an agency that regulates America's financial markets, polled Americans on financial literacy; two-thirds of respondents failed the test. Sadly, the number of people failing has actually been rising since the height of the financial crisis in 2009.[119] A Gallup survey on financial illiteracy had the same outcome as FINRA's: Americans were unable to answer basic questions about risk diversification, inflation, or compound interest.[120]

Is capitalism's dynamic ability to create opportunity and prosperity simply too complicated for Americans (especially younger people) to understand, leading to a preference for socialism's simple "equality of poverty"? No, they just aren't hearing both sides.

That so many young people strongly believe in socialism and central planning—and that so many teachers get away with advocating it—is a strong indictment of America's education system. Teachers' unions and the teachers themselves have reduced education in America, at all levels, to reading, writing, and redistribution. But mostly redistribution.

If they tested how well students understand the tenets of social justice or income inequality, my guess is that today's students' test scores would be much higher than what we're seeing for reading, writing, and arithmetic (let alone finance and economics). The Progressive agenda is simply what they're being taught.

Some Signs of Positive Change: Beyond the Propaganda

As bad as things are in America's Progressive classrooms, there are reasons to be hopeful. Many of the structural barriers that prevent students from getting a decent education are finally under threat.

First, technological change and shifting political headwinds have diminished the influence of once-powerful teachers' unions.[121] Should the Supreme Court's decision in the *Janus* case prohibit states from requiring union membership or paying union fees as a condition of employment, the power of public-employee unions, such as the teachers' unions, will thankfully decline.

School choice is also gaining bipartisan support among voters and politicians, and the failures of the current system are increasingly evident. The Obama administration, for example, set up a $7 billion fund that dumped money on failing public schools, which, by the administration's own account, "had no significant impacts on math or reading test scores, high school graduation, or college enrollment."[122] With results that bad, even some Democrats have come around to support market-based education reforms.

In 2016, Washington, DC's ultra-liberal city government teamed up with Paul Ryan and Congressional Republicans to preserve a successful school voucher program.[123] Such reforms give parents more control over who gets to teach their kids, which will make it more difficult for districts to employ radical, left-wing activists who propagandize rather than teach.

Not surprisingly, the Trump administration is pushing for major education reforms that could well upend the failed system. Trump's excellent choice for education secretary, Betsy DeVos, cut her teeth as a school-choice activist who advocated for voucher systems and charter schools. If there's any indication of the threat DeVos poses, it's how the teachers' unions responded to her appointment. Their fury was palpable. Randi Weingarten, the president of the American Federation of Teachers, described DeVos as "the most ideological, anti–public education nominee" in history.[124]

If Secretary DeVos successfully ends the public-school monopoly on education for disadvantaged students, there's a chance parents will be able to get their students out of schools run by Progressive activists. The reforms could cripple the teachers' unions and undermine the Progressive plot to use the education system to indoctrinate students. John Dewey's educational reforms and plans to inculcate socialist values in students will fail if students can opt out of the system.

Economics education is also starting to take off in America. Numerous market-oriented groups now exist to counter the influence of anti-capitalist propaganda in the classroom.

The California-based Foundation for Teaching Economics holds seminars that teach high-school students and teachers how to think like an economist.[125] During the Obama years, numerous student-activist groups like Turning Point USA and Students for Liberty started spreading capitalist ideas on college campuses, which counter the anti–free market narrative in the classroom. This kind of powerful pro-capitalism infrastructure is a relatively recent phenomenon.

There is even some hope in higher academia. The number of college students pursuing degrees in economics has surged in recent years.[126] Assuming they're not all students at the University of Massachusetts Amherst, their education will be a powerful antidote to the propaganda coming from the sociology, history, and humanities professors who constantly and ignorantly attack free markets.

All told, with the Trump administration's leadership, it's possible that the truth about capitalism might be returning to the classroom. There's only so much that anti-market propagandists can do to hide the failed history of central planning and socialism. The socialist orthodoxy on campuses and in classrooms is finally under siege from market-oriented educational reformers and a new presidential administration that seeks to institute businesslike reforms on America's failed system.

I believe that sooner or later they will succeed, and when they do, a new generation of American students will have the opportunity to learn about the great system they have inherited, the opportunities it gave to people like me, and the future it offers to all who believe in themselves and their country.

There is a reason people we discussed earlier in this book, like Madam C. J. Walker (the descendant of slaves) and Cornelius Vanderbilt (the descendant of an indentured servant), were able to succeed in this country in ways unimaginable anywhere else. It was our unique American capitalism, and we should teach that system's importance to American children as clearly as we teach the values of life, liberty, and the pursuit of happiness.

CHAPTER SIX

Entertainment: Rich Guy, Bad Guy

> *"[O]f all the arts the most important for us is the cinema."*
>
> VLADIMIR LENIN
>
> FOUNDER OF THE RUSSIAN COMMUNIST PARTY

Hollywood: Land of Dreams

The entertainment industry has become another essential ally in the Progressive's war on profit. While an important element of the Progressive propaganda machine, this alliance is both ironic and hypocritical. After all, Hollywood is the land of fame, fortune, and celebrity excess. Take a ride through west Los Angeles and you'll see hundred-thousand-dollar cars, limousines, paparazzi, and multimillion-dollar mansions.

That excess reflects Hollywood's status as one of the most aspirational cities on the planet. The film *Pretty Woman*, an iconic Cinderella story, ends with the exclamation that "this is Hollywood, land of dreams!" People from around the world flock there for a chance to make it big; a shot at the fame and fortune that come with a movie-star life.

Where else in the world could a struggling entertainer miss rent and face eviction this year, only to be shopping for a Maserati next year? One lucky break can make all the difference. Hollywood is a rags-to-riches story. Just ask the multimillionaire celebrities and entertainment industry magnates who live there.

On second thought, asking them might not be the best idea. I lived in Southern California for twenty-five years and can state unequivocally that some of the most successful people in Hollywood don't understand the economic forces that combined to provide them with their privileged lifestyles. They seem unable to grasp the reality that their immense wealth comes from a free market that places an astronomically high value on their talents as entertainers.

Not only do they fail to understand the system, they outright hate it—and want the rest of us to hate it. They inject this hatred into the popular entertainment they export to the rest of the country, if not the world.

The central contradiction at the root of Hollywood's hypocrisy is that the whole town is brimming with extremely rich socialists. Some millionaire celebrities publicly supported Progressive senator Bernie Sanders as he ran for president on a platform that boiled down to confiscating and redistributing wealth. Apparently unaware of this irony, Sanders's celebrity supporters publicly extolled the virtues of his socialist positions.

Even worse, some of Hollywood's richest celebrities openly advocate third-world socialism as a preferable alternative to the American free market.

While celebrity support for both Progressive candidates and socialist dictators is widespread, Hollywood's efforts to demean and demonize American businessmen and women know no bounds. On both TV and movie screens, businesspeople are portrayed as greedy, mean-spirited, and sometimes even sociopathic. They comprise a huge part of the villain class of stock movie characters, which puts them in such company as terrorists, gangsters, and Nazis.

The fairy tales and fiction that come out of Hollywood often make for enjoyable, riveting entertainment. However, the fiction that the free market is a tool of oppression and that Americans would be better off under socialism not only makes for poor entertainment, it's both patently false and downright dangerous. Nonetheless, filmmakers and celebrities pursue this Progressive narrative with vigor.

Progressives could find no better propaganda arm. The Left has long understood the entertainment industry's importance. As early as February 1922, Vladimir Lenin, founder of the Russian Communist Party, stated that "of all the arts the most important for us is the cinema."[1]

In the 1930s, Willie Muenzenberg was a leading figure in the Comintern, Moscow's front for worldwide coordination of the Left under Soviet control. Muenzenberg made the recruitment of Hollywood elites a priority, observing, "One of the most pressing tasks confronting the Communist Party in the field of propaganda is the conquest of this supremely important propaganda unit, until now the monopoly of the ruling class. We must wrest it from them and turn it against them."[2]

The Communist Party's success in wresting control of Hollywood was forestalled due to the actions of anti-communists such as Ronald Reagan, who was head of the Screen Actors Guild in the late 1940s. Nonetheless, it is hard to ignore the current success of Progressives in taking control of "this supremely important propaganda unit" to advance their agenda.

In fact, Hollywood's role in the Progressives' war on profit is as undeniable as it is hypocritical.

Feel the Bern

Take, for example, the case of Susan Sarandon—Oscar winner, star of such classics as *The Rocky Horror Picture Show, Thelma and Louise,* and *Bull Durham*, multimillionaire, and avowed socialist. Sarandon owns multiple New York City apartments, including a multimillion-dollar Greenwich Village condo. That condo is walking distance from her $3.2 million two-floor co-op in Chelsea, which she bought after her split from millionaire movie-star partner Tim Robbins.[3] In 2012, she bought a third apartment—a 2,500-square-foot pad in Brooklyn.[4] Her estimated net worth is in the tens of millions of dollars, which easily places her among America's richest people.

Susan Sarandon embodies the One Percent.

You wouldn't know any of this from Sarandon's politics. In 2016, she hit the campaign trail with Vermont senator Bernie Sanders. At a rally in Mason City, Iowa, Sarandon choked up as she introduced him at a rally.[5] She decried America's growing income inequality and blamed the country's economic woes on the rich.

When asked by *The Young Turks,* a left-wing media outlet, why she was so emotional about his candidacy, she remarked, "You have that percentage getting smaller and smaller that owns more and more, and people working so hard, you can't blame the Mexicans forever, you have to understand that it's not the immigrants that are creating this problem."[6]

It might seem strange that an extremely wealthy movie star with multiple million-dollar apartments in New York City was expressing concern about the concentration of wealth and even lecturing Americans on what they "have to understand." But it wasn't strange to Sarandon. In fact, her 2016 election odyssey only got stranger from there.

When Sanders dropped out of the race, Sarandon endorsed Green Party candidate Jill Stein. In a letter to the Stein campaign, she stated that she disapproved of Hillary Clinton because

Clinton didn't support a national $15 minimum wage and breaking up the big banks.[7] Stein filled the void: her position on the issues was somewhere to the left of and, if possible, more economically illiterate than Sanders's positions.

Stein promised to "end unemployment in America once and for all by guaranteeing a job at a living wage for every American willing and able to work."[8] The jobs program was going to place people in sustainable energy careers, clean manufacturing jobs, and mass transit positions.[9] If this type of government-dominated economy worked, the Soviet Union would be the world's leading economy, China would never have deserted socialism, and each night the lights would shine from North, rather than South, Korea.

Leaving the merits (or lack of merit) of Stein's promises aside for a moment, if Sarandon were really interested in Stein's economic plans, she could do something about it herself. She certainly has the money to help. If Sarandon simply sold her $3.2 million penthouse and moved permanently to her multimillion-dollar condo in Greenwich Village, she'd have millions of dollars in cash to donate or to invest in green jobs. With $3.2 million, she could pay a worker $15 per hour for eight hours per day, seven days per week for seventy-three straight years. Some of her poorer neighbors in New York would no doubt take her up on the offer.

Sarandon's story isn't unique. Bernie Sanders's campaign released a list of 128 celebrities who endorsed the Progressive socialist.[10] It was hardly a roll call of has-beens looking to revive their flagging careers by jumping in with the "cool" politician the kids seemed to like. There were some extremely rich, household-name celebrities on this list—people like Danny DeVito, who sold his Beverly Hills home for $28 million, and multimillionaire actor Mark Ruffalo.[11–12]

Ruffalo is both a socialist and a global warming alarmist, though when other activists pushed him to divest his holdings in companies that contribute to global warming, he opted instead to hold the stocks for a few more years.[13]

At the bottom of the celebrity endorsement list was the standard notice required by the Federal Election Commission, but with Sanders's own twist: "Paid for by Bernie 2016 (not the billionaires)."[14] Maybe there weren't billionaires on the list, strictly speaking, but there were plenty of Hollywood mega-millionaires. That still makes them richer than 99 percent of the country.

In a letter explaining why they chose to support Sanders, those same celebrities explained that Sanders had "a vision that pushes for a progressive economic agenda. It's a vision that creates jobs, raises wages, protects the environment, and gets big money out of politics." Apparently, their own "big money" is acceptable in politics.

Most of Sanders's movie-star supporters were the exact sort of people he claimed to be running against and demonized at every turn. Actor Daniel Craig donated $47,000 to a pro-Sanders super PAC.[15] Craig, too, is another One-Percenter who jumped on the Sanders bandwagon. Sony Pictures reportedly offered Craig $150 million for just two James Bond movies.[16]

Seth MacFarlane, the creator of *Family Guy* and other popular TV shows, acknowledged on Twitter that "Yes, I know we Hollywood liberals can be self-righteous, insufferable meatheads, but come on—Bernie Sanders would make an A+ president."[17] In 2008, MacFarlane signed a $100 million deal with Fox.[18]

Bernie Sanders decried people for being too rich if they worked for banks or hedge funds—or, presumably, restaurant chains—but had no problem with his own millionaire friends pitching in forkloads of cash. And these self-proclaimed supporters of a self-proclaimed socialist appeared totally ignorant of their own hypocrisy. The gulf between what they practice and what they preach is immeasurable.

How are these socialist-supporting celebrities able to accumulate multimillion-dollar fortunes in the first place? How can studios afford to pay them these enormous amounts? It's because the studios that employ them run their businesses as true capitalists: They do everything they can to generate revenue, reduce costs, and produce profits, just like big banks, hedge funds, or any other business that intends to survive.

For example, production companies often seek taxpayer funding for their mega hits through tax credits and rebates from the city or state in which they film. These are essentially cash payments for filming in that jurisdiction and can exceed the production company's state or municipal tax liability.

At the federal level, the American Jobs Creation Act of 2004, provides movie and TV producers an income tax deduction of 9 percent on taxable income from "any qualified film produced by the taxpayer" in the United States.[19] The point of this tax deduction is to keep the studios filming in the United States rather than moving production to foreign jurisdictions where labor costs and taxes are lower (a practice for which Progressives often criticize American corporations).

In other words, at the federal, state, and local levels, taxpayer dollars reduce filmmakers' costs through tax deductions, tax credits, and rebates, increasing the amounts available for the studios to attract and compensate their stars. Hollywood lobbies for these tax benefits, arguing that they create jobs in the jurisdictions in which they film.

The entertainment industry seems to understand that lowering taxes spurs economic activity when the tax benefits flow to them and their stars. However, when it comes to every other American, they are suddenly Progressive socialists supporting candidates who want income redistribution through taxation. Why is it a good thing to reduce taxes for the production companies that pay these socialist-supporting stars' salaries but evil capitalism for everyone else?

Though many stars make donations to charities (as do many corporations and entrepreneurs), why do these mega-rich socialist celebrities accept or keep more than they need for an average lifestyle? They could certainly donate the vast majority of their net worth to aid the poor and needy and still live very comfortable lives. Would a true socialist really amass hundreds of millions of dollars in personal wealth and choose to multiply it like a big bank CEO or a hedge fund manager?

Hollywood's Progressive socialists do.

While Hollywood's elite have supported some absurd political causes, none can match their unwavering support for pure, unadulterated socialism, an economic system that has inflicted untold suffering on those forced to live under it and has been abandoned by virtually every nation that has tried it.

Hugo Chávez: Hollywood Hero

An even more disturbing trend among the Hollywood Progressive set is, or rather, *was* their support for socialist dictators such as Hugo Chávez in Venezuela. Global jet setters, such as Sean Penn, Oliver Stone, and Danny Glover, would travel to the economically ravaged, repressive South American country to celebrate "economic justice."

Chávez never kept his political beliefs a secret. In 2009, speaking to a large group of unionists in New York City, Chávez stated that "the only way to save the world is socialism."[20] He detested free markets, believing that "the free market has messed everything up. What is labor flexibility for them becomes hungry children" (a remark that would later prove ironic). Nor did he attempt to conceal his support for communism, stating, "Their slogan is even more true now than in 1848, when Marx and Engels wrote the Communist Manifesto: Workers of the world, unite!"[21]

Oscar-winning actor Sean Penn (who has an estimated net worth of $150 million) was a well-publicized fan of Chávez's socialist policies and even hit the campaign trail with Chávez the year before his death. When Chávez died in 2013, Penn told the *Hollywood Reporter,* "Today the people of the United States lost a friend it never knew it had. And poor people around the world lost a champion."[22] He added, "Venezuela and its revolution will endure under the proven leadership of Vice President Maduro."

Oliver Stone, who made a fortune directing movies with left-wing themes, also mourned the death of Chávez. Stone told the *Hollywood Reporter* that Chávez was a "great hero."[23] There's no doubt Stone holds Chávez in high esteem. His 2009 film *Al Sur de la Frontera* (*South of the Border*) depicts the tender side of the Venezuelan strongman. The film is pure pro-Chávez propaganda and conveniently skips over his history of authoritarianism and human-rights violations.[24] Showing the Chávez regime's goons arresting judges and opposition politicians or shutting down privately owned television stations would hardly fit the narrative.[25]

But one celebratory documentary wasn't enough for Stone. In 2014, on the anniversary of Chávez's death, he released a second film titled *Mi Amigo Hugo* (*My Friend Hugo*). Venezuelan state-run media described it as "a human portrait of the leader of the Bolivarian Revolution."[26]

But neither Penn nor Stone match the enthusiasm that actor Danny Glover has for Venezuelan socialism. Glover, star of the

Lethal Weapon series of movies, has a long history of close relationships with Venezuela's socialist leaders. In 2007, the *Guardian* reported that Venezuela's government paid Glover $18 million to produce a film about the Haitian Revolution.[27] Chávez, who was Glover's close, personal friend, greenlit the idea. Chávez wanted to use Hollywood to showcase the evils of Western imperialism.[28] Fortunately for viewers around the world, the film was never released.

When Hugo Chávez died in 2013, Glover issued a statement, saying, "We all embraced Hugo Chávez as a social champion of democracy, material development, and spiritual well-being."[29] In 2014, Glover returned to Venezuela. At a political rally with Chávez's anointed successor, President Nicolás Maduro, Glover commemorated Chávez's "vision of a participatory democracy, one involving all citizens."[30]

After visiting Venezuela and meeting Chávez in 2013, socialist and Bernie Sanders–supporting filmmaker Michael Moore appeared to have found the country of his dreams, tweeting, "Hugo Chavez declared the oil belonged 2 the ppl. He used the oil $ 2 eliminate 75% of extreme poverty, provide free health & education 4 all."[31]

As Penn predicted, Maduro continued Chávez's policies. By December 2013, Maduro announced that Venezuela's inflation rate was 56.2 percent.[32] In 2014, violent protests roiled across Venezuela, challenging the Chávez-Maduro socialist policies as unban violence ran rampant and people were unable to purchase basic necessities, such as food or medical supplies.

Maduro, who got his start as a union activist, blamed "the parasitic bourgeoisie."[33] He promised "an economic offensive" against shopkeepers he called "capitalist parasites."[34] Apparently, the shopkeepers were attempting to stay in business and make a profit despite the then-current socialist policies that essentially insisted they sell goods at a loss. The *Washington Post* reported, "Some anguished shopkeepers cried as they watched their inventories snatched off the shelves at a fraction of their cost." This socialist offensive produced historically predictable results.

In August 2015, PBS reported the following: Food shortages "prompted some violence." Families of children with cancer demonstrated in front of a children's hospital, protesting "the country's shortage of chemotherapy treatments." Venezuela "has some of the highest HIV and teen pregnancy rates in South America," but there are tens of thousands of HIV-infected Venezuelans with "no access to antiretroviral drugs and condoms are scarce in the country."[35]

Within three years, the country's Supreme Court would render the National Assembly powerless, riots would break out throughout Venezuela, and the socialists would start cracking down on the opposition by arming their supporters.[36–37]

Just three years after Danny Glover visited the country to celebrate its participatory democracy, Maduro secured power in a sham election that left more than a dozen people dead.[38] Maduro replaced the National Assembly with a fake, party-run legislature that confirmed constitutional changes that essentially gave him dictatorial powers.

Venezuela's democracy collapsed, the currency's value plummeted, and the government started imprisoning bakers because of a bread shortage. In December 2016, Venezuela's inflation rate reached a record high of 800 percent.[39] Reminiscent of the Soviet Union prior to its collapse, the citizens of the socialist nation couldn't even buy toilet paper.

By May 2017, CNN reported, "Violence and unrest are tearing Venezuela apart. Lost somewhere in the spray of bullets and fog of tear gas are the stories of the dead."[40] In December 2017, the *New York Times* confirmed that "emergency rooms were being overwhelmed by children with severe malnutrition," including "the kind of extreme malnutrition often found in refugee camps—cases that were highly unusual in oil-rich Venezuela before its economy fell to pieces."[41] According to a January 2018 Reuters report, "Long supermarket lines and people eating from the trash are common sights."[42]

It's worth noting that the celebrities who love Venezuela, and seem to love owning multiple homes, never purchased a villa in the nation they are so eager to support. None of them, it seemed, ever had plans to actually move to the country. Can you blame them? When the country's full-fledged socialist government predictably went into economic and political collapse, the publicity-laden visits stopped. Penn, Stone, Glover, and Moore were nowhere to be found. Perhaps they retreated to their mansions in states such as California where, unlike Progressive Venezuela, the government has yet to seize private property.[43]

Socialism creates the very suffering socialists claim they will eliminate. To quote Chávez, although with a different intent: "What is labor flexibility for them becomes hungry children." Even Mao's communist China has adopted free-market principles and is no longer a purely socialist nation.

Yet, Hollywood elites who benefit tremendously from free-market capitalism continue to expound the virtues of socialism while retaining and expanding the benefits of their free-market success.

Why Socialism

Why do so many rich and successful celebrities believe in socialism? Perhaps because it's easy to support higher taxes and reduced income inequality when you have made your money and are sitting poolside in Beverly Hills. Socialist policies are far more likely to hurt the people trying to get rich than the people who are already rich.

That's how you end up with movie stars ruminating about a $15 per hour minimum wage, while they enjoy the opulent lifestyles of the Hollywood elite. A $15 minimum wage will never personally affect them. Nor will it affect them if small businesses from Seattle to Kansas City to Philadelphia have to lay off workers, automate positions, or shut down because they can't afford to stay open, leaving working-class Americans without jobs.

Publicly expressing a commitment to helping the poor is a win-win for celebrities, particularly if the method for doing so uses taxpayer dollars. They get to keep and grow their vast wealth while also earning credit in their Progressive social set for public professions of what Hollywood views as moral virtue. It's far easier to advocate helping the poor with other people's money than it is to give up your massive wealth and live like a true socialist.

For some celebrities, support of socialist principles may assuage feelings of guilt that come from believing they are undeserving of the wealth, fame, and accolades they receive. These individuals need to show the world they are far more than shallow celebrities living privileged lifestyles without regard for those less fortunate. Publicly supporting candidates who advocate taking from the undeserving wealthy and redistributing that wealth to those in need satiates their need for self-vindication. Simply redistributing their own vast wealth, rather than expanding it, seems not to have occurred to them.

Playing the part of a socialist by attending rallies with the likes of Bernie Sanders and Hugo Chávez, while balancing the reality of their outsized wealth, is a role well suited for people who make their livings by pretending to be someone they are not.

Blacklisting Conservatives

It used to be different. At one point, having extreme left-wing viewpoints would have gotten you blacklisted in Hollywood. People with ties to the Communist Party had their careers damaged or even destroyed.

In 1947, ten Hollywood professionals were asked to testify before the House un-American Activities Committee for suspected communist ties. They refused and were arrested for contempt of Congress. Hollywood's industry big shots issued a statement condemning those ten employees and pledging not to "knowingly" employ a communist ever again.[44] Hollywood was antibusiness even back then, but there was some balance. Progressives had not as yet totally co-opted the industry.

While the entertainment community often speaks of communist blacklisting with revulsion, today those same individuals have a blacklist of their own. Conservative celebrities in Hollywood regularly find themselves marginalized because of their views.

Author, comedian, and actor Orson Bean was blacklisted in the 1950s as a communist. Late in his career, he became a conservative and a Republican. Decades later, he told his son-in-law, the conservative writer Andrew Breitbart, that "it's harder now to be an open conservative on a Hollywood set than it was back then to be a Communist."[45] Bean also said that in the 1950s he "never felt hated by the ring-wing blacklisters. They just felt we were terribly wrong." But, "[t]hese days, the left doesn't just disagree with right-wingers—they hate them. People actually shudder when I tell them I'm a Republican."[46]

There are successful conservative actors with well-established careers who are willing to express conservative views. Clint Eastwood, Jon Voight, James Woods, Robert Davi, Tim Allen, and Gary Sinise are in this group. However, newcomers are unlikely to succeed unless they keep their right-of-center views to themselves. Even for these veteran actors, speaking out is a risky proposition that can destroy their careers.

Actor James Woods regularly expresses his conservative views on social media. In August 2017, he was asked whether there are "more #Repub actors than we know, and they all just remain quiet for fear of being shunned and blacklisted?" He responded, "Absolutely. The only reason I express my views is that I have accepted the fact that I'm blacklisted. Also I bought Apple stock in the 80's."[47]

Award-winning and outspoken actor Robert Davi experienced the impact of being on this blacklist. In August 2017, he stated, "Oh, there is certainly a blacklist these days. I recently had been looked at joining, ironically, the show, 'The Blacklist.' But because I was a vocal Trump supporter, this led to me losing that offer. Even my agent confirmed that to me. So yes, this is a reality we deal with." Unwilling to remain silent, Davi explained, "I'm comfortable no longer having a career."[48]

This anti-conservative bias compels Hollywood's conservatives to meet as members of a secret society called Friends of Abe, which keeps its rolls private to protect its members from vindictive studio bosses and agents. One Hollywood screenwriter, who tellingly refused to be named, told Fox News, "It has become personal, nasty even; there is a definite social blacklisting happening."[49]

Historically, it's never a good sign when people are forced to go underground with their political views.

In a March 2017 interview with late-night talk show host Jimmy Kimmel, actor Tim Allen discussed attending President Trump's inauguration. Ill at ease even discussing politics, he noted, "You gotta be real careful around here, you know. You'll get beat up if you don't believe what everybody believes." He then likened the political atmosphere in Hollywood to that of 1930s Germany.[50]

Allen was the star of the popular ABC comedy *Last Man Standing*. The show was a blue-collar comedy about a successful conservative businessman, his wife, and three daughters. Allen often engaged in "politically incorrect" humor with a conservative bent, although there were also liberals on the show. It was basically about family and was one of the few shows on network television where conservative viewers could avoid being inundated with liberal social and political beliefs.

The show was very popular. Deadline Hollywood reported that it was ABC's second-highest rated comedy, averaging 8.1 million viewers.[51] The overtly socially liberal comedy *Modern Family* was the highest-rated comedy, with an average of 8.7 million viewers. Allen's show was ABC's third most popular scripted series behind *Grey's Anatomy* (also blatantly socially liberal) and *Modern Family*. My wife and I have watched every episode of all three shows, and we are fans.

Despite its popularity, in May 2017, ABC announced that it was canceling *Last Man Standing* and renewing *Modern Family* for two more seasons. The show's fans (including me) were stunned. They weren't alone. On social media, Allen stated, "Stunned and blindsided by the network I called home for the last six years."[52]

The alleged fact-checking website Snopes looked into claims that the show was canceled because of Allen's political beliefs as expressed two months earlier on Jimmy Kimmel's show. Snopes stated that it was "unlikely that Tim Allen's politics were the *sole or primary reason* behind the cancellation of Last Man Standing" (emphasis mine).[53] When discussing whether Allen's political affiliations factored into the decision to cancel the show, ABC

Entertainment president Channing Dungey similarly stated that she "wouldn't say it was the *deciding factor*" (emphasis again mine).[54]

Sole, primary, or deciding, it clearly was a factor.

The message to conservative entertainers was even clearer: As was the case in the 1950s, if you want to work in Hollywood today, your politics matter.

Businessmen: The Stereotypical Villains

The consequence of monolithic, Progressive, anti-capitalist groupthink in Hollywood is, of course, movies that demonize those who achieve wealth and success (outside of Hollywood). Overtly or subtly, the message is the same. Pick a movie at random and there's a very good chance the moral of the story will be that rich people are villains with sinister plots to enrich themselves at the expense of everyone else.

If screenwriters ever treated minorities or women the way they routinely treat business characters, they'd be accused of racism and sexism. What other groups of people could writers, producers, and actors stereotype as out-of-touch, uncaring, dishonest, dismissive, or downright evil with no repercussions whatsoever? Very few, besides criminals, terrorists, Nazis, and maybe Russians.

This is because it's simply wrong to stigmatize entire groups of people based on stereotypes about their behavior. But businesspeople are not a protected class, and the screenwriters have a clear agenda. That's why the bad-guy businessman is so often cast as the villain in American cinema.

Within that category, these villains often emerge as one of four major caricatures: the greedy businessman, the psychotic businessman, the misplaced-priorities businessman, and the evil-mastermind businessman. We know them all because we see them all the time, from childhood through adulthood.

Greedy businessmen are the ones who want to get their hands on massive amounts of money, unencumbered by any pesky moral compass. We meet these characters most often around Christmastime.

The obvious prototype is Ebenezer Scrooge of *A Christmas Carol,* which obviously predates Hollywood. Scrooge is the caricature of a money-lending businessman who hates poor people. By the end of the story, Scrooge reforms and becomes a better person.

Few books have been made into movies more often than *A Christmas Carol* (Charles Dickens is, by the way, one of my favorite authors). The story makes a fair point, and the moral is positive. However, turning Scrooge into a stereotype for successful businessmen is neither fair nor positive.

For example, in *Scrooged* (1988), Bill Murray plays a greedy, selfish TV executive who wants to force his staff to work on Christmas. In the process, he fires people who stand up to him and denies them a Christmas bonus. The movie poster shows Bill Murray wearing a tuxedo and holding a cigar—the stereotypical rich-guy costume and prop.

Psychotic businessmen are exactly what they sound like: totally insane and amoral villains. They are obsessed with wealth and lack any semblance of morality. Patrick Bateman of *American Psycho* (2000) is the model for this villain.

Bateman is a super-rich New York investment banker. His interests and passions are all material. He wants reservations at the nicest restaurants; he is proud of his extensive music collection. Most of all, he is obsessed with the quality of his business cards. He is empty, vain, and vacuous. He also lacks a conscience.

When he sees a nicer business card than his own, he becomes enraged and kills a homeless man. Later in the movie, when he goes to lunch with someone else who also has nicer business cards, Bateman tries to kill him in the restaurant's bathroom. The entire story chronicles Bateman's life as a shallow, New York psychopath and presents a ham-fisted metaphor for the soullessness of capitalism.

The misplaced-priorities businessmen are generally good people who have lost track of what's truly important. They are distracted by money or their careers to the detriment of loved ones. You see misplaced-priorities businesspeople most often in children's movies.

In the children's film *Hook* (1991), based on the classic *Peter Pan,* Captain Hook kidnaps Peter Pan's children. The problem? Peter Pan grew up to be an intense, ruthless mergers and acquisitions lawyer hardly equipped with the skills needed to win a sword fight with Captain Hook. He's forgotten the inherent goodness of being Peter Pan, replacing it with the evils Progressives associate with the pursuit of profit. He needs to relearn what is right.

The evil-mastermind businessmen generally plot to take over something or engage in destructive behavior to serve their own acquisitive needs. James Bond's nemesis Auric Goldfinger is a perfect example of this kind of sinister character.

Goldfinger was a successful businessman with a love for golf and gold. In *Goldfinger* (1964), he plots to detonate a nuclear weapon underneath Fort Knox, rendering the gold radioactive (and therefore useless).[55] By ruining such a large reserve of gold bullion, he would cause a global financial collapse, sparking huge increases in gold prices.

Goldfinger had two weapons at his disposal: a nuclear arsenal and the central law of capitalism—supply and demand. With so much of the world's supply taken off the table, he was set to make a killing with his personal, untainted gold reserves.

Hollywood often uses these stereotypical businessmen as the foil in upfront attacks on free-market capitalism. For example, the movie *Glengarry Glen Ross* (1992) is a hundred-minute screed against American capitalism.[56] Set in Chicago in the 1980s, the movie opens with a stereotypical greedy businessman, played by Alec Baldwin, berating four real-estate salesmen for not selling enough of their properties. He gives them a one-month challenge: The next month's top seller gets a Cadillac. Second place gets a set of steak knives. Everyone else gets fired. It's brutal and ruthless. The point was to convey the harshness and inhuman quality of capitalism.

As is often the case, it was a "death of the American dream" story.

It's ironic, of course, that all the stars of the aforementioned movies make plenty of money for starring in these polemics against, well, money. And because we live in a free society—unlike the people of Venezuela—there is no government censorship horning in on their art and telling them what they can and cannot say about their country. So, the Hollywood machine can chug merrily along, turning out stories about the "death of the American dream" and how this country is too corrupt and greedy to survive—all while making money hand over fist doing it.

But they shut down Tim Allen and his co-stars for daring to make a show about decent family values.

Entrepreneurs in the Crosshairs

Hollywood also produces business movies based on "true" stories that go out of their way to portray entrepreneurs and innovators as contemptible.

Mark Zuckerberg is portrayed as an awkward social climber who is profoundly unlikable in *The Social Network* (2010).[57] The film suggests that he is an egomaniac who gained his success by stealing ideas and screwing over friends and business partners. Zuckerberg said, "There were pretty glaring things that were just made up about the movie that made it pretty hard to take seriously."[58] As with most stories, there are two sides to the tale of Facebook's founding, but making Zuckerberg into a clear villain seemed excessive.

The movie *Jobs* (2013) portrays Apple founder Steve Jobs as a ruthless sociopath who, among other things, leaves his girlfriend because she's pregnant.[59] In his review, critic Roger Ebert described the movie-version of Jobs as "an insensitive self-serving ass, especially when he refuses to acknowledge his out-of-wedlock daughter or denies compensation to deserving friends who helped build the Apple empire back when it was a two-bit operation in his dad's garage."[60]

Steve Jobs and Mark Zuckerberg might not be the world's best people, but their contributions to bettering our lives were, at the very least, significant and, in Jobs's case, immeasurable. They did not deserve to have the worst moments of their lives cherry-picked and demeaned in major motion pictures to create an image consistent with Hollywood Progressive-inspired stereotypes. Movies based on true stories should neither exclude nor diminish major life events to make the subjects look better, nor should they deliberately smear business figures to make them look worse.

Zuckerberg and Jobs made their positive contributions in a free-market capitalist economy and benefitted personally from their success. Begrudging them that success while praising socialist dictators who create little other than pain, misery, and poverty shows Hollywood's distorted scale of values.

One way to avoid criticism for exaggerating the entrepreneurs' personal character flaws is by highlighting the most genuinely deplorable figures in American business. The based-on-real-life story of Jordan Belfort, the protagonist of *The Wolf of Wall Street* (2013), did just that: it depicted a character who amassed a fortune through crime, deception, and fraud.[61] Unlike Zuckerberg or Jobs, Belfort actually was a bad guy who cheated and stole from the people who trusted him with their money.

Another way to avoid criticism for portraying real people as villains is to create one that's fictional. Perhaps Hollywood's greatest hit-job on business of any era came from Oliver Stone (before he made his Hugo Chávez hagiographies).

In the Reagan-era movie *Wall Street* (1987), Stone personified his paranoid loathing of capitalism in the fictional Gordon Gekko, an embodiment of the greedy businessman.[62] The film was a Progressive reaction to the economic success of the Reagan era (which Progressives has been unsuccessfully attempting to discredit for decades), and it introduced one of the slimiest businessman characters in the history of American film.

Gekko, a Wall Street financier, is a very rich guy. He's not rich from making or producing anything, but from "financial engineering," which is basically buying and selling companies for economic gain without regard for the consequences. Of course, he is neither happy nor fulfilled and certainly not a good person. But he has a lot to say about finance, much of which is harsh and inhuman.

In one scene, he calls a broker in the middle of the night, saying, "Money never sleeps, pal. Just made $800,000 Hong Kong gold."[63] At a shareholders meeting for a paper company, Gekko humiliates the corporate executives and drops his signature line: "Greed, for lack of a better word, is good. Greed is right. Greed works."[64]

Gekko enriches himself not through competitive free-market success but rather through illegal insider trading and nefarious plots to buy companies just to lay off the employees and pillage the assets for personal gain.

Wall Street offers an unrealistic and slanted view of American businessmen and women. Not surprisingly, given Stone's political views, it presents a black-and-white, good-versus-evil, socialism-versus-capitalism perspective. In 2010, before Venezuela's collapse into chaos, Stone admitted that the "anti–Gordon Gekko" was Hugo Chávez, saying, "One clarifies the other for me."[65] This limited and distorted viewpoint leaves little room for the decent, ethical, hardworking men and women that constitute the vast majority of America's business community.

Habitually highlighting the worst of the worst in both real-world and fictional business figures has a purpose: it creates a negative stigma against businessmen and women. Belfort and Gekko personify the stereotype. They lived the high life, complete with huge parties, mansions, private jets, models, cocaine, prostitutes, alcohol, and drunk helicopter rides. Hollywood writers and producers have resurrected these personas so often that many of their characteristics now seems cliché.

This feeds a fantasy narrative about businesspeople in general. Hollywood's hope is that audiences on their way out of the theater will think that they all do that sort of thing. A purely Progressive and destructive perspective.

TV as Propaganda

TV show portrayals of businesspeople and capitalism barely differ from the movies.

For example, *The Simpsons* gave us the fictional businessman C. Montgomery Burns. Burns is a mix between the greedy and the evil-mastermind businessman. He's the richest man in Springfield, the city where the Simpsons live, and he owns the nuclear power plant where Homer Simpson works. He's the Hollywood caricature of American business in every way: profit-oriented, selfish, greedy, and very rich.

In one episode, Burns blocks out the sun to drive up energy prices (and therefore make more money). Not that he needs it. *Forbes* magazine includes him on its list of richest fictional characters.[66] Burns lives in an elaborate mansion with a huge wall and security dogs (not unlike many of the Hollywood stars who profess to hate capitalism). He often forgets Homer Simpson's name, despite regularly interacting with him. He habitually bribes local officials and breaks rules with impunity. He is the brainchild of *Simpsons* creator Matt Groening, who is worth some $500 million, and in 2011, he dropped $11.7 million on a Santa Monica mansion with a tennis court and pool.[67]

Mr. Burns is not the only cartoon character obsessed with money. Sometimes they can be found in entertainment aimed at the very youngest viewers. After all, it's never too early to teach children about the dangers of capitalism and the degeneracy of rich businessmen.

The villain in *The Lego Movie* (2014) is named simply Lord Business.[68] Lord Business's evil plot is to develop an ultra-powerful super weapon that would literally glue all the pieces of Lego world together. It's unclear how that would make him richer, but it was an evil plan that needed to be stopped.

The fact that his name is Business basically implies that he is evil. Calling a character Lord Terrorist would accomplish the same goal. Luckily, a full cast of ordinary Lego people, led by a construction worker (How much more proletarian can you get?), rise up to thwart Lord Business. This is class warfare made fun for the youngest and most impressionable Americans.

In an adult context, *Dallas,* which aired from 1978 to 1991, features oilman J. R. Ewing, a psychotic businessman.[69] His rise coincided with Ronald Reagan's presidency, a time when capitalism was celebrated and business was booming. But Ewing is the opposite of everything that Reagan represented or believed about American businesspeople.

Where Reaganism holds that business is good for people because it increases standards of living and generates prosperity, *Dallas* shows that the influence of businessmen (like Ewing) is actually a bad thing. Ewing is petty, vindictive, ruthless, and uncaring. He would do *anything* to get his way, often resorting to illegal means. He has no issue engaging in intimidation, bribery, or the humiliation of his enemies. What Reagan celebrated, the *Dallas* screenwriters attacked.

Dallas aired on CBS and competed in its primetime timeslot with *Dynasty* on ABC.[70] They might as well have just run *Dallas* reruns on ABC, because the message was the same. *Dynasty* features two feuding families, both rich from oil money: the Carringtons and the Colbys. It too has plotlines showing how rich people are immoral, leading lives based on greed and corruption, challenging the Reagan Era zeitgeist.

Dallas and *Dynasty* represented Hollywood screenwriters hitting back at an era of material success and triumphant commercialism. Never mind that inflation was down and the economy was improving for working- and middle-class Americans—rich people were just so *mean*!

Trump: The Quintessential Successful Businessman

The same month that Oliver Stone released *Wall Street* and introduced Americans to Gordon Gekko, Donald Trump's book *The Art of the Deal* hit the *New York Times* bestseller list.[71] It was a best seller not because Americans want to be Gordon Gekko. Rather, they want the chance to get rich. That's been part of our spirit since the nation was founded. It is the source of Adam Smith's invisible hand that lifts us all through our mutual efforts to be the next Zuckerberg or Jobs or simply the next American to run their own business at a profit.

That spirit remains strong, even in the face of the media onslaught, because people know that America is a country where anyone can be successful. The system that Hollywood elites hate so much—American capitalism—has certainly done far more for them, and for our poor, than Chávez's Venezuelan system.

America is the country where a kid who grows up in a housing project can go to Harvard and end up making $1 billion as the CEO of Goldman Sachs.[72] That's exactly what Lloyd Blankfein did, but you probably don't know that because Hollywood never made a movie about it. It is the country where a young man named Carl Karcher, who has an eighth-grade education, can buy a hot-dog cart and turn it into an international restaurant company. You didn't see that movie either.

There are college dropouts who strike it rich, folks who go from nothing to everything, and people who start business empires that provide a living for hundreds of thousands of other people. There are even grandsons of immigrants and sons of car salesmen who end up running major restaurant chains.

In 2016, Hollywood's hostility toward capitalism found its clearest expression in the reaction to Donald Trump's run for the White House.

At the outset, Trump offered little for them to hate. He had a reality TV show. He ran as the most socially liberal Republican in history. He was the first presidential candidate to wave a rainbow flag at a campaign event.[73] (As recently as 2008, Barack Obama was still pretending to support traditional marriage.[74])

Trump seemed agnostic on transgender rights. Trump properties opened up bathrooms to anyone who wanted to use them.[75] He included a transgender participant in a Miss Universe beauty pageant.[76]

When he bought Mar-a-Lago, he opened it up to Jews, gays, and African Americans, which was controversial at the time.[77]

He didn't have a long history of socially conservative positions and, in fact, was consistently attacked by Republican rivals during the GOP primary for not being conservative enough. You'd think he was the type of Republican Hollywood would want.

The problem was that Trump was the wrong kind of rich. He turned loans from his father into a New York City–based global real-estate empire.[78] His businesses employ thousands of people. He had a television show about business. He owned and ran golf courses and hotels around the world. He owns a customized Boeing 757 with gold-plated seat belts.[79] He authored books like *The Art of the Deal* and *How to Get Rich*. He is the embodiment of American success.

His success tortures the Hollywood liberals who can't stand free-market capitalism. As noted above, in Hollywood Tim Allen and Robert Davi suffered the career consequences of supporting him. Nearly two dozen ultra-rich celebrities promised to leave the country if Trump was elected. At least two of them, Jon Stewart and Cher, said they'd leave Earth.[80–81] George Lopez, Lena Dunham, Snoop Dogg, Barbara Streisand, Raven Symone, and Miley Cyrus all started looking at places in Canada. Samuel L. Jackson said he'd move to Africa.

Like socialism itself, so far none of them have followed through on their promises.

The Mainstream Media

You might wonder what a discussion of the news media has to do with Progressives in entertainment. But in recent years, the American media has shown itself unwilling to fulfill its supposed goal of impartially keeping citizens informed. In abdicating this responsibility, they have placed greater emphasis on sensationalism than on truth, and as far as I'm concerned, have crossed over and placed themselves firmly in the entertainment camp.

A traditional tenet of journalism has always been that there is a need to maintain non-biased objectivity when reporting the news. Objectivity is the centerpiece of press credibility. The Society of Professional Journalists' Code of Ethics provides guidance for journalists in "seeking truth and providing a fair and comprehensive account of events and issues."[82] This requires that journalists "be honest, fair and courageous in gathering, reporting and interpreting information" and that they "[e]xamine their own cultural values and avoid imposing those values on others."

Nonetheless, research has long indicated that the national press leans Left, more decidedly so in recent years.[83] The media's coverage of President Trump's first one hundred days in office removed any doubt on this point. The national press has joined the Progressive war on free-market capitalism. It has taken sides to such an extent that its coverage is often little more than entertainment intended to meet the emotional needs of the Left.

A report from the Harvard Kennedy School's Shorenstein Center on Media, Politics and Public Policy analyzed news coverage during President Trump's first one hundred days. It considered coverage in the *New York Times, Wall Street Journal,* and *Washington Post*; the main newscasts (not talk shows) of CBS, CNN, Fox, and NBC; and three European news outlets (the UK's *Financial Times,* the BBC, and Germany's ARD). To the surprise of no one who was paying attention, the coverage was 80 percent negative versus 20 percent positive.[84]

For previous presidents, the Harvard study found the coverage was far more balanced: Barack Obama, 41 percent negative, 59 percent positive; George W. Bush, 57 percent negative, 43 percent positive; and Bill Clinton, 60 percent negative, 40 percent positive.[85] While these numbers obviously favor Progressive President Obama, there was at least a semblance of balance. That balance no longer exists. As the report stated, "the sheer level of negative coverage gives weight to Trump's contention, one shared by his core constituency, that the media are hell-bent on destroying his presidency."

The study found that CNN's and NBC's coverage of President Trump was 93 percent negative and 7 percent positive. According to the study, "CNN and NBC's coverage was the most unrelenting—negative stories about Trump outpaced positive ones by 13 to 1 on the two networks."[86]

CBS wasn't much better with coverage 91 percent negative and 9 percent positive. The *New York Times* was 87 percent negative and 13 percent positive. The *Washington Post* was 83 percent negative and 17 percent positive. The *Wall Street Journal*, whose coverage tends to be more on economic issues, was 70 percent negative and 30 percent positive.

There was an exception. One network appears to have been more fair and balanced. While still negative, Fox News coverage was only 52 percent negative to 48 percent positive. The Harvard study referred to Fox's coverage as "A Ray of Sunshine."[87]

The study advised that "the news media need to give Trump credit when his actions warrant it." It noted that the public has a "low level of confidence in the press" and believes "that journalists are biased." Given the liberal slant in the coverage, it's difficult for any reasonable person to conclude otherwise.

This "weakens the press's watchdog role" as evidenced by the fact that the "news coverage of Trump's first 100 days...changed few minds about the president, for better or worse." As a result, "[t]he nation's watchdog has lost much of its bite and won't regain it until the public perceives it as an impartial broker, applying the same reporting standards to both parties."[88]

Currently, that clearly is not the case.

An October 2017 study by the Pew Research Center produced similar results. It examined the tone of the media's coverage of President Trump's first one hundred days. Pew examined over three thousand news stories from radio, television, and the Web. It found that "only about one-in-ten stories (11%) delivered an overall positive assessment of the administration's words or actions. Four times as many (44%) offered a negative assessment, while the remaining 45% were neither positive nor negative."[89] So, overwhelmingly negative.

The question is, why does the national press act this way?

In part, it's the fury of outraged expectations. The Left—and the press is most definitely part of the Left—really believed that Obama's two victories meant they had the country under lock and key. Of course, objectively, they shouldn't have believed it. As noted, following Obama's election, the Democrats lost over one thousand elective offices nationwide. You would have thought that was a clue.

The press simply overrated President Obama. To win his big victory in 2008, he campaigned as a vague goodwill centrist. He also benefitted enormously from the disenchantment with President George W. Bush and the financial crisis. Senator John McCain was far from the most effective Republican candidate. Really, any reasonably competent Democratic politician would have won by as much as Obama did, and many would have won by more.

Obama won reelection in 2012 because he used the advantages of incumbency to drive out his vote. Bush had done the same thing in 2004, and he made the same mistake Obama made: They both thought that because they were grudgingly reelected, the country approved of their leadership and them. For Democrats, Obama's mistake led to the loss of majorities in every branch of government.

Nonetheless, the Left (including the press) is still convinced that the direction of history is in their favor. They are Progressive, after all. They believe history is progressing toward an inevitable goal. They identify what they want with what history wants. They identify what they subjectively view is right as objectively and broadly accepted as right. As discussed, the tremendous irony is that history is moving so decidedly against them. Whatever else happens, our children will live to see the day when the Left, as we've known it and certainly as we know it now, is tossed off the stage of history as a failed relic.

The larger cause of the Left's and the media's hatred of Trump may be that Trump so obviously disdains them: their moral authority, their identity politics, and their control of the culture. President Trump is not the kind of person who hides his contempt in order to get along. He bluntly and mercilessly exposes their hypocrisy and turns it back on them.

Trump is the mirror image of Progressives, without their ridiculous and unhinged hatred of their own civilization. He is dismantling the big-government redistributive infrastructure the Progressives have been building since Woodrow Wilson decided government should put successful people in their place. And when the press unfairly attacks him for doing so, he calls them out. He's generated a movement that does the same thing.

That's why they hate him, and that's where the entertainment begins.

The Great Irony

Why is all of this a big deal? Should we really care if a few rich actors or out-of-touch journalists have the wrong idea about America and capitalism?

Yes, we should, and we must, because whether we like it or not, these groups are positioned to tell America's story. For too long, they have been willfully getting that story wrong.

For Hollywood and elsewhere in the media world, the story lines are black and white. What makes one person rich makes others poor. Wealth is an immoral, zero-sum game with winners and losers, good guys and bad guys. Businesspeople are the villains and only achieve success by harming others. It's the patently false Occupy Wall Street message that you can't be successful because the One Percent are hoarding all the benefits of success.

They insist on ignoring the benefits of our exceptional American capitalist system and attempt to distort our own image of our nation. Hollywood elites promote this narrative directly and subtly on TV and at the movies, and in what they say, although rarely in what they do in their pursuit of fame and fortune.

These celebrities seem unable to understand that outside of their liberal confines lives a nation of strivers, people who understand that, as a tide lifts all boats, economic growth and prosperity elevate everyone, rich and poor. Despite Hollywood's best efforts, these hardworking Americans understand that earning your success—making a profit—doesn't automatically turn you into an immoral jerk. These are the people who elected Donald Trump as president, despite Hollywood's best efforts to the contrary.

Americans are inherently business-oriented people who want—Heaven forbid—to get rich. It's certainly not that they want to be Hollywood caricatures—greedy, psychotic masterminds with misplaced priorities. Many just want to make enough to buy a home and send their children to college so that their children have a shot at a better life (and maybe even a shot at making a few million).

Our free-enterprise system offers people the opportunity to succeed and keep the benefits of that success. It's why people from around the world are knocking down doors to get here. In fact, it's why people with dreams of fame and fortune go to Hollywood.

The great irony in all of this is that the lives people like Susan Sarandon and Sean Penn take for granted are exactly the lives millions of Americans strive for every single day. It is a luxury of wealth to be able to campaign with socialist politicians and know that, no matter what, you're still going to have more money than almost everyone else. It is a luxury of wealth to hypocritically moralize about how the top One Percent of Americans have too much wealth while owning a Hollywood mansion or a handful of multimillion-dollar New York City apartments.

Those who worry about making rent every month can't afford to waste time on such matters. They're too busy working hard to make a little money and maybe a better life for themselves and their families, to live the American Dream. Despite their best efforts, the Hollywood elites will be unable to shame them out of it. That's the real moral of the story.

But, they will keep trying. The Progressives' Hollywood propaganda machine will continue to spew anti–free market movies and TV shows. They will continue to advance a socialist agenda that demonizes our free-enterprise system while they reap the benefits of wealth and fame. And, they will do so until the American people simply stop watching.

CHAPTER SEVEN

The Democrats: From Decency to Demagogues

"I didn't leave the Democratic party, the Democratic Party left me."

PRESIDENT RONALD REAGAN

The Battle Lines

With Donald Trump in the White House, the supporters of American capitalism have taken back power that's been kept away from them for far too long. By defeating Hillary Clinton, they stopped the forces of Progressivism from taking this country down a path of no return. Trump's positive actions to free American businesses from regulations and grow the economy in ways that benefit American workers instead of foreign corporations are already having positive effects. That's because Trump's Republican, capitalist vision for America is, at heart, a positive vision.

The Republicans' goal is simple: for individuals and companies to keep more of the money they make because it's their money and they know how to invest it better than the government. This goal reflects the simple belief that a free people, given the opportunity to succeed and to keep the benefits of their success, will produce greater prosperity than a repressed people forced to work for what government bureaucrats consider the public good (a belief well supported by the economic results in the former USSR, Cuba, North Korea, and Venezuela as well as China's venture into a more open economy).

To get this done, Republicans want to reduce the size and influence of government in our lives and lower taxes across the board, for everyone from individuals to families to small-town grocers to nationwide restaurant chains. They know that when it comes to economic growth, creating jobs and generating the tax revenue to pay for infrastructure, defense, the social safety net, and any other government functions, it is American businesses and their employees who will accomplish that.

When Democrats attack business, they are attacking everyone who has a private-sector job. Having a job in the private sector makes you a businessperson as much as any hedge fund manager. I was in business as much when I was painting houses as when I was the CEO of a restaurant company.

If Republicans want to get government out of the way so businesses can succeed, that means good things for employees, employers, and, ultimately, for the national economy. Lowering taxes on individuals and families frees up money for more consumer spending. Lower taxes and regulatory costs make capital available for businesses to invest, generating growth, creating jobs, and pushing our economy further along. Economic growth produces more tax revenue even at lower tax rates.

Being the "party of business" should be, and is, a good thing. In fact, it's an excellent thing.

But Trump's win in 2016 was still not a total victory for capitalism. The Progressives took the loss to Trump especially hard, and because of that, politics has become more polarized than it has been for decades.

The Democratic Party, which lurched to the Left under Barack Obama, is continuing to move in that direction. The Democrats' message to American entrepreneurs and business owners since the Obama administration has been simple: You owe your success to the government. As President Obama clearly stated, "Somebody helped to create this unbelievable American system that we have that allowed you to thrive. Somebody invested in roads and bridges. If you've got a business, you didn't build that. Somebody else made that happen."

Ironically, American business was Obama's unidentified "somebody," the community that provided the funding for those roads and bridges. And the businesses of today will be the "somebodies" who generate the tax revenue needed to pay for the infrastructure of tomorrow.

The dollars somebody invested to build those roads and bridges came from the profits American businesses generate and the wages and salaries they pay their employees for performing the jobs they create. Granted, our elected officials and government bureaucrats authorize and manage the construction of roads and bridges, but even they depend on this same business-generated tax revenue to make these projects happen (and for their own paychecks).

Who did President Obama think paid his salary while he was in office? Yes, it was the American people, but our businesses are just collections of Americans working together to provide goods and services for profit and generating the tax revenues without which government would be unable to function.

Understandably, Obama's "you didn't build that" comment rankled the business community across our nation. (I still occasionally wear my "You Didn't Build That" T-shirt from the Romney campaign.) It was, and is, an accurate reflection of

Progressive-socialist ideology. For Progressives, government is the "somebody else" who "made that happen."

Even with Obama out of office and Hillary Clinton's unanticipated defeat, Democrats are showing no signs of backing off from their failed antibusiness vision. If anything, they are doubling down, moving further to the Left as Progressive apparatchiks like Senators Bernie Sanders and Elizabeth Warren jockey to control their party's future. With Progressive socialist Tom Perez as Democratic National Committee Chair and the ultra-leftist Keith Ellison (a Progressive Democrat with Communist Party ties) as DNC Deputy-Chair, the party's direction seems clear.

As the rest of the world abandons socialism, American Democrats are embracing it.

In fact, given the success of Sanders's insurgent presidential campaign as well as the popularity of unvarnished socialism among our younger generations, it is hard to imagine that whoever eventually controls the Democrat machine will point the party anywhere but the Left, perhaps to a degree we have never experienced in this country.

When voters sent Donald Trump to Washington, Republicans gave the Oval Office possibly the most business-savvy occupant it has ever had. Republicans have traditionally favored the candidates with business experience over the activists, academics, and career politicians the Democrats like to toss up. For example, Mitt Romney was a very successful businessman who came close to making Obama a one-term president in 2012.

But Trump was different, as became increasingly obvious in the months leading up to the November 2016 election. Having never served in political office a day in his life, Trump spent the past several decades building up an impressive real-estate empire, not to mention an extremely profitable personal brand. If anyone could understand how to run government like a business, he could.

To an almost stereotypical degree, the contenders in the 2016 election—a career businessman and a career politician—accurately reflected the current state of their respective parties. Hillary Clinton's total lack of private-sector experience was a welcome attribute in a Democratic Party that has set out to vilify businesses and businesspeople at every turn. As a businessman with real-world economic experience, Trump was her polar opposite. The battle lines were clearly drawn.

But there was a time when the Democrats' ranks were not so rigidly aligned. In not-so-distant memory, the notion of a pro-business Democrat was not as absurd as it might seem today. In fact, while the Left would just as soon ignore it, the modern-era Democrats, under whom our economy thrived, primarily governed like pro-business conservatives and the country benefitted from it.

Kennedy and Clinton: When Democrats Understood the Economy

Few Democratic presidents enjoy the level of prestige among members of both parties as John Fitzgerald Kennedy. The thirty-fifth president of the United States was young, dashing, a war hero, quick-witted, and, alongside his glamorous wife, Jackie, seemed destined to prove what he declared in his inaugural address, that "the torch has been passed to a new generation of Americans" ready to face the challenges of the post–World War II era. I have a framed copy of Kennedy's inaugural address that I got when I was ten years old hanging in my office to this day.

His tragic assassination assured his place in our national memory. The political Left especially lionizes him. The Left often described President Obama as "Kennedyesque," the ultimate liberal laurel.

But one of Kennedy's most significant political achievements, an effort that greatly benefitted the American economy, is rarely mentioned as part of the Left's Kennedy myth. Perhaps that's because it involved a bold policy move at odds with today's liberal orthodoxy: a dramatic tax cut to generate economic growth and jobs.

When Kennedy declared at his inauguration that Americans would "pay any price, bear any burden, meet any hardship, support any friend, oppose any foe to assure the survival and the success of liberty," many of his fellow citizens were dealing with the burdens and hardships of a tough economy. The country was struggling to recover from several bouts of recession from the late 1950s into the 1960s.

While Kennedy's inaugural address focused almost exclusively on America's role in world affairs, particularly the struggle against communism and the ever-present threat of nuclear war with the USSR, the 1960 presidential campaign preceding it featured much debate about domestic economic affairs.

Kennedy told an Allentown, Pennsylvania, audience in October 1960, "As an American I am not satisfied to pass through in a period of 8 years, a recession in 1954, a recession in 1958, and now in 1960 to have only 50 percent of the steel mills of Pennsylvania and the United States operating, to have 100,000 steel workers out of work, to build 30 percent less homes this year than last year."[1] He closed those remarks by asking the audience to "give us the opportunity to get America moving again."

Reminiscent of President Trump's "Make America Great Again" campaign theme, "Getting America moving again" became a common refrain for Kennedy on the campaign trail. He earned the opportunity to do just that when he defeated Vice

President Richard Nixon in the election that November. But what did Kennedy consider the proper way for his administration to help boost the American economy?

Ted Sorensen, a Kennedy aide who went on to write the president's official biography after his death, gives us a glimpse of his early economic thinking: "Young Jack Kennedy probably didn't learn much economics in high school—few do—or, for that matter, anywhere else."[2] It was, and still is, a great shame that economics is barely taught in high schools. According to Sorensen, while at Harvard college, Kennedy got a "C" in basic economics but reported in letters home that "he was operating on a 'budget' and occasionally dabbling in stocks," both solid free-market tendencies.[3]

He maintained that same fiscal responsibility while serving in the Senate, working "to keep at least his household operations within the confines of his Senate salary."[4] It was also during his time as a senator that he demonstrated a willingness to go after one of the supposedly sacred pillars of the Democratic political establishment: the unions.

In a 1957 speech in Lynchburg, Virginia, then–Senator Kennedy railed against the "cancer of labor racketeering" and attacked corrupt union bosses. "Labor racketeers are using their positions with a union to practice extortion, shake-downs and bribery," he declared, "threatening strikes, labor trouble, physical violence or property damage to employers who fail to give them under-the-table payments, personal gifts or other contributions which the union members never see."[5] It is difficult to imagine the "Kennedyesque" Barack Obama standing up to his union backers in a similar manner.

Sorensen also reports that Kennedy enjoyed cross-examining his own one-time economics professor, Russ Nixon, over Nixon's involvement with a union that had communist ties.[6] Kennedy understood that the communist threat was philosophical and economic as well as military.

According to Sorensen, when Kennedy reached the White House, he "was generally more cautious on spending than the Republicans thought but more liberal than his tight-fisted handling of the Budget indicated."[7] At least, that's how Sorensen put it in the official biography. Author Ira Stoll reports that sometime later, and in a more private setting, Sorensen painted a different picture. "Kennedy was a fiscal conservative," the speechwriter said later. "Most of us and the press and historians have, for one reason or another, treated Kennedy as being much more liberal than he so regarded himself at the time...in fiscal matters, he was extremely conservative, very cautious about the size of the budget."[8]

Stoll's book on Kennedy, *JFK, Conservative,* argues that the thirty-fifth president leaned far more to the right on a variety of issues than his liberal champions today would care to admit. While his staunch anti-communism and his religious faith speak for themselves, his economic record as president demonstrates a willingness to consider conservative economic policy proposals.

What's more, he acted on them. His lack of indoctrination in liberal economic ideology during his early life and career, from high school to college to the Senate, doubtless contributed to his open-mindedness as president. As we will see, it was ultimately the country that benefitted.

President Kennedy's first efforts to right the struggling economy employed reliably liberal methods, probably because they came from the reliable liberals in his policy circle. Larry Kudlow of CNBC and Brian Domitrovic, who studied the fiscal policy links between two significant presidencies in *JFK and the Reagan Revolution: A Secret History of American Prosperity,* point out that Kennedy's Council of Economic Advisors was "stacked...with

Keynesian professors from the top universities" who advocated fighting the problem by (predictably) growing government.[9]

Their ideas, according to Kudlow and Domitrovic, included "a huge panel of new spending initiatives, a slew of additional post offices, national-park programs, hospital-construction projects, veterans benefits" and more.[10] Unfortunately, while these efforts increased federal spending by 15 percent in the first two years of the Kennedy presidency, they predictably produced little economic benefit; the economy grew by a tepid 2.6 percent in 1961.[11] The national unemployment rate remained high and the stock market shaky, neither of which were good signs. Even the official history as recounted by the Kennedy Presidential Library admits that "by 1962, Kennedy's domestic political fortunes seemed bleak."[12]

Salvation came in the form of a plan put together by perhaps the unlikeliest member of the Kennedy cabinet: Treasury Secretary C. Douglas Dillon. Dillon was both a career businessman—a Wall Street investment banker, no less—and a committed Republican. He had even served in the Eisenhower administration, first as ambassador to France and later as undersecretary of state. Appointing him to the post of treasury secretary was an inspired choice by Kennedy. More than a nod to bipartisanship, it showed his willingness to have voices in the room that prevented his White House from becoming a liberal echo chamber.

Dillon's plan was to aggressively slash tax rates across the board for individuals and businesses. The income tax at the time ranged from 20 percent to a shocking 91 percent on top earners, and the corporate tax rate stood at 52 percent.[13] Dillon advised the president that this heavy tax burden created "severe disincentives to work and invest," restraining economic growth.[14]

Kennedy listened to this free-market wisdom and took it to heart. In December 1962, he spoke at the Economic Club of

New York and pointed out the "paradoxical truth that tax rates are too high today and tax revenues are too low," arguing that "the soundest way to raise the revenues in the long run is to cut the rates now." "The purpose of cutting taxes now," he explained further, "is not to incur a budget deficit, but to achieve the more prosperous, expanding economy which can bring a budget surplus."[15]

Anyone who is skeptical about Kennedy's conservative economic credentials can see and hear the president himself extolling the virtues of tax cuts as a means to generate economic growth on YouTube. Entitled *Income Tax Cut: Kennedy Hopes to Spur Economy,* this video is simply inspiring.

In the video, President Kennedy proposes "an across the board, top to bottom cut in both corporate and personal income taxes," including the "long needed tax reform that logic and equity demand."[16] But it's Kennedy's explanation for how this tax cut would impact the economy that is most revealing.

According to Kennedy, the billions of dollars his proposed bill would "place in the hands of the consumer and our businessmen" would "have both immediate and permanent" economic benefits. "Every dollar released from taxation that is spent or invested will help create a new job and a new salary. And these new jobs and new salaries can create other jobs and other salaries and more customers and more growth for an expanding American economy."[17]

Of course they would.

Today, Kennedy could easily pass for a Republican. Obama could have spared our nation years of anemic economic growth had he actually been more Kennedyesque.

Cutting taxes was one of the Kennedy administration's top domestic priorities in 1963. Their plan was to bring income taxes down to a range of 14 percent to 65 percent and to drop the corporate tax rate to 47 percent.[18] Naturally, this plan met with some resistance from within Kennedy's own camp, but he remained fervently committed. One economic adviser, the arch-Keynesian John Kenneth Galbraith of Harvard, was against it. Kennedy bluntly told him to shut up.[19] If only other presidents had done the same.

Overcoming congressional objections was another problem, since any bill to cut taxes must originate in the House and then pass the Senate. Sounding very 2017, Democrat senator Albert Gore, Sr., of Tennessee groused that the cuts in the top tax rates were a favor to "fat cats."[20] He unknowingly presaged his son, who droned on during the 2000 presidential campaign about the "wealthiest one percent."

Kennedy reportedly called Gore Sr. a "son of a bitch" multiple times during a closed-door meeting, and grumbled, rightly, that "if we get a good recession next summer, it's not going to do him much good, is it?"[21]

Kennedy did not live to see the next summer, but he did live to see his tax plan pass the House in September 1963. As it worked its way through the Senate that fall, the president took a trip to Texas to lay the groundwork for the 1964 campaign. His tax plan was going to be a key component of his reelection strategy.

In one speech, sounding like a consummate economic conservative, he touted "cutting personal and corporate income taxes by some $11 billion . . . to assure this Nation of the longest and strongest expansion in our peacetime economic history."[22] But this speech never went beyond the written page. Kennedy was on his way to deliver it in Dallas when he was assassinated on November 22, 1963.

The new president, Lyndon Johnson, was a keen political operative and very much at home dealing with the Senate. Under his watch, the Kennedy tax cuts survived and passed the Senate a few months later, in February 1964. The results were immediate and dramatic. GDP growth jumped to 5.8 percent in 1964 and was up to 6.6 percent in 1966, while the unemployment rate was slashed from 5.2 percent to 3.8 in the same period.[23]

Unfortunately, while Johnson helped bring the Kennedy tax cuts into being, his own Progressive social policies were responsible for undoing much of their positive effects. Once Johnson's administration came into its own, it became clear that he was much more of a big-government ideologue than his predecessor.

Johnson raised taxes again in 1968.[24] By 1969 the country had entered a recession, the first of four that would strike the nation's economy until the Reagan tax cuts of the 1980s.[25] However, the record was clear: Kennedy's tax cuts had performed as the now-deceased president had predicted, generating a "more prosperous, expanding economy." Unfortunately, it simply placed the economy on a solid footing going into Johnson's massive government expansion.

It was during this time, under Johnson's Great Society domestic policy initiatives, that the modern "welfare state" as we know it in the United States came into being. But decades later, it was, to the surprise of many, another prominent Democrat who sought to reform that welfare state as well as enact other positive, market-based initiatives.

On July 24, 1963, while Kennedy was busy working the House to get his tax cuts passed, he took some time off to visit in the Rose Garden with several young men from the Boys Nation program, run by the American Legion. One sixteen-year-old from Arkansas, by his own account, "muscled his way" up to the front of the crowd and was able to shake the president's hand.[26] That boy's name was William Jefferson Clinton, and decades later, when he occupied the Oval Office himself, he reflected that meeting Kennedy "had a very profound impact" on his life, and that the event was "something that I carried with me always."[27]

Indeed, he carried it with him during his run for president in 1992, when a photo of his handshake with Kennedy became a staple of his campaign. As he ran his campaign, Clinton certainly tried to capture the Kennedyesque image of a dynamic new leader seeking to represent a younger generation, in this case the baby boomers. Like Kennedy, Clinton was exciting and dashing—*too* dashing in some ways. But Clinton also shared another trait with Kennedy: He was a Democrat willing to buck his party's orthodoxy for the good of the country.

Running against a sitting president, moderate Republican George H. W. Bush, Clinton was careful not to present himself to voters as a left-wing ideologue. Instead, he sold himself as a "New Democrat," a moderate, centrist politician who seemed to recognize that Americans preferred the government restraint and prosperity of the Reagan era to the excesses of further-left liberals like Jimmy Carter and Lyndon Johnson.

One campaign commercial called Clinton and his running mate Al Gore "a new generation of Democrats" who "don't think the way the old Democratic Party did" and "rejected the old tax-and-spend politics." One of Clinton's key campaign promises in 1992 was a pledge to "break the cycle of welfare dependency" and "end welfare as we know it," a far cry from the days of the Great Society.[28]

Even so, Bill Clinton—again, like Kennedy—began his time in office by governing as a fairly standard Progressive liberal. He made a failed run at passing government-run health-care legislation (called "HillaryCare" thanks to First Lady Hillary Clinton's heavy involvement). In 1993, he and the Democratic-controlled Congress passed legislation that raised taxes on everything from corporate profits to top earners' income to Social Security checks to gas.[29]

But the 1994 midterm elections changed the political landscape literally overnight. The Republicans swept into control of the House and the Senate for the first time in decades. With Newt Gingrich from Georgia now installed as Speaker of the House, by 1995 it was clear that Clinton would have to make good on his moderate campaign promises if he stood a chance at reelection in 1996.

At a 1995 campaign event where he discussed his 1993 tax increases, Clinton initiated his political recovery by stating, "Probably there are people in this room still mad at me at that budget because you think I raised your taxes too much. It might surprise you to know that I think I raised them too much, too."[30] It surprised more than the assembled donors. According to the *New York Times*, "[a]ngry Democrats accused him of repudiating a package they had stuck their necks out to pass without a single Republican vote."[31] It was not your typical Democrat's stump speech. But Clinton, my generation's consummate politician, was just getting started.

On January 23, 1996, Clinton delivered perhaps his most memorable State of the Union address (notably, the presidential election would take place in November of that year). "We know big Government does not have all the answers," he declared. "We know there's not a program for every problem." He extolled his administration's efforts to "give the American people a smaller, less bureaucratic government in Washington . . . one that lives within its means." After that remarkably conservative warm-up, he delivered one of the most famous lines ever uttered in a State of the Union speech.

President Clinton said simply, "The era of big government is over."[32]

Across America, Progressives listened in shock and despair. President Wilson and both Roosevelts were rumored to have rolled over in their graves. The rest of America breathed a sigh of relief.

This obviously marked a significant departure from the Clinton administration's early years and a return to the centrist attitude that got him elected in the first place. Historian Michael Beschloss called it "a skywritten acknowledgment, by someone who in another age might have liked to govern as a liberal Big Government Democrat, that the Age of Reagan was so overwhelming that even a Democratic President had to work within its limits."[33] Later that year, President Clinton was reelected.

However Clinton may have wanted to govern in his ideal world, he was a pragmatist, and the political reality brought about by the 1994 Republican takeover of Congress reflected the fact that the American people wanted to replicate the Age of Reagan. And who could blame them?

The same year he declared an end to big government, Clinton went to work with the Republicans in Congress on a project that would tangibly reduce government's size and scope: the landmark welfare reforms of 1996.

Speaker Gingrich's *Contract with America,* the cornerstone of the Republicans' successful campaign to retake the House in 1994, had promised to enact much needed welfare reform, consistent with Clinton's 1992 campaign promise to "end welfare as we have come to know it."

Clinton was clear in his 1996 State of the Union address that while big government was not the solution to every problem, "we cannot go back to the time when our citizens were left to fend for themselves." Republicans agreed and calibrated welfare reform to make sure that nobody was left behind, stuck languishing on government welfare rolls as they eked out a bare-bones existence.

In 1996, Congress passed and Clinton signed the Personal Responsibility and Work Opportunity Reconciliation Act. The bill's reforms required those on welfare to go out and get work, but they also provided the job training and other assistance needed to help make the welfare-to-work transition go as smoothly as possible. Other measures like tax credits and subsidies for childcare helped fill the gaps.[34]

Instead of a permanent way of life, welfare became a temporary way to help working families get back on their feet. Of course, to the liberal ideologues this was nothing less than heresy. The Left regarded reducing anyone's dependence on the government and nudging them toward work in the private sector as unconscionable. Especially because Clinton worked out the plan with the help of Republicans, including the much-reviled Speaker Gingrich, Clinton was accused of making "a pact with the devil."[35]

As it turned out, rather than "a pact with the devil" the Clinton welfare reforms turned out to be a gift from heaven. These reforms were responsible for meaningful improvements in the lives of individuals and families around the country. As more and more welfare recipients found jobs, the total number of Americans on welfare fell by 60 percent.[36]

For some of the most vulnerable low-income Americans—the mothers of children born out of wedlock—the benefits were especially staggering. According to analysts at the Brookings Institution, between 1996 and 2000, the poverty rate among this group dropped by about a third, while the number of those women who held jobs increased by about a third.[37] This was not a coincidence.

In 1997, Clinton went on to sign a Republican bill that reduced capital gains taxes from 28 percent to 20 percent. The bill's proponents intended to create a surge in capital investment to generate economic growth. They were not disappointed, according to economist J. D. Foster at the Heritage Foundation. In fact, "[b]y 1998, the first full year in which the lower capital gains rates were in effect, venture capital activity reached almost $28 billion, more than a threefold increase over 1995 levels, and by 1999, it had doubled yet again."[38]

While there is dispute as to who gets the credit and for what period of time, it is clear that because of the policies put in place by President Clinton and Congressional Republicans led by Speaker Gingrich, the country experienced its first budget surplus since 1969 for each of the fiscal years 1998 through 2001.[39]

Late in his presidency, Clinton presided over another free-market reform for which the Progressive Left has yet to forgive him: the massive deregulation of the financial services industry. In 1999, he signed into law the Gramm-Leach-Bliley Act. The brainchild of three Republicans—Senator Phil Gramm from Texas and Representatives Thomas Bliley from Virginia and Jim Leach from Iowa—Congress passed this legislation with significant bipartisan support in both houses even though it was designed to free businesses from regulations that had been imposed during FDR's New Deal government-expansion bonanza.

In the wake of the 2008 financial crisis, however, Progressives were quick to say that this deregulation was to blame. This is simply not the case. The truth is that the crisis would have been far worse without it. In fact, by unfettering banks and financial firms and allowing them to enter into mergers more easily, Gramm-Leach-Bliley actually helped stabilize the finance industry during this crucial period. As George Mason University economist Tyler Cowen points out, "in the crisis times the diversification has done considerably more good than harm."[40]

Bill Clinton himself defended his record as the crisis unfolded, and to his credit, reaffirmed his support for the bipartisan deregulation efforts. "Phil Gramm and I disagreed on a lot of things," he said, "but he can't possibly be wrong about everything." He supported the plan, and didn't consider it a free gift to Republicans: "This wasn't something they forced me into."[41] Whether the Left likes it or not, the financial crisis could have been a lot worse without Clinton's bipartisan deregulation efforts.

I spoke at an Adam Smith Society event sponsored by the Manhattan Institute in early 2015 with Clinton's former deputy assistant for domestic policy, William Galston, in the audience. Afterward, he approached me to discuss what I had said. During our discussion, he asked if I realized "that during the Clinton years we shrank the size of government intentionally, and took a lot of criticism from within our own party for doing so." I did know it, and I told him I thought it was both courageous and smart.

Whether Bill Clinton actively supported conservative fiscal policy or simply went along with Republicans for political reasons is an open question. But, it is beyond doubt that, by the time his presidency ended, the heavy hand of government on the economy had been reduced. One crucial measure of the size of government makes this very clear: federal spending.

According to the *Wall Street Journal,* when Clinton took office in 1991, federal spending made up 21.7 percent of the total US economy. Spending as a share of GDP decreased steadily throughout the Clinton years, and it was down to 17.6 percent by 2000.[42]

It has not reached such reasonable levels since.

By bringing federal spending down, Clinton was true to the promise he made on the 1992 campaign trail that he had "rejected the old tax-and-spend politics" of earlier Democrats. He worked with Republicans to reduce capital gains taxes, balance the budget, and generate economic growth. He brought Americans who had been living on government handouts into the workforce and removed cumbersome regulations burdening a major sector of the economy.

At nearly every turn, he was besieged by elements in his own party for daring to trust the power of the free market. And yet, in the final estimation, he was clearly doing something right. Under Bill Clinton, GDP grew at an annual average rate of nearly 4 percent.

Obama's Lurch to the Progressive Left

Unfortunately, today's Democratic Party is no longer the party of either Bill Clinton or John F. Kennedy. With the election of Barack Obama in 2008, the Democrats lurched to the Left, returning to their Progressive roots with a vengeance. And they show no signs of shifting back toward the center.

Much has been written, in this book and beyond, about President Obama's dismal economic record, brought about by raising taxes during a touchy economic recovery while expanding government through a Wilson-inspired myriad of executive orders and regulatory actions, on top of the economically crippling Obamacare and Dodd-Frank legislation.

For eight years, the business community lived in fear of what growth-hobbling economic action was coming next. As a result, wages stagnated, paths to the middle class were closed, and income inequality increased. GDP growth hovered around 2.1 percent annually during the seven and a half years from the end of the recession in June 2009 to the end of the Obama presidency in January 2017. For the last year of his presidency, GDP was 1.5 percent.

In early 2017, the Commerce Department estimated that the

US economy grew by an average of just 1.5 percent while President Obama occupied the White House. Since 1930, only Herbert Hoover's administration amassed a worse record, and the Great Depression started on his watch.[43] That's not a terribly flattering comparison.

Unlike Clinton or Kennedy, Obama failed to see the error of his ways and continued to pursue Progressive economic policies throughout his presidency

In the midst of the 2008 campaign, Obama famously told Joe "the Plumber" Wurzelbacher, "I think when you spread the wealth around, it's good for everybody."[44]

In a sense Obama did not intend, I agree with this sentiment. While I prefer spreading wealth through capitalism rather than compulsion, I would not want to live in an economic system that failed to "spread the wealth around." Neither did my grandfather, which is why he moved to the United States.

Like most Americans, I support the government using the wealth the free-enterprise system creates to benefit the poor or disadvantaged who truly need it. I grew up in a lower-middle-class neighborhood. I went to school with kids whose families couldn't make it on their own. They needed help to get on their feet.

As President Clinton stated in his 1996 State of the Union address, while big government clearly is not the solution to every problem, "we cannot go back to the time when our citizens were left to fend for themselves." Welfare must be calibrated to make sure it is helping those in need, lifting people up rather than condemning them to a life of poverty on government welfare rolls.

Like the bipartisan welfare reform passed during the Clinton years (and, to a great extent, repealed during the Obama years),[45] programs designed to get the able-bodied off of welfare and back into the workforce can have a very positive impact on peoples' lives. On the other hand, programs that lock people into government dependence can have a very negative impact. But no one receives help unless the rest of society produces enough wealth to help them. We can't redistribute wealth we don't have.

The great benefit of a capitalist economy is that it vastly enhances the opportunities available to everyone and therefore vastly increases the number of people who enjoy prosperity through their own efforts, while at the same time creating tremendous additional wealth to support the charitable impulse, whether that impulse expresses itself through public programs or voluntary private charity.

Again, my own history is an example of that. I have grown wealthy because of the advantages afforded by capitalism at every stage of my life, and that wealth enables me and my family not only to have a high standard of living, but to pay much more in taxes and give much more in charity than would have been possible had I grown up in any other country with any other economic system.

However, whenever the government raises taxes or increases regulations, it tends to undermine the wealth-creating ability of a capitalist economy. That doesn't mean that higher taxes or additional regulations are necessarily wrong, but it does mean that they come with a real cost to real people, and especially to those people whose individual circumstances make their hold on economic security more fragile.

Any politicians who fails to recognize this will, time and again, hurt the people they are supposed to represent, just as President Obama's economic policy hurt, most of all, the poor and disadvantaged. For example, despite seven and a half years of recovery, the number of people receiving Supplemental Nutrition Assistance Program benefits (food stamps) increased by 32 percent during the Obama presidency from 33.5 million people in 2009 to 44.2 million in 2016.[46] Having repealed President Clinton's work requirement for welfare, and with anemic economic growth failing to produce good-paying jobs, the poor and disadvantaged suffered during the Obama recovery.

It is a perverse irony that the economic equality Progressives demand, and the big government they want, is only possible in a country with the one economic system that produces sufficient wealth to fund their efforts—capitalism—a system they, at best, distrust and, at worst, despise.

Near the end of the Obama administration, the president visited Argentina, where he offered some interesting insights into his economic thinking in a speech to young people:

> *So often in the past there's been a sharp division between left and right, between capitalist and communist or socialist. And especially in the Americas, that's been a big debate... Those are interesting intellectual arguments, but I think for your generation, you should be practical and just choose from what works. You don't have to worry about whether it neatly fits into socialist theory or capitalist theory—you should just decide what works.*[47]

I am very comfortable making economic policy based on what works, but what President Obama failed to see is that the debate on what works is, outside of higher academia, over. Capitalism works. Capitalism "spreads the wealth around" by creating a middle class. Capitalism makes both welfare and charity possible. True socialism makes them impossible.

That truth is by no means the end of the debate about economic policy, but it is the indispensable beginning. A government in confusion about the success of capitalism and the failure of socialism is, at best, going to produce the kind of economic stagnation that characterized the United States during the Obama years.

Yet Progressives are moving further away from that truth than ever, and they are taking the Democratic Party along with them.

The Rise of America's Sandernistas

In the race among Democrats to succeed Obama, the party's comfort level with socialism has only increased. Of course, the chief example of this is the surprise surge in support for Vermont senator Bernie Sanders, an Independent (not even technically a Democrat) who identified himself as a proud "Democratic Socialist" in the primary campaign.

Though Sanders has been hailed for putting a clever but cranky, grandfatherly face on socialism, most of his life has been dedicated to supporting radical redistributionist policies, in which cause he has allied himself with radical groups and policies.

As mayor of Burlington, Vermont, in the 1980s, he guided a "foreign policy" for the city because, as he put it, "as progressives, we understood that we all live in one world." In practice, that meant supporting the violent Sandinista communist rebels in Nicaragua and designating a "sister city" in the Soviet Union. In 1988, he traveled to the Soviet state with his wife to enjoy a sort of "honeymoon" before its collapse.[48] He even reportedly hung a Soviet flag in his office.[49]

Not surprisingly, Sanders's political idol (and possibly the model for his campaign) is the early twentieth-century socialist leader and Marxist admirer Eugene Debs. Sanders produced a record album celebrating Debs in 1979, in which he proclaimed that "Debs was hailed by many as a prophet, a Moses—a man who would lead the American working class out of the desert of capitalism, and into the promised land of socialism."[50]

While Debs ran his multiple campaigns for president knowing they were futile efforts, he did hope they would spark a socialist revolution. Perhaps in honor of that spirit, Sanders keeps a plaque honoring Debs on the wall of his senate office.[51]

In 2011, Sanders made his preference for failed socialist policies very clear, although it would take a few years and Venezuela's horrific economic collapse to prove the point. In an article entitled *Close The Gaps: Disparities That Threaten America*, Sanders stated that, "These days, the American dream is more apt to be realized in South America, in places such as... Venezuela... where incomes are actually more equal today than they are in the land of Horatio Alger. Who's the banana republic now?"[52]

As Venezuela implodes, we might again ask: who is the banana republic now?

Sanders's policy recommendations as a presidential candidate painted a vision for the United States almost as collectivist as those of the Marxists he idolizes. Its centerpieces included a fully government-run health-care system, free college tuition, and using the force of government to break up banks he deemed too big.

The question naturally became, how to pay for all this? For Sanders, the answer was easy. An analysis by the *Washington Examiner* during the campaign found that Sanders's proposed policies would be responsible for raising taxes by nearly $20 trillion over ten years.[53]

Of course, Sanders did not become the Democratic Party's presidential nominee. That distinction went to Hillary Rodham Clinton.

Although clearly a Progressive, Hillary Clinton at least did not publicly identify as a Democratic Socialist. And though Sanders eventually endorsed and campaigned with her, she had some harsh words for Sanders in her post-campaign book *What Happened.* Despite the large percentage of primary voters who chose him as their candidate, Clinton declared that the Vermont senator "isn't a Democrat." "He didn't get into the race to make sure a Democrat won the White House. He got in to disrupt the Democratic Party."[54]

Clinton worked hard to differentiate herself from Sanders, but as a consummate politician, she was hardly immune to the obvious support he was getting, especially from younger members of the party.

Clinton had played fast and loose with economic philosophy before. In 2014, she mystifyingly told a Boston crowd, "Don't let anybody tell you that, you know, it's corporations and businesses that create jobs."[55] After two days of Republican criticism, an aide claimed that she left some words out of the sentence and meant "to talk about tax breaks for corporations and businesses."

How the sentence was supposed to read is anyone's guess. But, according to *Politico,* some Democrats who backed Clinton saw through this ruse and said privately that "she appeared to be trying too hard to capture the [Senator Elizabeth] Warren rhetoric and adjust to the modern economic progressive language."[56] If that was her goal, she certainly succeeded.

In 2016, she proudly and openly embraced the Progressive label, marketing herself to voters as "a progressive who likes to get things done." Her policy proposals would disclose that those things she intended to get done included increasing the size and power of government, increasing taxes, and punishing businesses for the sin of making a profit.

When defending a proposal for a federally mandated family

leave program during a Democratic primary debate, she proclaimed, "We should not be paralyzed by the Republicans and their constant refrain 'big government this, big government that,' except for what they want to impose on the American people. I know we can afford it because we're going to make the wealthy pay for it."[57]

The United States already operates under a very Progressive graduated income tax system (the much vilified One Percent pay nearly 40 percent of all federal income tax revenue while the top 10 percent pay 71 percent).[58] Nonetheless, the wealthy remained a favorite target of Clinton's. She also apparently forgot that it was her husband's own refrain about big government—specifically, ending it—which helped cement his legacy as a successful Democratic president.

But neither Obama's Progressive policies nor the Clinton/Sanders fight to outdo each other for Progressive credibility helped the Democratic Party in the long run. Between 2008 and 2016, voters gave Republicans majorities in the House, in the Senate, among state governors and legislatures, and finally, the presidency, leading to a conservative majority on the US Supreme Court.

But that has not stopped the Progressives from lurching more and more to the failed socialist policies of the past.

Bernie Sanders returned to the Senate, and in September 2017 introduced a new bill to change America's health-care system to a single-payer, government-run program. The Huffington Post pointed out that the last time Sanders tried to introduce this bill in 2013, "he had no support from his colleagues. But in a clear sign of the idea's increasing popularity, as well as Sanders' influence within Progressive politics, 16 Democratic senators co-sponsored the bill."[59] Is it possible that the Sanders insurgency during the campaign has motivated senate Democrats to move even further left than they were when President Obama was in the White House?

Among the supporters of Sanders's bill were several rising Democrat stars in the Senate who are rumored to be considering challenging Trump for the presidency in 2020, including California senator Kamala Harris, New York senator Kirsten Gillibrand, New Jersey senator Corey Booker, and Massachusetts senator Elizabeth Warren.[60]

Warren, in particular, has built herself up as a Progressive force in the Democratic Party for some time. In fact, Warren beat Obama to the "you didn't build that" game. Before he made that infamous declaration in 2012, Warren told an audience during her first (unsuccessful) senate campaign in 2011 that "there is nobody in this country who got rich on his own. Nobody."[61] Apparently her point was that these successful people all owe us something, and she intended to use the government to collect that debt.

Once she made it to the Senate, she continued to rail about how "the biggest financial institutions figured out they could make a lot of money by cheating people" and how markets don't work for "real people."[62] Painting businesses as cheaters and alienating "real people" from the markets that affect almost everything in their daily lives is essential to the Progressive agenda, and Warren is widely seen as the natural heiress to Bernie Sanders's Far Left mantle if he chooses not to run for president again.

Her high profile is already causing Warren to face some difficult questions. In September 2017, a local radio host in Boston confronted the senator, whose own net worth is estimated in the millions, about her tendency to "rail against the One Percent" while she, in fact, is a member of that group, accusing her of hypocrisy. Warren proceeded to describe her modest upbringing, but when the host pressed her about her current wealth, all she could do was protest, "It's not hypocrisy!"[63] Well, it is.

The Progressive Future

Whether it's Warren, Harris, Booker, or even Sanders leading the charge for the Democrats in the future, their deep devotion to lock-step Progressive ideology, with its vilification of capitalism and American business, should remain a matter of concern for all Americans. They seem willing to double down on Far Left ideas, directly in contrast to some of the most revered and successful Democratic administrations of the past.

Without a major shift in their party, we may never again see a Democrat with the courage to enact major tax cuts like John F. Kennedy or declare war on big government like Bill Clinton. The era of pragmatic government with room for market-based reforms might be over, and the era of the Progressive demagogues dominating the Democratic Party might be here to stay.

CHAPTER EIGHT

Economic Inequality and the Ruse of Democratic Socialism

"The inherent vice of capitalism is the unequal sharing of blessings. The inherent virtue of Socialism is the equal sharing of miseries."

SIR WINSTON CHURCHILL

Economic inequality

Since the global financial crisis, economic inequality has emerged as one of America's preeminent political issues. In 2008, President Obama stated, "When you spread the wealth around, it's good for everybody." In 2013, he labeled economic inequality "the defining challenge of our time."[1]

But Senator Bernie Sanders has gained the most political leverage from this issue. His website boldly states, "The issue of wealth and income inequality is the great moral issue of our time, it is the great economic issue of our time, and it is the great political issue of our time."[2]

He proposes addressing this issue through "democratic socialism"—greatly expanding government benefit programs, massively increasing taxes, and expanding the regulatory state. That platform nearly propelled him to the Democrat Party's presidential nomination in 2016.

While some level of economic inequality is inevitable in any free society, this issue resonates because economic inequality has been increasing, although far less than you have been led to believe. We need to understand the extent to which such inequality exists, why it is increasing, and how we can effectively reduce it.

When your only tool is a hammer, every solution needs a nail. Sanders's economic inequality solution is to use government (the socialist's only tool) as the hammer and redistribution (their principal solution) as the nail. Democratic socialists propose empowering government while taking power from those who create wealth. Their solution is simply for government to coercively redistribute wealth until there is parity.

Problem solved! Well, not really.

Driving that redistribution nail diminishes individual initiative and dampens the entrepreneurial spirit, destroying both opportunity and prosperity. When you remove the incentive to create wealth, you diminish wealth creation. You can divide what wealth there is, but if no one is creating wealth, there soon won't be much to divide.

Individual opportunity and initiative drive successful economies and lead to the better-paying jobs that spread wealth organically, reducing economic inequality without the perverse effects of government coercion. Economic inequality results from too little opportunity or incentive for people to improve their lives.

So, how do we create opportunity and reduce income inequality? The answer is obvious. We create opportunity by incentivizing economic growth. That tide, that creator of opportunity that lifts us all, is economic growth.

Nothing in the human experience incentivizes economic growth or spreads its benefits more broadly than capitalism. The Progressives' redistributionist policies, on the other hand, hobble capitalism's dynamic economic energy.

A 2015 New York Times/CBS News poll found that the majority of Americans were aware of growing economic inequality and believed that the government should do something about it.[3] The question is what exactly should the government do? Is the best solution to redistribute existing wealth or to incentivize economic growth and opportunity?

The question itself suggests the answer.

The Solution Clearly Is Not Traditional Socialism

For much of the world during the twentieth century, the answer to economic inequality was socialism. Anti-capitalist zealots claimed that if the government nationalized industries, confiscated wealth, eliminated private property, and controlled the distribution of goods, nations could achieve true equality and justice for their people. Utopia, they promised, was just a worker's revolution away.

In reality, socialism led to totalitarian regimes, mass murder, and devastating poverty. One credible estimate places the number of Marxist-socialist victims at one hundred million, making it "the greatest catastrophe in human history."[4] For those who survived, the wealth gap between affluent government elites and the impoverished masses was immense.

In the former Soviet Union alone, over eleven million citizens died of famine.[5] None of them were high-ranking government officials.

More recently, in socialist Venezuela, the government is using food to control the political opposition.[6] Children are literally starving.[7] All of this is happening in what was, as recently as 2001, South America's richest nation.[8] Judging by recent photos, President Maduro, his family, and his political allies are doing just fine.

In the words of British Prime Minister Margaret Thatcher, "Socialist governments traditionally do make a financial mess. They always run out of other people's money."[9] These comments were the basis for a well-known adage often attributed to Thatcher: "The problem with socialism is that eventually you run out of other people's money." The exact quotation may have been inaccurate, but the underlying point remains strikingly accurate.

No socialist nation realized the promised egalitarian utopia. In 1991, the Soviet Union collapsed and separated into fifteen different states.[10] Between 1989 and 1993, reformers in communist Cuba realized that the country had to institute market-based reforms to stay solvent.[11] In 1992, Deng Xiaoping began implementing price reforms and privatization of state-owned enterprises in China.[12] By 2001, China was a member of the World Trade Organization with a more market-based economy.[13]

Traditional socialism unequivocally and undeniably failed. Today, even the avowed socialist Senator Bernie Sanders, who spent his honeymoon in the former Soviet Union and has Eugene Debs's photo on his office wall, no longer believes government should own the means of production.[14] History certainly supports his belief.

Faced with traditional socialism's failure but unwilling to concede capitalism's superiority, those who would elevate the collective (i.e., the government) over the individual needed to rebrand their socialist ideals to gin up the masses' revolutionary spirit. In effect, they needed to put lipstick on a pig.

Their lipstick of choice is known as democratic socialism.

The Solution Clearly Is Not Democratic Socialism

For politicians, describing oneself as a socialist remains a political problem even today. Senator Sanders is well aware that when he uses the word *socialist*, there are "some people" who "aren't comfortable about it."[15] So, when he's asked about being a socialist, Sanders attempts to clarify that he's talking about something else.

"Tell me what it means to be a socialist," prodded liberal Vox.com journalist Ezra Klein in a 2015 interview with the senator. Sanders corrected him immediately, saying, "A democratic socialist."[16] It happened again when CNN anchor Anderson Cooper asked him, "How can any kind of socialist win a general election in the United States?" Sanders replied, "Well, we're going to win because first, we're going to explain what democratic socialism is."[17]

However, explaining the ideology of democratic socialism is easier said than done.

When asked to define democratic socialism, Sanders makes no effort to explain it in the way that one would explain an economic theory. Rather, he vaguely responds that "democratic socialism means that we must create an economy that works for all, not just the very wealthy."[18]

If that sounds like a platitude that harkens back to the class warfare of traditional socialism, that's because it is.

In practice, Sanders's democratic socialism is a government benefits program whereby voters elect politicians who will give them things such as free college, free health care, free childcare, shorter hours, higher wages, more time off, and so on. All these benefits are to be handed out by an expanded and empowered government. Who will pay for all these wonderful bribes? Well, of course, the rich will pay.[19]

If that sounds like a traditional Progressive agenda, that's because it is.

The "free stuff" side of democratic socialism is where its proponents get very specific about what they would do. Sanders, for example, released his own budget plan in March 2016 that would have instituted a single-payer health care system in addition to providing fully funded, long-term care services; "free" college; paid family leave; and even expanded Social Security.[20]

The next year, he introduced a $3.4 trillion "Medicare for all" bill in Congress, which would have massively expanded government-run health care in America. The *Washington Post* noted that under his proposal, "everything from emergency surgery to prescription drugs, from mental health to eye care, would be covered, with no co-payments."[21]

Of course, it's not really free. The details of how to pay for it are where democratic socialists stop being specific. The Office of Management and Budget estimates that the federal government's total revenue for 2018 will be $3.65 trillion, just slightly more than the $3.4 trillion Sanders's proposed health-care plan alone would cost per year.[22]

But when he introduced his universal health-care scheme, Sanders failed to include any funding mechanism, telling reporters "rather than give a detailed proposal about how we're going to raise $3 trillion a year, we'd rather give the American people options."[23] That's double-speak for "We don't want to tell you how we're going to pay for this plan because, if we did, you wouldn't support it."

In fact, the Associated Press polled Americans on whether they supported Sanders's proposal, and 39 percent said they did. Asked whether they'd continue to support it if their taxes went up, more than two-thirds of the supporters changed their minds.[24]

When Sanders released his 2016 budget that would have provided everything from "free" health care to expanded Social Security, he at least tried to explain how he'd pay for it. He proposed increasing the top marginal personal income tax rate from 39.6 percent to 54.2 percent. The problem is that even if he taxed the rich at 100 percent of their incomes, the revenue would be insufficient to pay for what he promised.[25] The rich simply don't have enough money, which is why every country that's created a cradle-to-grave welfare state has levied high taxes on the middle class, and in some cases, even the poor.

Unquestionably, Sanders's democratic socialist agenda would significantly increase taxes for working- and middle-class Americans, and he knows it. Unfortunately, not everyone does. Sanders prefers to keep it that way.

The problem of paying for his proposals has dogged Sanders throughout his career. At a 2017 CNN televised town hall debate on health care, a Danish citizen told Sanders that "my sense is still that you would like to spend as a Scandinavian but not tax as one, is that right?"[26] Sanders, caught off guard by the question, first noted that "you raise some very good points" before quizzing the Dane on how much free stuff he gets.

Sanders failed to explain how much everyone, including the middle class, would have to pay for all these "free" government benefits, but he finally conceded that "nothing is free. Taxes are high. You're right."[27] Republican senator Ted Cruz, who was debating Sanders at the time, remarked that it was a "rare moment of candor in Washington."[28]

While the monies Sanders predicted his massive tax increases would bring in were insufficient to pay for his programs, when the nonpartisan Tax Foundation scored Sanders's plan, they found that they actually would bring in far less than he predicted.

His estimates failed to account "for decreased economic output in the long run."[29] The Tax Foundation found that Sanders's high taxes on investment and capital would lower economic output by nearly 10 percent, and almost everyone's income would go down.[30] No surprise here, unless you're a democratic socialist or a Progressive.

The perverse incentives that higher taxes on labor, investment, and success create, would inevitably reduce growth by producing a climate in which business success is extremely difficult, discouraging would-be entrepreneurs from even making the effort. Without the entrepreneurial spirit that generates economic growth and tax revenue, Sanders's democratic socialism, like traditional socialism, would run out of other people's money.

Given Sanders's inability to explain how democratic socialism would be any more effective in funding its various government benefit programs than traditional socialism, the question is whether democratic socialism is an innovative, coherent concept to effectively address economic inequality or simply a rebranding ploy, a ruse, an effort to garner votes, re-empower a failed socialist ideology, and advance the Progressives' agenda.

To answer that question, we need to understand how Senator Sanders's democratic socialism would work beyond enumerating the giveaways. How would it generate the revenue necessary to fund all the free benefits Sanders would have government distribute? How would democratic socialism avoid the cardinal pitfall of traditional socialism? How would it avoid running out of other people's money?

In short, what distinguishes democratic socialism from traditional socialism?

A Distinction with Little Difference

Democratic is the adjective that distinguishes Sanders's socialism from traditional socialism. The word *democratic* is important because, historically, socialism has been imposed on people rather than being the result of democratic elections. So, knowing how Sanders defines *democratic* is enlightening.

In a 1987 interview, Sanders identified himself as a member of the "progressive coalition," and offered this definition: "Democracy means public ownership of the major means of production, it means decentralization, it means involving people in their work. Rather than having bosses and workers it means having democratic control over the factories and shops to as great a degree as you can."[31]

In other words, the system that had been in place in the Soviet Union for seventy years and was on the verge of collapse.

By November 2015, Sanders ostensibly changed his position on public versus private ownership of American businesses. In a 2015 speech attempting to define democratic socialism, Sanders stated point blank, "I don't believe government should own the means of production."[32]

So, unlike the failed command-and-control socialism of the twentieth century, at least Sanders's democratic socialism doesn't call for nationalizing companies like Amazon, Ford, and Apple or shutting down the stock market. It doesn't make government the direct employer of our nation's workforce. As near as one can discern from Sanders's explanations, this is the factor that most clearly distinguishes Sanders's democratic socialism from traditional socialism.

But, how much of a distinction is it? Rather than *owning* the means of production, under democratic socialism the government would *control* the means of production through a myriad of statutes and regulations.

Looking at the list of issues requiring government action on Senator Sanders's website is revealing. While appealingly phrased, his democratic socialism would have government dictate how businesses compensate their employees by setting the wages and benefits they must provide. It would manage their environmental, energy, labor, training, and financing options through government departments, executive orders, and regulations. It would control business profits as well as the earnings of those who ostensibly own or run their businesses through taxation (massive taxation). It would then redistribute these tax revenues to the masses through Sanders's myriad of government benefit programs.

Traditional socialism's primary fault was that it eliminated the incentive for individuals to be productive, destroying both economic growth and opportunity. Without economic growth, it collapsed under its own weight.

Would this subterfuge of substituting pervasive government control for government ownership really avoid the pitfalls of traditional socialism?

It would not.

Through statutes, regulation, taxation, redistribution, and a Wilsonian-inspired bureaucracy, democratic socialism would virtually eliminate the incentive for entrepreneurs, innovators, and the leaders of private-sector firms to succeed, much like traditional socialism. The government would control what business owners could and could not do, how much profit their businesses could earn, and how much or how little they could personally retain from their efforts.

Democratic socialism would turn business owners into the equivalent of managers reporting to government overseers. Government would run the economy like a super-CEO, from the top down, but without a good CEO's vested interest and business knowledge.

If that sounds like traditional socialism with lipstick, that's because it is.

The Progressives have been working to put America on this democratic socialist path to economic stagnation and decline for decades. President Obama moved us as close as we've ever been to this vision in which government levies high taxes on personal and business income and, by varying degrees, regulates the way businesses operate.

As a result, by the time President Obama left office, working-class Americans faced anemic economic growth resulting in limited job opportunities, stagnant wages, and a diminishing middle class. Perhaps not surprisingly, this increased the income inequality to which President Obama, Senator Sanders, and their Progressive allies so object.

The obvious way to reverse this trend is to encourage the individual initiative that inevitably leads to private-sector growth and the opportunity for people to improve their circumstances. Our history has repeatedly demonstrated the ability of free-market capitalism to generate that growth and broadly spread the benefits. But democratic socialists would put President Obama's policies on steroids, making our nation even more Progressive and democratically socialist, which is far more punishing for business.

Why?

Socialism's Essential Misconception

The essential misconception of socialism (both democratic and traditional) is that wealth is static. This misconception enables the assumption that government can take wealth from those who produce it and redistribute it without impacting the amount of wealth available to distribute. In other words, it assumes that people will create wealth even if the government eliminates the incentive to create it by transferring the benefits of doing so to others. This assumption justifies the belief that government can slice our economic pie into smaller and smaller pieces without impacting the size of that pie.

In this fictional world where the economic pie never shrinks, it makes sense to address economic inequality by having government simply take from those who produce wealth and redistribute the benefits of their success to others. However, this approach has two very fundamental flaws.

First, wealth is fluid, not static. Those who create wealth react to incentives either by causing wealth to increase or allowing it to dissipate. As socialism irrefutably proves, if you discourage those who create wealth, wealth will diminish.

Second, by divvying up a diminishing economic pie into smaller (but more equal) pieces until there is no pie left to divide, socialists eventually run out of other people's money. As a result, in the unfortunate countries where it has been tried, socialism invariably produced the equality of poverty.

In reality, increasing opportunity—the opportunity to improve your life—is the only way to successfully reduce both poverty and economic inequality. Opportunity, in turn, only increases meaningfully when there is economic growth. The key to reducing economic inequality is to incentivize economic growth while assuring that people have equal access to the available opportunities. That is the vision of American capitalism.

Addressing income inequality by simply dividing existing wealth without addressing the need to incentivize economic growth is like giving an aspirin to someone with a brain tumor. It may make them feel better for a short time, but the underlying problem will still kill them. Economic growth, President Kennedy's tide that lifts all boats, cures the underlying problem by creating opportunity while reducing poverty.

In all of human history, capitalism is the only economic system that has ever successfully incentivized self-sustaining and broad-based economic growth. Only personal economic incentives in a healthy free-market economy can produce the expansive growth that lifts people out of poverty, raises their standard of living, and reduces income inequality.

Traditional socialism proves that policies designed to spread the wealth (or the misery) more equally may reduce income inequality, but they will neither grow the economy nor reduce poverty. Government is incapable of mandating economic growth or artificially reproducing its benefits. Government policies can incentivize or discourage growth, but it takes the human initiative that capitalism unleashes to create it.

Sanders's policies are based on government-controlled wealth redistribution. None are based on the notion that democratic socialism will incentivize economic growth, creating the opportunities necessary to lift people out of poverty.

This is hardly surprising. Both democratic and traditional socialists would use government to compel the equality of outcomes—what socialists call justice—rather than to inspire prosperity.

It's Been Tried

Despite socialism's inevitable failure everywhere it has been tried, Sanders treats the Nordic countries as the models for reform because the redistributionist aspect of his policies appear to have been more successful there than in, say, Venezuela, North Korea, or Cuba (not to mention Spain, Greece, and Italy).

"We should look to countries like Denmark, like Sweden and Norway, and learn from what they have accomplished for their working people," Sanders said on the campaign trail.[33] Denmark is the example of choice. The liberal website Vox gleefully noted that both Democratic candidates in 2016 "want to make America look a lot more like Denmark."[34]

The irony is that voters in Denmark are increasingly electing politicians committed to making it look more like America.

DENMARK

While democratic socialists offer Denmark as the quintessential example for how their system can succeed, Danish leaders are quick to disavow Sanders's brand of socialism as "too leftist."

In a 2015 speech to Harvard's Kennedy School of Government, Denmark's prime minister Lars Løkke Rasmussen remarked, "I know that some people in the US associate the Nordic model with some sort of socialism, therefore I would like to make one thing clear. Denmark is far from a socialist planned economy. Denmark is a market economy."[35]

One Danish economist told CNN, "When I hear Bernie Sanders talk about himself as a democratic socialist, it's a little bit 1970s. The major political parties on the center-left and the center-right [in Denmark] would oppose many of the proposals of Bernie Sanders on the regulatory side as being too leftist."[36]

In fact, on the Heritage Foundation/*Wall Street Journal*'s 2018 Index of Economic Freedom, Denmark ranks twelfth, ahead of the United States at eighteenth. On business freedom, Denmark scored a 92.5, while the US, after the eight years of the Obama administration (and less than a year under President Trump), scored 82.7.[37] (In 2008, the pre-Obama United States ranked fifth freest overall and scored a 91.7 on business freedom.[38]) One can only wonder how much further the US would drop during a Sanders presidency.

Yet, Denmark does have some policies that are consistent with Sanders's welfare-state benefits vision. For example, the

Danish government covers almost all health and education costs for everyone.[39] Doctor visits come with a small co-pay, and university students get a stipend to attend school. Hospital services are free. Taxpayers cover job training for the unemployed, and people get paid when they lose work, get sick, or go on parental leave.[40] The government covers both childcare and elder care.[41]

But someone has to pay for it. Danes are taxed at the highest rates in the developed world. The average personal income tax from 1995 to 2017 in Denmark was 60 percent.[42] This is not a Progressive tax that falls squarely on the rich, either. There basically are no rich people in Denmark, so the burden falls on the middle class. Denmark's top tax bracket kicks in at roughly $55,000 a year.[43]

Danes also pay a 25 percent value-added tax on purchases, and companies face a corporate income tax. To fill in the gaps, Denmark charges an 8 percent tax to pay for health care (deducted from income before other taxes are calculated), property taxes, an inheritance tax on the wealthy, and a gift tax.[44–45] Until recently, the government imposed a 150 percent tax on cars, which made an entry-level Ford the price of a mid-level BMW.[46]

Denmark's cost of living further diminishes the value of the income Danes are able to retain after paying all these taxes. Denmark is one of the most expensive places in the world to live. According to Numbeo's *Cost of Living Index by Country for 2017 Mid-Year,* Denmark has the sixth-highest cost of living out of 115 countries worldwide.[47] Mercer's Cost of Living Survey of the world's cities lists Denmark's capital, Copenhagen, as having the twenty-fourth-highest cost of living out of the 209 cities it surveyed.[48]

As you would expect, this system of high taxes, a high cost of living, and generous government benefits creates incentives for people not to work.

In 2013, Danish newspapers discovered "Carina," a single mother of two who had been on welfare since she was sixteen years old because, she discovered, the welfare system allowed her to have more disposable income than if she worked full-time.[49]

Not long after, they found Robert Nielsen, nicknamed "Lazy Robert" by the press, who admitted on television that he managed to buy an apartment with welfare checks he'd been collecting since 2001.[50]

But their situations aren't unique. As reported in the *New York Times,* a study by the municipal policy research group Kora "found that only 3 of Denmark's 98 municipalities" had a "majority of residents working in 2013."[51] That number was 59 municipalities as recently as 2009.[52]

According to the *Times,* "Denmark's long-term outlook is troubling," and few experts in Denmark believe it "can long afford the current perks."[53] Part of the problem is the portion of Danes not in the workforce. But they also face an aging population and a depressed economy.

As you would expect, without the incentive to materially improve your circumstances to the extent there is economic growth, it is truly anemic. Between 2007 and 2017, Denmark's annual growth rate never rose above 2 percent and was often below 1 percent.[54]

Slow economic growth plus an aging workforce have made Denmark's social welfare system unsustainable, forcing the government to scale back benefits and consider proposals to cut student stipends, unemployment benefits, and other reforms, proving Margaret Thatcher right once again. When the likes of Sanders and Warren praise the Denmark-style welfare state, this is the part of the story they don't tell.

Even with a reduction in benefits, Denmark still needs to find a way to get people to work. By 2017, faced with the inevitable problems of a Progressive welfare state, Denmark's politicians decided on new reforms to make it "more attractive to work" there.

They decided on broad-based tax cuts for workers at all income levels.[55] The government released plans to lower the top rate to 44 percent, slightly less than what a top-bracket earner currently pays in California.[56]

When they proposed the reforms, Danish Finance Minister Kristian Jensen channeled his inner Ronald Reagan or JFK and told reporters that the tax cut is "important for the economy and it's to the highest degree a boon for hardworking Danes, who will be able to keep more of their earnings.[57]

To pay for these tax cuts, the Danish government also proposed a new round of benefit cuts. The ruling party wrote in its 2017 manifesto, "We want to promote a society in which it is easier to support yourself and your family before you hand over a large share of your income to fund the costs of society."[58] That also has a familiar ring.

A small homogeneous nation, Denmark will keep much of its welfare system intact with comparatively high taxes, but instead of America looking "more like Denmark," as Vox gushed, the Danes are finding it necessary to move their system (which is already free-market based) closer to something that looks much more like ours.

SPAIN AND GREECE

By way of comparison, while Denmark is the best-case scenario for democratic socialism's approach to government benefits, in Southern Europe the situation is quite different and more typical.

In 2004, Spain's Socialist Worker's Party rose to power with promises to build a welfare state that rivaled those in Northern Europe.[59] Once in power, the party expanded universal health care, raised the minimum wage, created scholarships for college tuition, paid for housing for young Spaniards, covered childhood health-care costs, paid women to have kids, and financed care for the elderly.[60]

In less than a decade, the entire scheme collapsed. Seven years after rising to power, the Socialist Worker's Party's main concern was averting bankruptcy by controlling government spending, cutting pensions, raising the retirement age, cutting pay for government workers, undermining unions, and cutting many of the benefits on which they campaigned.[61] Their promises were unmanageable in real life. The costs were unsustainable. And after the financial crisis, Spain faced a downgraded credit score and mandatory austerity measures.[62]

Greece's experiment with democratic socialism went even worse than Spain's. Greek politicians promised lavish pension and benefits packages to Greek workers, often in exchange for votes.[63] Greece lacked some of the other perks of Northern European socialism, but compensated for it with an elaborate (and generous) pension system that paid out benefits to nearly everyone.

As recently as 2008, many Greeks were retiring in their mid-fifties on the public dime.[64] Government benefits, poor growth, and high taxes discouraged Greeks from working. At one point, 25 percent of Greek workers and more than 60 percent of Greek youth were unemployed.[65]

To pay for the social programs, Greece ran up a massive debt and lied about the numbers. In 2009, the Greek government admitted falsifying its national accounts and vastly underestimating its debt.[66] The statistician who made honest revisions to Greece's debt numbers was later prosecuted by the government, a sign that perhaps there's a bigger problem of corruption in the country.[67]

Ratings agencies slashed the country's debt rating and Greek bond yields soared above 11 percent.[68] The International Monetary Fund and the European Union offered three bailouts on the condition that Greece reign in spending and cut social programs. The reforms led to nearly a decade of austerity measures, leading to widespread rioting and bank runs.[69]

To pay down its debt, Greece's parliament increased taxes at least five separate times.[70] Higher income taxes and a value-added tax (24 percent) weren't enough to satisfy the country's creditors, so Greece implemented or increased levies on coffee, cigarettes, beer, fuel, gas, heating oil, natural gas, TV subscriptions, broadband, and hotel stays. The government extended the VAT to apply to ice cream, air rides, ferry rides, packaged food, and restaurants.[71] High property taxes forced many older Greeks out of their homes. With their pensions slashed, they couldn't afford to pay their tax bills.[72]

One Greek citizen told the *Guardian* that "the only thing that is not being taxed is the air we breathe."[73]

The crippling tax rates have forced businesses out of the country. According to the *Wall Street Journal,* the number of companies in Greece fell by 27 percent from 2008 to 2016.[74–75] The economy hasn't grown in a decade.[76] The average household owes more money than it makes, and 75 percent of Greeks can't pay their bills on time.[77–78]

After nearly a decade of crisis, just 3.7 million Greeks were working in a country of 11 million people.[79] With no growth, fewer businesses, and a smaller workforce, it's unclear how higher taxes could ever lead Greece out of its crisis. Thatcher's maxim prevailed once more: The Greeks literally ran out of other people's money.

Measuring Economic Inequality

As Senator Sanders repeatedly makes clear, the socialist justification for abandoning free-market capitalism in exchange for democratic socialism is our nation's economic inequality, which he identifies as the great moral, economic, and political issue of our time. Barack Obama called economic inequality "morally wrong."[80] People who spend time reading America's leftist newspapers or listening to cable news shows are likely to think there are robber barons running away with the American economy. The *New York Times,* for example, ran more than 250 stories on income inequality in 2016 alone.[81]

It isn't true.

There are two elements to economic inequality, income and wealth. Income is what you earn from your work or investments plus what you receive from the government in the form of benefits. Wealth is what you own: your assets, such as a house, stocks, bonds, savings, retirement accounts, your car, and so on. While they are related (high incomes often lead to wealth accumulation, and investments can produce income), it's important to understand the differences.

INCOME INEQUALITY

The Left often misleadingly uses pre-tax earnings when discussing income inequality. In fact, Bernie Sanders's website currently contains (as of February 2018) a graph purporting to show that "the gap between the very rich and everyone else is wider than at any time since the 1920s."[82] It is titled "Top 1% Share of Total Pre-Tax Income." "Pre-Tax" being the key word.

Back in the world of economic reality, our highly Progressive tax system reduces the take-home incomes of top earners, reducing the gap between rich and poor.[83] A 2016 report on income inequality by the Congressional Budget Office (CBO) entitled *The Distribution of Household Income and Federal Taxes, 2013,* states that federal taxes "reduce income inequality, because the taxes paid by higher-income households are larger relative to their before-tax income than are the taxes paid by lower-income households."[84]

In 2015 (the most recent year for which data is available), the top 1 percent of taxpayers paid 39 percent of all personal income tax, the top 10 percent paid 71 percent and the bottom 50 percent paid only 3 percent.[85] Taxes reduce the pre-tax incomes of higher-income taxpayers. Ignoring our Progressive tax system's impact distorts the data, making income inequality appear worse than it is.

Government benefits are another variable Progressives often ignore. Sanders, of course, currently includes a pie chart on his website purporting to show that "58 percent of all new income since the Wall Street crash has gone to the top one percent."[86] This chart is supported by a study, which notes that it excludes "government transfers" from its income definition (and acknowledges that it is measuring pre-tax incomes).[87]

When you factor in the various government welfare programs already in place in the United States, the gap between the rich and poor drops even more significantly than when you look to after- (as opposed to pre-) tax income. These programs include Social Security, Medicaid, Medicare, SNAP (food stamps), veterans' benefits, and so on.

The CBO Report states that "[g]overnment transfers reduce income inequality because the transfers received by lower-income households are larger relative to their market income than are the transfers received by higher-income households." In fact, "[t]he equalizing effects of government transfers were significantly larger than the equalizing effects of federal taxes from 1979 to 2013."

When analyzing income inequality, it is disingenuous to ignore both government policies that reduce the incomes of high-earning Americans (our Progressive tax system) and government programs that redistribute a significant portion of those tax revenues to lower-income Americans (our welfare system), increasing their incomes and narrowing the economic inequality gap.

To determine the extent of economic inequality, the CBO Report relies on a standard measure of inequality known as the Gini coefficient. It then compares income inequality before and after the impact of taxes and government benefits. When you factor in our Progressive tax system and government transfers, the CBO Report notes that America's income inequality on the Gini index declines by a whopping 26 percent.[88] That's a significant difference.

Looking at the dollar difference between the top 20 percent of earners and the bottom 20 percent on a pre-tax and pre-benefits basis, in 2013, the lowest 20 percent of earners made an average of $15,800 while the top 20 percent made an average of $253,000.[89] If you factor in taxes and government transfers, income for the bottom 20 percent rises to $24,500 on average and the top falls to $195,300, reducing the gap in dollars between these quintiles by 28 percent.[90]

A November 2017 in-depth academic research paper by nonpartisan researchers David Splinter (an economist at Congress's Joint Committee on Taxation) and Gerald Auten (an economist at the Treasury Department's Office of Tax Analysis) found that income inequality has increased even less than the CBO concluded and far less than liberal economists have claimed.[91]

Splinter and Auten found that prior studies by French economists Thomas Piketty and Emmanuel Saez, the primary source for Progressives' income inequality claims, presented "a distorted view of income inequality levels and trends."[92] In concluding that the top 1 percent's share of income increased substantially between 1960 and 2015, Piketty and Saez relied upon tax return data that failed to "account for the effects of major tax reforms, income sources not in the individual income tax base, and changes in marriage rates."[93]

Applying their "measure of broad pre-tax income," including "government transfers," rather than the 11 percent increase Piketty and Saez estimated, Splinter and Auten's found that the top 1 percent's share of pre-tax income increased "about 2 percentage points," about 80 percent less than Piketty and Saez estimated.[94] Looking at after-tax income, the top 1 percent's share increased about 1.6 percentage points, about 85 percent less than Piketty and Saez estimated.

Splinter and Auten concluded that using "consistent and broad measures of pre-tax and after-tax incomes," the "changes in the top one percent income shares over the last half century are likely to have been relatively modest."[95]

As stated in a policy analysis on economic inequality by Michael Tanner of the Cato Institute, "many of the most common beliefs about [income inequality] are based on misperceptions and falsehoods" as they ignore the reality that "[t]ax policy and social welfare spending substantially reduce inequality in America."[96] While the gap between rich and poor has increased, it has increased far less than Progressives or the media would have you believe. In fact, a few years of meaningful wage increases could significantly reduce that gap.

WEALTH INEQUALITY

Wealth inequality has been increasing in recent years. However, wealth is not a zero-sum game. The rich getting richer does not necessarily mean that the poor are getting poorer. In fact, while stock and real-estate values have been increasing, benefitting those who own these assets, the poverty rate has also been declining.

Wealth inequality deserves a closer look.

The CBO issued a separate report in 2016 entitled *Trends in*

Family Wealth 1989 to 2013. Over this period of time, it found that "[t]he share of wealth held by families in the top 10 percent of the wealth distribution increased from 67 percent to 76 percent, whereas the share of wealth held by families in the bottom half of the distribution declined from 3 percent to 1 percent."[97]

With the value of stock and real estate materially improving, this is hardly surprising. Typically, people need wealth to acquire stocks and real estate. As such, wealthy people have more of these assets than poor people. But stock and real estate increasing in value does not mean that the rich are taking from the poor.

Perhaps the biggest impact on wealth inequality in recent years has come from the Federal Reserve holding interest rates artificially low for over a decade to stimulate the economy. Much of the wealth creation in our nation has come from increased value in the stock market (as the returns on stocks are better than the returns on interest-bearing investments, driving up demand and prices) and increased real-estate values (as low interest rates incentivize real-estate purchases, driving up demand and prices).

Gains in the stock market in particular have impacted wealth inequality as the major indexes boomed after the recession.[98] The US stock market, measured by S&P 500 returns, rose 235 percent while President Obama was in office.[99] Through at least the first year following President Trump's election, that boom has accelerated.

The Federal Reserve reported that, in the second quarter of 2017 alone, the value of stocks rose by $1.1 trillion and the value of real estate rose by $600 billion.[100] In the third quarter of 2017, the Federal Reserve announced that the value of stocks increased an additional $1.1 trillion and real estate rose an additional $400 billion as the markets continued to hit record highs and demand for homes remained high.[101]

As a result, the net worth of households and nonprofits rose to $96.9 trillion, a record high and an increase of $29.1 trillion in household wealth over the prerecession high.[102] However, you needed to own stocks or real estate to participate in the increase.

It's important to keep in mind that increasing wealth inequality does not necessarily result in increasing poverty. For example, in 1989 when there was less economic inequality than there is today, the poverty rate for families was 10.3 percent.[103] Despite increasing economic inequality, by 2016, the poverty rate was down to 9.8 percent.

Conversely, during the recession, when economic growth went negative, the assets of the wealthy declined in value as the stock and real-estate markets both declined and the poverty rate increased, peaking at 11.8 percent for each of the years from 2010 through 2012. While a rising tide lifts all boats, a declining tide lowers them.

Again, wealth is not a zero-sum game. The poor do not necessarily get poorer just because the rich get richer, nor do the poor get richer when the rich get poorer.

In a healthy economy, rich and the poor alike should get richer as the economic tide lifts all boats, increasing standards of living at every income level.

Economic Inequality in America

Progressives, including democratic socialists, have greatly exaggerated the extent of economic inequality in America, its causes, and its impact.

While there are certainly exceptions, America's rich earn their wealth. Generally speaking, they are neither lazy nor indolent inheritors of great wealth passed down generation to generation by a permanent ruling class. In fact, it's common for rich Americans to lose their wealth, particularly inherited wealth.

Research shows that 70 percent of inherited family money is gone by the end of the second generation in America.[104] Of the families that amass huge amounts of wealth, few retain that wealth over many generations. The Cato Institute's Michael Tanner pointed out that in 1982, thirty-eight people from the Du Pont and Rockefeller families were on the Forbes 400 list. By 2016, just one of them remained (a 100-year-old Rockefeller).[105]

There isn't a permanent class of robber barons hoarding all the money.

With respect to new wealth, is it really a negative if individuals like Henry Ford or Steve Jobs enrich all our lives and are rewarded for it? Of course not. To the extent they lift everyone, from those who would otherwise live in poverty to those at the top, the outsized benefits of capitalism that can lead to economic inequality can also produce extremely positive results.

This is particularly true if there is economic and social mobility, allowing those who succeed to move from one economic class to another. Luckily, there is still a decent amount of economic mobility in the United States.

Research by the Brookings Institute, a centrist think tank in Washington, DC, found that of the poor Americans who (1) finish high school, (2) get a full-time job, and (3) wait until age twenty-one to get married and have children, 98 percent escape poverty and 75 percent join the middle class.[106] Failure to accomplish those three things has more to do with culture than economics, and many poor do rise up.

Americans generally rise up or get rich by creating. Tanner points out that the best path to riches is to be an entrepreneur or an innovator. Like Ford and Jobs, the super-rich *make stuff*.[107] That's how Donald Trump got rich, too—by *building* things.

Of the ten richest Americans, only one is a professional investor.[108] Of those billionaires, most got rich by creating things that improved life for everyone; imagine life without Apple, Microsoft, Google, Facebook, or Amazon.[109] Those companies produced the majority of America's ten richest people.

Yes, success in the financial sector is one way to become a billionaire, and the financial sector serves a number of very valuable functions. However, success in tech, media, energy, food services, fashion and retail, real estate, manufacturing, and sports also create wealth. Each of those industries has created more than a dozen billionaires.[110]

In the words of Pew Research, "what is considered poor here is a level of income still not available to most people globally."[111] Nonetheless, there is poverty in the United States. As a rich nation, we can afford to, and should, address it.

Government welfare programs have played a role in reducing income inequality by elevating incomes for those at the bottom of the income scale. However, it is good to keep in mind that, for those who can work, government largesse can have unintended negative consequences, as was the case in Denmark and in the United States prior to President Clinton's and Speaker Gingrich's welfare reforms.

Unfortunately, the negative consequences returned when President Obama gutted the Clinton/Gingrich welfare reforms.

When I was the CEO of CKE Restaurants, Inc., I saw these unintended consequences firsthand during the Obama presidency. Our restaurant crew members were declining promotions to shift leader positions because the increase in income would disqualify them for food, housing, medical, or other government benefits. These promotions were the first step on the ladder to becoming a general manager, potentially making up to $80,000 a year.

Following local minimum wage increases (particularly in California), other employees refused additional hours or requested fewer hours to keep their incomes below the cutoff for receiving benefits.

In the policy community, this loss of benefits upon hitting a certain income level is called the "welfare cliff." Unfortunately, it encourages benefit recipients to earn less so they don't go over the cliff and lose valuable government benefits. This is simply people responding to incentives. If you will lose valuable benefits and make less money by working more, in all likelihood, you will work less and keep the benefits.

Individuals are eligible for food stamps until their incomes exceed 130 percent of the poverty line, or $15,000 per year. For Medicaid, eligibility runs out at 138 percent of the poverty line. Those who receive these benefits often find that it makes sense to work fewer hours and earn less so as not to cross these income thresholds and maintain their government benefits. As a result, the welfare cliff has the adverse effect of locking those it is intended to help in a cycle of poverty and government dependence.

One way to fix this problem is with welfare reform that includes a work requirement, like Clinton and Gingrich implemented.

Another option is the Earned Income Tax Credit (EITC), which provides government assistance to those in need but then dials down the assistance amount over time as the individual's earned income increases. While benefits decrease as a person's income increases, the benefits never decline at a faster pace than income increases. As a result, these individuals always make more as they earn more so the incentive is to work more, not less. The EITC is already helping millions of Americans and could be reformed and expanded to help millions more.

Much of the current structure of welfare programs unintentionally locks people into poverty, which increases income inequality. That's not good for the economy, but more importantly, it's not good for the men and women who need government assistance but want to make better lives for themselves and their families. The current system is failing them. Our welfare system should act as a safety net, not a cage. It should encourage the self-respect and dignity that come with earned success and a job.

The Solution Is Good-Paying Jobs

The majority of Americans earn their income from wages, and wages have stagnated. An analysis by Pew Research found that the average hourly wage's purchasing power was about the same in 2014 as it was in 1979.[112]

According to the CBO, in 2013, the top 1 percent made 38 percent of their income from capital income and gains. The bottom 40 percent earned just 1 percent of their income from those sources, making most of their money from wage income instead.[113]

In recent years, government policy has been a major cause of wage stagnation. Wages stagnate when trade policies send jobs outside the United States, lax enforcement of our immigration laws and liberal immigration policies increase the supply of labor, and Progressive economic policies stymie job-creating economic growth.

This is not to disparage the economic arguments in favor of free trade and liberal immigration policies. Both have the impact of reducing prices, making goods more affordable for larger numbers of people. Well-negotiated trade policies should also open markets for American companies, creating more domestic jobs. However, working-class Americans of all racial and ethnic backgrounds have borne a disproportionate share of the costs from bad trade deals and lax enforcement of our immigration laws.

As businessman and author Edward Conard notes in *The Upside of Inequality: How Good Intentions Undermine the Middle*

Class, trade and immigration polices lower "the relative incomes of the middle and working classes."[114] On the other hand, those who are already wealthy or retired as well as those already on government benefits "enjoy lower-priced goods without suffering the cost of lower wages."[115] Free trade and liberal immigration policies have reduced job opportunities, spreading "a limited amount of income over a greater number of workers," which slows wage growth.[116]

According to the Bureau of Labor Statistics, there are five million fewer Americans working in manufacturing jobs than there were thirty years ago.[117] Free trade might sound good on paper, but when a town loses its economic engine thanks to a factory moving to Mexico or China, the residents might have a difficult time understanding the benefits. They live with the negative consequences every day.

The same goes for liberal immigration policies or the failure to enforce our existing immigration laws. Working-class Americans looking for jobs (possibly because of that lost factory) have a hard time seeing the benefit of bringing in excessive amounts of cheap labor from beyond our borders. These immigrants are willing to work for less, and thus they price Americans out of good-paying jobs.

Working-class Americans helped elect President Trump based on his promise to improve trade and immigration policies. But, even with improved policies on trade and immigration, we will still need economic growth to create good-paying jobs that lift people from one economic class to another. Under President Obama, the government discouraged that growth by overregulating and overtaxing businesses. This is another reason wages stagnated.

Businesses can increase their profits by growing (increasing revenue) or cutting costs (decreasing expenses). Either works. When the economic incentives encourage growth, they invest and grow. When government policies discourage growth through regulation and taxation, they cut costs. In other words, policies that reduce the incentive to generate profits by confiscating and redistributing those profits discourage growth and kill jobs.

Economic growth creates jobs, and when companies are hiring, it increases the demand for workers, raising wages. Cutting costs to compensate for increased regulation and taxation increases profits, but it also kills jobs (particularly good-paying jobs), reducing the demand for workers.

When businesses compete for workers, wages increase. When workers compete for jobs, wages decrease. If you want wages to move up, increase the demand for workers. It isn't rocket science.

The Rising Global Tide

In 1960, Hong Kong's economy produced just $429 worth of goods per person in today's dollars. In 2016, Hong Kong produced more than $43,000 worth of goods per person, making it one of the wealthiest places in the world[118] despite having almost no natural resources (like Venezuela's oil reserves).

With levels of inequality higher than the United States, Hong Kong has still managed to make life better for everyone.[119] The poor there earn nearly ten times what the GDP per capita was in 1960.[120]

Growing the economic "pie" for everyone is what distinguishes capitalist policies from socialist policies. In places like Hong Kong or America, everyone benefits from shared prosperity when innovators, risk-takers, and entrepreneurs have the proper incentives to grow wealth.

This phenomenon of growth extends far beyond the United States and Hong Kong. Free-market capitalism has been lifting people out of poverty and spreading prosperity for two centuries.

Angus Maddison was a British economist who specialized in quantitative macroeconomic history, including the measurement and analysis of economic growth and development.[121] Since his death in 2010, The Maddison Project has continued his highly respected work on "measuring economic performance in the world economy."

In 2012, Derek Thompson, who writes about economics and labor issues for the *Atlantic,* published a chart utilizing the Angus Maddison data and showing "the full 2000 year sweep of the world through GDP/capita" (annual gross domestic product per person).[122] In a 2016 article entitled "How Capitalism Changes Conscience," Jonathan Haidt, a psychology professor at New York University's Stern School of Business, aptly described this chart as "the most important graph in the world."[123] Truly, it is compelling.

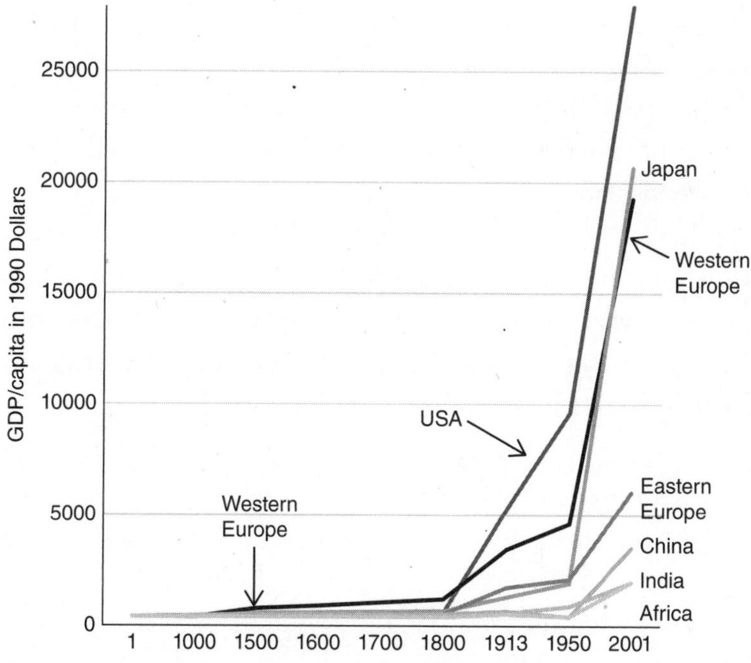

What Professor Jonathan Haidt calls "the 'hockey stick' of rapid recent prosperity," citing Derek Thompson (2012), using data from Angus Maddison. (Source: https://www.humansandnature.org/culture-how-capitalism-changes-conscience)

As Haidt stated, this graph "shows us how capitalism changed the West and Japan in the blink of an eye, and it foretells a similar transformation in the rest of the world. Billions of people are rising out of poverty" and "will be as wealthy as Americans are today."[124]

Current data supports Haidt's conclusion. Capitalism has created unprecedented global prosperity since the world's major socialist economy (i.e., the Soviet Union) collapsed. The world's other major socialist economy (i.e., China) transitioned to state-run capitalism.

In 1990, nearly 40 percent of the world population lived in extreme poverty, on less than $1.90 a day. By 2015, just 9.6 percent did.[125] In the interim, economies around the world experienced massive amounts of liberalization and growth. In China alone, 720 million people escaped extreme poverty between 1990 and 2015, according to the World Bank.[126]

In the past three decades, we have witnessed the greatest explosion of prosperity in human history, and because of it, the world is richer now than it has ever been.

Neither traditional nor democratic socialism deserve any credit whatsoever for this incredible improvement in the human condition. It was all due to the spreading ideals of American free-market capitalism and the creation of unequal prosperity for all rather than socialism's equality of misery and poverty.

CHAPTER NINE

Defending Capitalism: A CEO's Guide

"The only thing necessary for the triumph of evil is that good men should do nothing."

EDMUND BURKE

Progressives are attacking President Trump with intensity rare even in today's partisan political environment. They are using every weapon in their extensive arsenal to obscure his success and demean him personally. As I noted early on, it isn't his failure they fear. In fact, they would welcome it. Their fear is that he will succeed in reducing the size and influence of government, returning power and prosperity to the American people. The early signs are very good. If he can keep it up, he may actually make America great again.

However, as his policy successes become increasingly harder to deny, the Progressives will only intensify their attacks. His economic success stands witness to the negative impact Progressive policies have for every American. The comparisons to Obama's failed big-government policies are too fresh in the minds and wallets of working- and middle-class Americans to be ignored.

The president needs defenders. So does the American

economic system. Overcoming the Left's formidable media presence is a daunting task, particularly with the support it receives from Progressive politicians, the icons of the entertainment industry, and left-wing academics. But there is a group of individuals with the experience, credibility, and presence to defend capitalism even against these odds: America's entrepreneurs and CEOs. Those who have seen capitalism work its magic from the inside can best explain how it creates opportunity and prosperity for all Americans, putting the lie to the Left's narrative of victimhood and oppression and challenging their self-identification as defenders of the underclass.

My principal regret with the success of the Progressives' attack campaign that killed my nomination for secretary of labor is that other CEOs may be reluctant to risk standing up for the system from which we have all so obviously benefitted. Of course, that is exactly what the Progressives hope will happen.

Why CEOs Matter

Looking to business leaders for advice on economic issues simply makes sense. They entered the highly competitive commercial arena and prevailed, learning in the process how to make a profit, create jobs, and spread prosperity. Modern-day presidents have relied on their counsel to varying degrees.

When President Barack Obama formed his first cabinet in 2009, a survey in *Forbes* looked at the percentage of all cabinet secretaries with private-sector experience in each administration going back to 1900. Republican cabinets tended to be more stocked with business leaders. Eisenhower's had the most, followed closely by Reagan's. Not surprisingly, the lowest percentage belonged to President Obama, an administration during which Progressives and the wider political Left employed a heavy hand against those in business.

The Obama administration was also a time of economic transition and—not surprisingly, given his Progressive policies—anemic growth. With economic expansion stalled, Americans were stuck with limited job opportunities, stagnant wages, a diminishing middle class, and, as a result, increased income inequality. Working-class and lesser-skilled workers were desperately seeking job opportunities and increasingly feeling disconnected from the American Dream.

In 2010, the White House projected that annual gross domestic product (GDP) growth would "accelerate in 2011 to 3.8%" and "exceed 4% per year in 2012–2014."[1] In reality, GDP languished at an annualized growth rate of 2.1 percent from the end of the recession in June 2009 through the end of the Obama presidency, never making it to even 3 percent for any calendar year.

This was precisely the time when policymakers should have been soliciting the opinions of business leaders to plot a better way forward. Yet, during the Obama administration, the primary goal was to grow government, redistribute wealth, and advance the Progressive agenda at any cost. They didn't want to let a crisis go to waste. With the country mired in the anemic economic growth that resulted from Progressive, antibusiness policies, any CEO who stood up to defend the free-market alternative presented a particularly difficult problem—they might actually be heard.

Credibility

The Progressives' core problem is credibility. Successful business leaders enter the economic policy debate with real-world experience and the high level of credibility that brings. Meanwhile, the Left's policies are often grounded in ideology and supported by friendly academics at think tanks or universities.

That can set up a conflict between what politicians and academics would *like* to see happen *in a perfect world* (ideology) and what business leaders' experience tells them *will* actually happen *in the real world* (reality). A reasonable observer, as are most American voters, would conclude that the side with real-world experience carries more weight in this credibility fight. For Progressives, that's a problem.

This credibility gap makes successful business leaders who believe in free markets a threat to the Left's coalition of activists, politicians, and ivory tower academics. Progressives face an uphill battle when engaging in substantive policy debate with business leaders who have experienced firsthand the power of capitalism and its positive impact on working- and middle-class Americans.

Progressives are like spectators who have never played baseball claiming an understanding of strategy superior to that of the manager whose team just won the World Series. It can be done, but you might look ridiculous, and nobody watching at home will believe you.

The Progressives' solution is to abdicate substantive debate for a shoot-the-messenger approach right out of Saul Alinsky's Progressive bible *Rules for Radicals.* Alinsky's thirteenth and final rule states, "Pick the target, freeze it, personalize it, and polarize it." *Personalization* is the key concept in these battles. During the Obama presidency, expressing opinions that ran counter to Progressive policies was a risk few CEOs were willing to take. Those who did often ended up in the Progressives' gun sights.

In the Crosshairs

John Mackey, CEO of Whole Foods, was given the full treatment of Alinsky's thirteenth rule in 2009. Mackey published an op-ed in the *Wall Street Journal* entitled "The Whole Foods Alternative to Obamacare: Eight things we can do to improve health care without adding to the deficit." Mackey acknowledged that "[h]ealth-care reform is very important" but argued for "less government control and more individual empowerment."[2]

His eight commonsense reforms included providing the same tax benefits for individuals' policies as are currently available for employer-purchased policies; allowing insurance companies to sell insurance across state lines; enacting tort reform; and reforming Medicaid to provide greater patient empowerment, choice, and responsibility. Almost as an aside, he noted that eating better would improve overall health and further reduce health-care costs.

Mackey was and remains a very successful CEO, running a Fortune 500 company (until Amazon acquired it) focused on more healthful eating alternatives and employing over seventy thousand people. The Whole Foods brand was, quite frankly, readily identifiable and popular with socially and environmentally conscious liberal consumers.

As he composed his thoughtful op-ed, Mackey no doubt imagined people on both sides of this debate would appreciate and rationally consider his recommendations. He almost certainly thought people would view his aside on eating more healthfully as a noncontroversial, commonsense observation on a subject where he had obvious credibility (an observation that also happened to be supported by medical science). He was about to learn the errors of his ways.

Jumping to Obamacare's defense, the leftist media attacked.

Following Alinsky's thirteenth rule, they "personalized." They trained their fire not on Mackey's suggested reforms, but rather on Mackey personally for having the audacity to recommend that people watch what they eat.

The Huffington Post published an editorial that perfunctorily dismissed Mackey's eight substantive proposals to improve health care as "standard conservative talking points."[3] In an op-ed revealingly entitled "Whole Foods CEO: 'The Whole Foods Alternative to Obamacare'—Just Eat Whole Foods!" it argued that Mackey only entered this debate to increase his profits. It attacked Mackey's motives for speaking up as selfishly profit-based. The substance of his arguments, of course, was hardly worth discussing.

The *Talking Points Memo* website followed suit, saying, "Whole Foods is the solution to all of America's health care woes."[4] As threats of a boycott rose, *Time* magazine asked "whether Mackey's missive was a bold entrance into a polarizing political debate, or a shortsighted business blunder that will only alienate his customer base."[5]

By convincing people that Mackey's substantive proposals were just a ruse to promote his business, the Left hoped to discourage people from considering his points and to discount their merits by focusing attention on Mackey's purportedly selfish profit-based motives for speaking up. Freeze it, personalize it, and polarize it.

Similarly, in 2012, pizza chain Papa John's CEO and founder John Schnatter told his shareholders that increased costs associated with the implementation of Obamacare would cause his franchisees' restaurants to raise prices "11 to 14 cents per pizza, or 15 to 20 cents per order."[6] He also noted that, to keep costs down, they would need to reduce some employees' hours below Obamacare's thirty hours per week coverage cut off.[7]

In the highly competitive restaurant business, where profits are measured by pennies on the dollar, businesses have little choice but to pass government-imposed cost increases on to their customers. In effect, these cost increases are a "silent tax"; businesses pass the costs of a government program on to consumers through price increases rather than having the government do so directly by imposing an actual tax. Politicians look like the good guys protecting those in need by imposing the costs on evil businesses. In either event, it's the American people who bear the costs, either as consumers or as taxpayers. Whether they pay more at the restaurant register or to the IRS, the money is still coming out of their pockets.

The only way businesses can avoid passing such silent taxes on to consumers is by otherwise reducing their costs. In Schnatter's case, one way of reducing the burden of Obamacare was cutting employees' hours below the number at which they must provide cost-increasing Obamacare coverage.

Why take the risk of entering this debate? Schnatter said, "Unfortunately, I don't think people know what they're going to pay for" with Obamacare.[8] Schnatter was attempting to inform people about the silent Obamacare tax the government would pass on to them and the real-world consequences that workers would face when Obamacare forced businesses like Papa John's to impose that silent tax.

This was a warning from a successful CEO that Obamacare was going to have economic consequences for consumers in ways they might not fully understand. He did not intend to attack health-care reform in general, and also said it was "good news" that full-time employees were "going to get health insurance."[9]

His reward: The political Left went on the attack, targeting Papa John's products and Schnatter himself.

On Comedy Central's left-leaning show *The Colbert Report,*

Stephen Colbert said people would not pay "another cent" for a Papa John's "hot turd" pizza.[10] Later, as host of *The Late Show* on CBS, he would attack President Trump with similar eloquence, this time with a homophobic vulgarism. But he was wrong about Papa John's success. The small-business owners who ran Papa John's franchises across the country went on selling their pizzas very successfully.

Still, the liberal attack continued. The online academia publication Inside Higher Ed described Schnatter as a "Moral Monster."[11] Others, including the blog site Freak Out Nation and Ed Shultz on MSNBC's *Big Ed Show,* criticized Schnatter's comments as well as his success, lambasting both his net worth and the size of his home.[12] Although he rose to wealth by starting a business out of a broom closet in his father's tavern, according to Freak Out Nation, Schnatter's "partisan views made while living in his sprawling mansion, clearly are not in the interest of the middle class."[13]

The Left reacted by calling for a boycott.[14] One thread on the social news site Reddit commented, "There are plenty of places to get cheap s*** pizza in the world. Anyone else on reddit ready to boycott Papa John's?"[15] The up-votes and comments poured in by the thousands.

As subsequent experience has demonstrated, Obamacare was never going to work as structured. It eventually entered a death spiral, predicted by many, where people were unable to keep their insurance or their doctors; insurance companies withdrew from the exchanges after losing hundreds of millions of dollars; Obamacare's co-ops went out of business; and both insurance premiums and deductibles soared. President Clinton even called it "the craziest thing in the world."[16] Reality prevailed over ideology, and it is the American people who continue to pay the price.

Perhaps listening to the CEOs who foresaw many of these problems would have helped.

Well before President Trump nominated me to serve as his secretary of labor, I also learned through personal experience how the bells of liberal outrage will toll for CEOs willing to speak up when they see the folly of Progressive economic policies. I have been roundly criticized by the Left for speaking out about the problems with Obamacare and the negative impact on working-class Americans that will come from dramatically increasing the minimum wage. Perhaps my most telling experience with the Left personalizing an attack came from comments I made on the threat automation poses for lesser-skilled American workers.

In March 2016, I gave an interview to Business Insider about issues facing the restaurant sector and American businesses in general. Among other things, we touched on automation and its impact on entry-level jobs. I expressed my concern that politically motivated government mandates supposedly intended to help American workers were going to accelerate automation and price workers out of their jobs.

Dramatic minimum-wage increases, the burdens of Obamacare, and paid-leave legislation were increasing labor costs for businesses, making each worker more expensive. From the perspective of both a CEO and a former minimum-wage employee, I explained that this made automation a more economically viable option at a time when young Americans in particular needed entry-level jobs.

The benefits of automation for a business's bottom line help explain the problem. For example, since automated ordering kiosks don't earn wages or benefits of any kind, restaurant owners would be tempted to use them to replace order-takers when faced with mounting labor costs.

My concern was that by incentivizing automation, these government mandates were hurting some of the most vulnerable people in the workforce, eliminating jobs for the lesser-skilled workers they were supposed to protect. My argument was that policymakers should stop pricing working-class Americans out of their jobs by slapping burdens on their employers.

This, apparently, was too much nuance for the Internet to comprehend. Left-leaning websites and individuals immediately began attacking me as a heartless CEO intent on replacing hard-working Americans with robots.

Business Insider ran the interview with the headline "Carl's Jr.'s CEO says he dreams of a day when human workers are obsolete."[17] This was the polar opposite of what I said and what I wanted. My comments arose out of my concern that the government was pushing restaurants in the direction of automation, something I didn't want to happen. Having gotten my start in restaurants scooping ice cream at Baskin Robbins, I wanted others to have that same chance to get on the ladder of opportunity.

The article appeared in other outlets under headlines like "Fast-food CEO says he's investing in machines because he can't afford to pay workers."[18] That is something I never said. The Russian propagandists at RT titled their article "Order up: Robots may take over Carl's Jr."[19] I never even mentioned robots in the interview and, as the article notes, specifically said you could not automate all the jobs at Carl's Jr. *Fortune* ran an article titled "This Fast Food CEO Wants to Replace Workers with Robots."[20] Not only did I never say this, but there are no robots that could replace our workers.

A few phone calls got some of the headlines belatedly revised, but it was too late to repair the damage. The Twitter-verse filled with comments from people who read and quoted the Twitter-ready false headlines and criticized me for what they believed was my compensation. Beyond attacking me personally, they demeaned the quality of our food and then, of course, called for a boycott, actions which could only insult or hurt the workers they seemed so keen to defend.

Interestingly, while many of our competitors have installed automated ordering kiosks to reduce labor costs, our company never did while I was CEO. Nonetheless, during my confirmation process, liberal media outlets and politicians routinely and falsely claimed that I supported replacing workers with robots.

In January 2018, after numerous restaurant chains had announced their intent to automate positions due to increased labor costs, Business Insider wrote another story on the subject and was kind enough to quote me warning of this consequence back in 2016.[21] Better late than never, I guess.

The Chilling Effect

While the Left was "personalizing" my remarks rather than addressing their subsequently confirmed substance, the people who knew the most about the issue understood exactly what I was saying. In the midst of this controversy, the CEO of another large restaurant chain called me to express his support. Like me, he faced the danger of automation replacing employees almost every day.

He enthusiastically told me, "You nailed it. I can't believe people don't see what's happening. Great comments. If we don't stop the insanity, they'll put us all out of business." I thanked him and mentioned that I was being attacked on Twitter and would appreciate his support. He replied, "I can't do that. Then they'll attack me and my business."

There was the chilling effect at work. I reminded him that he'd just expressed concern about being put out of business.

If he agreed that these government policies were really hurting our businesses and our employees and threatening the jobs of younger, lesser-skilled workers, shouldn't he speak out? I reminded him that the restaurant industry is where a lot of young Americans get their first entry-level job experience, enabling them to go on to any number of careers. In effect, for decades our industry has trained America's workforce.

He said that of course he agreed but all he could do was offer to "help anonymously," as he was concerned with how his Board of Directors and shareholders would react to an attack on him or his brand. I thanked him for the call and went back to work.

I would certainly have appreciated the support, but I understood his reluctance. In this highly politicized age, where reputations can be made and destroyed on social media platforms that didn't even exist a generation ago, CEOs face a veritable minefield. As the Left is well aware, engagement with our customers on Facebook, Twitter, Instagram, and the like is increasingly critical to our success.

With the ability to drum up nearly instantaneous online outrage mobs, smear campaigns, and threats of boycotts, the Left has made it very dangerous for successful CEOs who believe in free markets to speak up on economic or political issues. As part of their larger effort to demonize making money, owning a business, or trying to maximize profits, America's leftist influencers in politics and the media have engaged in a concerted effort to silence and discredit those with whom they disagree, including business leaders who question the negative impact of their policies on workers.

Unfortunately, their scare tactics are succeeding. The chilling effect of their intimidation tactics was on full display when my fellow CEO called and offered his anonymous help. When people call you an uncaring monster every time you open your mouth, the temptation is to keep it shut. My friend was supportive, but he didn't want to be in the Progressives' crosshairs. If we are to restore our nation's economic well-being, it is essential that America's CEOs not allow the Left to intimidate them into silence.

I offer these examples of attacks on CEOs to illustrate the diversity of left-wing attacks and the lengths to which they will go to discredit anyone who disagrees with their Progressive policies. Even the truth is not a safe harbor. Actually, it isn't even relevant. The misleading narratives and outright false claims concerning me accelerated during my confirmation process, but they started years earlier and have been employed to silence many a CEO frustrated by the negative impact of Progressive policies. Freeze it, personalize it, and polarize it.

The Best They've Got

This handful of examples show what can happen when CEOs dare to enter the policy arena and question the Progressive Left. Certainly, people could have rationally disagreed with any of our opinions. None of us would have objected to a debate on the substance either of our concerns or proposed solutions. I believe each of us would have welcomed open discourse. We had positions we believed we could defend. But the Left's tactics for silencing us could tolerate no substantive policy debate.

Rather than engaging in open discourse, left-wing individuals, groups, and publications chose to attack our motives and our success, attempting to bury the substantive policy issues rather than addressing them. But this attack on wealth or the desire to generate profits is simply a Progressive ruse. Their concern is policy, not wealth. Even the most highly motivated profit-seekers can easily avoid these attacks on their wealth and motives simply by towing the Progressive line.

I have already discussed the multimillionaire socialists in the entertainment industry. The business community has a few of these itself. Consider those in the business world who have used every opportunity the free-enterprise system offers to create enormous wealth but are nonetheless Progressive icons.

Multibillionaire investor George Soros stands at the center of the liberal pantheon due to his support for leftist causes and candidates, despite his own insider trading conviction and widely acknowledged currency speculation. The Left praises multibillionaire investor and CEO Warren Buffet, one of the richest people in the world, for his Progressive positions such as the so-called "Buffet Rule" that advocates higher taxes on the wealthy. Billionaire Tom Steyer receives Progressive accolades for his support of leftist candidates and causes, particularly environmental causes and efforts to impeach President Trump, despite having earned his wealth as a dreaded hedge fund manager.

Clearly, the desire to generate profits and create personal wealth is no impediment to having an opinion on politics or economics if that opinion supports the Progressives' agenda. But is this the most effective way to overcome the economic obstacles facing the American people?

In a rational world where politicians and policymakers were actually trying to find the best solutions to our pressing economic problems, people on both sides of policy debates would appreciate, encourage, and consider experience-based opinions regardless of politics. The absence of input from business leaders who support our free-enterprise system empowers an elite group of Progressive politicians and academics to set economic policy without the practical experience necessary to foresee the consequences. For Progressives, empowering this elite group is exactly the point of engaging in such personal attacks.

The reality is that derogatory, nonsubstantive attacks are the Progressive Left's best, if not their only, effective alternative. Were there convincing substantive responses to the points CEOs like Mackey, Schnatter, and myself raised about Progressive economic policies, our opponents certainly would have employed them rather than demonizing and attempting to discredit us personally while disparaging our businesses.

Their Fear Is Not That Trump Will Fail, But Rather That He Will Succeed

Silencing the opposition is hardly a new strategy. History is rife with examples of political movements incapable of succeeding on substance but seizing power and control by silencing those who opposed them. History also demonstrates that, once in power, such movements are incapable of solving their society's problems or generating wealth for any but the ruling elite.

Unfortunately, these personal attacks can be very effective in silencing dissent from Progressive ideology. For CEOs willing to speak up, such attacks can threaten their reputations, the continued success of their businesses, and perhaps their jobs.

So, experienced and successful business leaders sit on the sidelines frustrated, discouraged, and silently forced to navigate poorly conceived and unnecessary government roadblocks. The result is needlessly ineffective and destructive policies that mire economic growth in the bog of ideology rather than releasing the dynamic entrepreneurial energy that can only exist in a capitalist free-market economy. President Trump is actively and successfully reducing or eliminating many of those destructive policies and freeing the private sector to grow. He could use more support from the CEOs whose businesses and employees are benefitting.

But CEOs who want to advise the president have learned that the more successful President Trump is at reducing government's size and scope, the more they and their companies will be subjected to intense pressure from Progressives not to support him. That has been evident almost since President Trump took office.

Shortly after his inauguration in January 2017, President Trump created two business advisory councils, the American Manufacturing Council and the Strategy and Policy Forum. The members of these councils were some of America's top business leaders. Before long, these business leaders felt pressure from the Progressive Left to resign.

In March, protestors held a rally at Disney's annual shareholders meeting and presented over five hundred thousand petitions demanding that CEO Bob Iger quit the president's business council. Iger told shareholders that he thought it "was in the best interests of our company and of our industry, to have an opportunity to express points of view directly to the President of the United States and to his administration."[22] He went on to say that he did not consider that his "membership in that group in any way endorses or supports any specific policy of the president or his administration." Rather, he believed it was "a privileged opportunity to have a voice in the room." Iger subsequently resigned from the Strategy and Policy Forum following the president's decision to withdraw from the Paris Climate Accord.[23]

In April, a Silicon Valley investor took out full-page ads in the *Washington Post* and the *New York Times* urging Tesla CEO Elon Musk to "dump Trump." Musk also met with opposition from some Tesla customers for his involvement on the councils.[24] Musk had clear policy differences with the president but stated that he would remain on the councils because "[a]dvisory councils simply provide advice and attending does not mean that I agree with actions by the Administration."[25] He also later resigned when the president withdrew from the Paris Climate Accord.

In August 2017, in the wake of the negative publicity following the president's handling of the violence and chaos at a white supremacist demonstration in Charlottesville, Virginia, other CEOs began to resign from the councils. In response, the president disbanded the councils tweeting, "Rather than putting pressure on the businesspeople of the Manufacturing Council & Strategy & Policy Forum, I am ending both. Thank you all!"[26]

Of course, that didn't satisfy the mob. Protestors subsequently marched on the Manhattan headquarters of both J. P. Morgan and Blackstone.[27] They wanted J. P. Morgan CEO Jamie Dimon (who had served on the council) and Blackstone CEO Stephen Schwarzman (who had chaired the Strategy and Policy Forum) to intensify their opposition to President Trump.

Certainly, there were CEOs who felt compelled to resign from the business councils due to policy or personal differences with the president. However, it's also clear that each of them was subjected to significant pressure from the Progressive Left to disassociate themselves from the president. That pressure certainly had an impact on their decisions. This is pressure to which CEOs are particularly vulnerable as they look to the entire political spectrum to sell their services or products. It is most effective when employed against CEOs with a left-leaning customer base such as Tesla.

One would think those on the Left would want the voices of CEOs who share their views on issues like climate change or immigration heard in the White House. Clearly, that is not the case. But why? The answer is fear. There is intense fear on the Progressive Left that President Trump will succeed. The early success of his economic policies has only shown the Left that their fears are justified.

Progressives learned their lesson well from President Reagan's undeniable free-market economic success. GDP soared at an annualized growth rate of 4.4 percent from the end of the recession in November 1982 through the end of Reagan's time in office. Should President Trump implement free-market policies with anything approaching these historic levels of success, it will be decades before Progressives can obfuscate economic reality and convince Americans to once again subject themselves to the devastating consequences of a Progressive big-government agenda. President Obama's eight years of failed economic policies would only serve to magnify the benefits of a successful Trump presidency.

Progressive efforts to drive a wedge between business leaders and the president are based on this fear rather than any concern that the president's policies might fail. Despite the benefits economic prosperity would have for Americans, despite the historically proven ability of free-market principals to drive that prosperity, Progressives will continue to oppose President Trump's efforts because his success represents an existential challenge to both their agenda and their identity.

Our nation needs open input from business leaders who have the practical real-world experience necessary to understand both what will work economically and the consequences of policies that will not. As we saw under President Obama, the absence of such input opens the door for Progressive policies that rely on the benevolence of big government while limiting the potential for individual innovation, accomplishment, and self-esteem.

It's Worth the Risk

To generate the economic growth that would benefit all Americans, we need creative and effective free-market policy solutions. Input from proven business executives can help us find them.

These are the individuals who successfully overcome obstacles to economic growth as a part of what they do every day. It is a part of who they are, and it has become a part of who we are as a people. Without input from experienced and successful business leaders, our economic policies will reflect the utopian dreams of an inexperienced and unrealistic Progressive intelligentsia committed to the belief that they know how to run our businesses and our lives better than we do.

Even with President Trump in the White House and Republicans in charge of Congress, the Progressives enjoy continued prominence out of power, kept alive by the liberal media complex, loyal adherents in academia, political candidates, and governments-in-waiting. In fact, Progressives may even be more dangerous as outsiders since that is their traditional status, at least in America.

In or out of government, Progressives know that if their brand of tyranny is to prevail, it must first defeat the American business community. For this reason alone, these derogatory personal attacks on business leaders will continue. The good news is that such attacks are the best they've got. On substance, they cannot win.

This is why it's more important than ever for America's CEOs to fearlessly speak up despite personal attacks. If we are to grow our economy, curtail the expansion of government, and create the jobs and careers that lead workers to the middle class, it is essential that business leaders have the courage to say what they know to be true. They need to acknowledge what is at risk and assume the civic and moral obligation to speak out. There is simply too much at stake for business leaders to allow themselves to become intimidated, cowering victims.

I'm well aware that CEOs need to protect their companies and their stakeholders. When the Left attacks, your Board of Directors gets nervous as the email complaints start coming in. Your shareholders wonder if your comments will negatively affect the company's value. The reality is that commenting or advising on issues of public policy has never been without risk.

But CEOs can reduce the risks by thinking and acting proactively.

A Practical Guide to Proactive Support for Your Principles AND Your Brand

After years of attacks from the Progressive Left, I've learned a few lessons that I hope can help prevent other entrepreneurs and CEOs who speak up from going through what I did.

1. It's important to understand that over the eight years of the Obama administration, Progressives and their allies have succeeded in leaning the country more to the Left. Extreme leftist elements have taken over the Democratic Party. This will likely be the case for the foreseeable future.
2. CEOs must resist the natural instinct to try to appease the mob. Appeasement often fails even in the short term and certainly fails in the long term. Once CEOs demonstrate that they are susceptible to pressure they will get more pressure (as Jamie Dimon at J. P. Morgan and Stephen Schwarzman at Blackstone have witnessed). Aggressors keep attacking unless and until they believe aggression is ineffective.

3. CEOs should adopt policies regarding political input and involvement. They should emphasize that these policies are based on principle and that the policies will be followed regardless of pressure. These policies could include:

    a. That the company and its representatives will offer advice to any sitting public official regardless of party about matters affecting the company specifically, its segment of the economy, and the economy in general.
    b. That offering such advice says nothing about whether the company or its representatives support the public official generally and should not be taken as a political endorsement.
    c. That the company recognizes there are many diverse schools of thought among its constituencies regarding politics, and the company respects all those views and the people who hold them.
    d. That every employee of the company, from the production floor to the executive suite, is entitled to participate as individuals in the political process, and that no one will be penalized at the workplace for doing so, provided that the employee conducts himself or herself lawfully.
    e. That the company is a business enterprise and will market its products and otherwise conduct its business affairs without regard to politics.
    f. That the company reserves the right to participate in advocacy or elections as it determines is necessary to protect its customers, employees, and shareholders, and always in accordance with law.

No policy solution is perfect. I offer these suggestions as a means to provide at least some rational protection from political attacks regardless of their source. Empowering our nation's business leaders to speak out will always be critically important.

The failure to do so enables those who derive their power from big government to destroy not only our businesses but the very free-enterprise system that empowered the American people and set the stage for our nation's unprecedented success. We cannot allow that to happen, and we cannot waste the opportunity we have to organize the business community around President Trump, who truly appreciates our perspectives.

There is already some momentum among the CEO community to get the voices of America's CEOs heard. the Job Creators Network (JCN) is one of the leaders in this effort. JCN is a nonpartisan group, founded by free-market advocate Bernie Marcus, the (cofounder and former CEO of Home Depot) and run by free-market CEO Alfredo Ortiz. It offers CEOs a platform to tell their stories about how bad government policies have negative consequences that are often overlooked in today's political climate.

Like me, JCN believes that the best defense against bad government policy is a well-informed public. Its Employer to Employee education program provides materials for CEOs to educate their employees, helping them understand how regulations, taxes, and mandates affect their paychecks.

If America is to regain its economic momentum and lead the way to worldwide prosperity, its business leaders must stand ready and willing to defend capitalism and the free-enterprise system. The reality is that America desperately needs its CEOs to speak up and defend a system they understand better than any left-wing activists, politicians, or academics. This is the reason big-government Progressives work so diligently to silence them and the reason their voices must be heard.

I understand the risks because I've lived them. I put myself and my ideas out there early on, and, yes, I've been attacked for it. But the risks are small when compared to the threat big-government Progressives pose to America's promise of economic freedom and individual opportunity secured through limited government.

A Low-Risk, High-Return Opportunity to Make a Difference

The 2017 Republican tax cuts present a significant opportunity for CEOs to stand up for business-friendly legislation that benefits all Americans. When these tax cuts became law in December 2017, American workers got a pay raise. That's a message employers can and should convey to their employees.

The impact of lower individual tax rates first hit employees in February when the new withholding tables took effect. Typical workers with an annual salary of $50,000 saw about a $100 monthly increase in their paychecks, more if they had children. It might be crumbs to coastal elites like Nancy Pelosi, but for the four-fifths of Americans who live paycheck to paycheck, rest assured, it made a difference.

For millions of workers, the benefits of the Tax Cuts Bill went well beyond reduced withholding. Within a month of it becoming law, over two hundred and fifty employers announced increased compensation for millions of employees, all because of the business tax cuts.

If you are an employer who has yet to increase your employees' compensation, you should do so. They surely must wonder where your extra profits are going. All they have been hearing from the Democrats and the mainstream media is that the rich are getting tax cuts at their expense. It certainly couldn't hurt to let them know it isn't just your profits that have increased. Their paychecks are also larger and benefitting from the Republicans' tax cuts.

If you are one of the employers who increased your employees' compensation, let them know why. Also, let them know those paychecks are even larger than they would otherwise have been because the federal government is taking a smaller percentage of their increased earnings. They have benefitted from tax cuts, both business and personal, that the Democrats and their media allies characterized as "Armageddon" and "a Disaster," claiming they are only for the rich. Let them know just how untrue that is.

The reality is that the Left so successfully misrepresented what Republicans were doing that, prior to its passage, about 66 percent of Americans thought the Tax Cuts Bill would increase their taxes or that they would stay the same. However, even according to the left-leaning Tax Policy Center, about 80 percent of Americans will see a tax decrease in 2018.[28] While their withholding may be lower, employees may not see the full benefits of these tax cuts until their taxes are due next April. It would be a mistake to assume that employees are reading the positive coverage in the financial press or the company's press releases.

CEOs have a bully pulpit, credibility, and the business as a common point of reference with employees. Neither they nor their employees will benefit from their silence. Use that bully pulpit to let employees know how the Republican tax cuts actually impact both them and the business. Send something out personally that tells them the truth.

If this Trump economic boom is to continue or even accelerate, we need to elect pro-business Republicans in November. Keep in mind that not a single Democrat voted for these tax cuts. That's another point to make with employees. If employees hear directly from CEOs how these tax cuts and President Trump's pro-growth economic policies are benefitting them, it could make a difference.

Otherwise, employees may well continue to buy into the Left's false narrative of tax cuts for the rich. I don't see that narrative dissipating. Its all they've got. In that event, employees may well credit the Democrats for trying to protect them and give Republicans none of the credit they deserve. Should that occur, Democrats will retake power in Washington and there will be no further business-friendly legislation.

The fact is that what CEOs have to say matters, if they have the courage to speak up.

CHAPTER TEN

The Tide Is Turning

"We need somebody who can take the brand of the United States and make it great again. Ladies and gentlemen: I am officially running for president of the United States, and we are going to make our country great again."

PRESIDENT DONALD J. TRUMP
CAMPAIGN KICKOFF, JUNE 2015

An Historic Election

Following the 2016 presidential election, I was speaking with a friend who is the CEO of a major trade organization. Trump's win was certainly historic, but we were wondering if the Trump presidency to come would have historical significance. Would it matter in the long run?

My friend lamented that, for the last eight years, President Obama had implemented Progressive policies through legislation, executive orders, and regulations that expanded government's size, power, and influence. In the past, Progressive legislative gains had proven difficult, often impossible, for Republicans to reverse.

Could President Trump set our nation back on the course of incredible growth and prosperity that capitalism can produce, or would we remain on the path of stunted growth, poverty, and disintegrating families that inevitably result from socialism. We wondered, whether President Trump could withstand the Progressive forces aligned against him.

Could he really "Make America Great Again"?

In this sense, the Trump presidency is part of an ongoing historic struggle dating back to Woodrow Wilson and Teddy Roosevelt. This struggle pits those who, like our Founders, believe in limited government and individual liberty against Progressives who, like Wilson and the Roosevelts, would impose big-government collectivism.

What will President Trump's role be in that struggle? Early on, it appears that it will be significant. That's just what the country needs.

By defeating Hillary Clinton, President Trump had unexpectedly stopped the Progressives in their tracks, at the very least delaying what the Left views as the inevitable trend toward socialism. Can President Trump reverse over one hundred years of Progressive gains? Can he even reverse the significant gains Progressives achieved under President Obama?

Obama's Failed Progressive Legacy

On November 4, 2008, voters elected Barack Obama president of the United States. He ran as if he were a left-leaning moderate. He was not. He was a big-government Progressive.

For the next eight years, the Obama administration waged war on business and enlarged government to a size and scope FDR would have envied. At first, with the Democrats in control of both the legislative and executive branches of government, he would do so by statute. Once Republicans regained control over the House of Representatives in 2010, he would do so by executive orders and regulation, exercising raw executive power with Wilsonian aggression.

In February 2009, Democrats passed a Progressive, Keynesian-style economic stimulus bill authorizing over $800 billion in federal government spending for supposedly "shovel-ready" projects to revitalize the economy. Obama released a report by his administration's economic advisers, projecting that this stimulus spending would keep unemployment below 8 percent. (It was 7.8 percent when Obama took office in January 2009.[1]) He described the report as a "rigorous analysis," which he released "so that the American people can see exactly what this plan will mean for their families, their communities, and our economy."[2]

The stimulus bill passed without a single Republican vote in the House and three Republican votes in the Senate (including Arlen Spector, who would soon switch party alliance to the Democrats).

Two years later, Obama would chuckle as he admitted, "Shovel-ready was not as—uh—shovel-ready as we expected."[3] As for the unemployment rate, it shot up to 10 percent by that October and wouldn't dip below 8 percent again for the next forty-three months. As the *Washington Times* pointed out at the time, the "stimulus" was little more than "a bailout for lobbyists and a vehicle for political paybacks."[4] The failed investments like Solyndra and Fisker spoke for themselves.

In March 2010, without a single Republican vote in the House or the Senate, the Democrats enacted Obamacare, achieving a long-held Progressive goal by placing government bureaucrats in charge of our health care. Ironically, if not deceptively, called The Affordable Care Act, it created compulsory health-care mandates for individuals and businesses alike, dramatically increased the costs of health insurance, drove young people out of the market, and discouraged businesses from hiring full-time employees.

Not wanting to let a crisis go to waste, four months later, Obama signed into law the Dodd–Frank Wall Street Reform and Consumer Protection Act, simply known as Dodd-Frank. It passed with a mere three Republican votes in the House and three in the Senate. Senator Christopher Dodd and Representative Barney Frank, who played major roles in bringing about the Great Recession, authored this legislation. It saddled the financial sector with the most regulations it had seen since the Great Depression. But like most big-government efforts, it backfired. The so-called "too big to fail" banks actually got bigger, while the community banks (the ones that typically fund small businesses) suffered. The smaller banks couldn't afford the massive regulatory and compliance costs imposed by Dodd-Frank, but the big banks could.[5]

It's worth noting that the Obama administration's policies were so unpopular, and Obama himself so personally distant from Congress, that he was unable to achieve any additional legislative enactments during the following six years of his presidency. In 2010, voters returned control of the House of Representatives to Republicans and Obama's legislative onslaught mercifully came to an end. However, that did not stop the president from furthering his regulatory agenda.

During Obama's term, the Federal Registry of Regulations reached nearly one hundred thousand pages, the longest in history.[6] A report by the National Association of Manufacturers noted that "U.S. federal government regulations cost an estimated $2.028 trillion in 2012 (in 2014 dollars), an amount equal to 12 percent of GDP."[7] The Heritage Foundation reported that regulations from the Obama era racked up costs of some $100 billion per year by 2016.[8]

Obamacare regulations perpetuated a statutory scheme that never had a chance of succeeding. The Labor Department, under then-Secretary (at this writing, DNC Chair) Tom Perez, passed a flurry of business-hobbling regulations. The National Labor Relations Board advanced the unions' interests, the EPA drove up energy costs, and for the first time ever, the Internet faced FCC regulation.[9]

The courts eventually overturned many of these regulations. The Trump administration has gotten rid of more since coming to power, and they've only just begun. But some regulations have survived, and even those that didn't survive created such uncertainty in the business community that they hobbled economic growth.

Because of this growth-blocking Progressive power grab, even though he was rolling over exceptionally low economic growth coming out of a major recession (making any amount of growth appear more impressive), and despite his administration's projections of over 4 percent GDP growth, Barack Obama had a dismal average GDP growth of just 1.5 percent, as measured when he left office in January 2017.[10]

But, in fairness, as this legislative and regulatory onslaught demonstrates, economic growth was never the Obama administration's primary goal. Rather, the primary—and Progressive—goals were first, to expand government, and second, to redistribute wealth.

He accomplished his first goal. Through statutes and regulations, Obama expanded government beyond anything that had come before. However, by stifling economic growth, Obama's Progressive policies predictably caused wages to stagnate, closed paths to the middle class, and froze both working- and middle-class Americans out of whatever benefits the economy was able to offer.

It wasn't capitalism that created these barriers to advancement for those who wished to rise. It was the Progressive policies from a president and political party intent on increasing government's size and power. This party railed against income inequality while causing it to increase. Policies sold as beneficial to the middle-class all but destroyed it. In the 2016 presidential election, both working- and middle-class Americans responded.

The Country Takes a New Direction

Hillary Clinton promised to continue the Obama legacy. Donald Trump promised to end it.

Perhaps less surprisingly than the left-leaning media might suppose, on November 8, 2016, for the first time in history, America elected a businessman with no political experience as president of the United States. And not just any businessman. It was Donald Trump, a billionaire businessman, famous for wheeling-and-dealing in New York City real estate. Americans knew him from *The Apprentice,* the television show where he pitted contestants against one another on business-related challenges, and from his best-selling books, like *How to Get Rich* and *The Art of the Deal.* As Trump's saying goes, "You're fired." This time, it was Barack Obama and Hillary Clinton who were out of a job.

To even get to the White House, Trump first had to overcome America's two reigning political dynasties, the Bushes and then the Clintons. Few thought he could, but working- and middle-class Americans knew there was a problem in our nation and they wanted a president with the courage, tenacity, and self-confidence to stand up to an establishment that had ill-served their interests.

America also needed a president willing to stand up to the increasingly Far Left Democratic Party, unions shackled to Progressives and desperate for relevance, an education system mired in failed left-wing ideology, an entertainment industry that despised the capitalist principles of which it so vigorously took advantage, and a mainstream press so Far Left that the center looked reactionary.

To the Progressive Left, Trump's victory was shocking. Up until Election Day it seemed certain he would lose. The Progressives and their allies were convinced that demographics and the tide of history had turned irreversibly in their favor. They held the same beliefs about socialism's ultimate success before the Soviet Union fell. In 2016, they were wrong, again.

Had they been right, Hillary Clinton would be president and the Obama Administration's progressive assaults, both statutory and regulatory, would have remained in place, becoming a part of American culture much like FDR's Depression-era New Deal reforms. With the government in control, Progressives would have marginalized American businesses, allowing them to function only to the extent necessary to generate tax revenue and to keep the populace content enough not to vote Progressive politicians out of office.

When it didn't happen and Trump won, the liberal outrage was palpable. In an open letter to his daughters, liberal screenwriter Aaron Sorkin warned that "economists are predicting a deep and prolonged recession."[11] CNN predicted that a Trump victory would "almost certainly tank" the stock market.[12] The day after Trump's win, the *Economist* stated that "the election could presage a longer slump" in the market.[13] *Newsweek* writer, and former *New York Times* reporter Kurt Eichenwald admitted that he preemptively sold all his stocks and converted all his investments into cash.[14]

Again, they were wrong. Trump's election was a turning point for our nation. Working- and middle-class Americans repudiated Barack Obama's failed Progressive policies. They rejected the Washington establishment and the reigning political dynasties.

Nearly a decade of overregulation and poor governance drove the American people to hand the reins of power over to a businessman who promised to make America great again.

Within less than a year, the economy boomed. As soon as Trump was elected, business optimism soared. In his first year, the stock market hit record highs an average of every four days.

His successful efforts to deregulate drove economic growth to an average of 3 percent in the first three full quarters of his presidency. The economy created over two million jobs, and the unemployment rate hit a seventeen-year low while job openings and household wealth hit historic highs. Based simply on passage of the tax reform bill, hundreds of employers across the country announced increased compensation and bonuses for their employees plus billions of dollars in planned investments in growth. America was back in business.

The Businessman Wins

Even before his election, Trump's run encouraged people. Some of the optimism came from his background. Like many on Wall Street, he's a New Yorker. Trump properties dot the Manhattan skyline, and he's been a fixture of the city for decades. Months before the election, one New York business owner told the *New York Times,* "I think Donald is fantastic, and he's going to beat Hillary and be the next president."[15] Billionaire investor and fellow New Yorker Carl Icahn endorsed Trump early on, claiming, "You need somebody that understands business, and I think he understands it."[16]

Trump was different, and people liked that. Unlike ordinary politicians who buy into the Progressives characterization of businessmen as unscrupulous and undeservedly wealthy, or act ashamed of their success, Trump touted his wealth on the campaign trail: "I'm not using donors. I don't care. I'm really rich," he said in his announcement speech.[17] Unlike traditional Republicans, he used his success to appeal to mailmen and teachers. "Our country needs a truly great leader, and we need a truly great leader now. We need a leader that wrote 'The Art of the Deal.'" The message worked and delivered victory on Election Day.

Unlike most politicians who've spent most of their lives campaigning for something or other, Trump doesn't have to rely on ideological arguments in support of capitalism and the free market. He's lived it for decades. He woke up and went to bed dealing with real-life capitalist forces every single day.

In 1971, he took over his family's business, renaming it The Trump Organization and refocusing its real-estate deals in Manhattan.[18] Within five years, Trump was making plays for some of the biggest properties in New York. In one of his early deals, he bought the Grand Hyatt hotel near Grand Central Station, negotiated a forty-year tax abatement and somehow managed to navigate New York's complex building codes.[19] In 1980, he expanded to the casino industry in Atlantic City, New Jersey. By the late 1980s, he owned The Plaza, one of New York's most prestigious hotels.[20] He built hotels, apartment and commercial buildings, and Fifth Avenue's iconic Trump Tower.[21]

He also experienced setbacks. In the early 1990s, his empire came crashing down as the economy sputtered and his revenue streams dried up. At his low point, Trump's company was $9 billion in debt and his personal debts were close to $1 billion.[22] While walking down the street with his ex-wife Marla Maples, Trump said, "I pointed to a homeless man and said, 'This guy is worth $900 million more than me.'"[23] He sold his yacht and his airplane and struck a deal with his lenders to save his company.[24]

Before long, he resurrected his business. He added licensing to his real-estate empire. Thanks to creative restructuring, he paid down his debts. By 2016, The Trump Organization was the forty-eighth largest privately owned company in America.[25] By Inauguration Day, his company employed more than twenty-two thousand people and had revenues of nearly $10 billion a year.[26] He owned luxury golf courses, hotels, wineries, and other properties in some of the nicest parts of the world.

Along the way, Trump tried his hand at various other businesses: Trump Ice, Trump financial, Trump books, Trump Model Management, Trump Steaks, and even Trump Vodka. Department stores sold his line of neckties and menswear and even a couple of fragrance lines.

His career embodies the entrepreneurial spirit that made America flourish, and it paid off for him. He isn't a perfect person and makes no effort to appear as one. Refreshingly, what you see is what you get. He is also a successful person. As of February 2017, *Forbes* estimated that he was worth $3.5 billion, by far the richest person to ever become president of the United States.[27]

It's no surprise then that, after his election, Trump staffed his administration with other men and women with business experience. His first cabinet had the highest percentage of CEOs in decades, and he was the only president since the 1980s not to appoint a single PhD.[28] After the liberal media criticized him for putting too many businesspeople in his cabinet, Trump responded, "I want people that made a fortune. Because now they are negotiating for you, OK? It's no different than a great baseball player or a great golfer."[29]

Still, the media complained that it was the richest cabinet in history, and it was.[30] But Trump wasn't ashamed of that. He wanted people with real-world experience, not out-of-touch intellectuals.

Once again, Trump was doing the opposite of what his

predecessor, Barack Obama, chose to do. The *New Yorker* described Obama's cabinet as a "team of brainiacs" while the *New York Times* called them "a team of whizzes."[31–32] Forty percent of Obama's initial appointees had Ivy League degrees, and others had degrees from Stanford and Oxford.[33] The overwhelming majority had no executive business experience at all, including Obama himself.[34] His was the first cabinet in a century to have a secretary of commerce and a secretary of the treasury with no major previous business experience.[35] The Obama administration's failure to produce real economic growth and widespread prosperity was all but predictable.

Yet for all that the Trump administration has accomplished early on, there's still much that threatens his agenda. In Washington, Trump faces new threats unlike anything he's seen before. In his business, Trump had nearly unlimited control over his company's direction. In Washington, he's had to deal with checks and balances. Worse yet, he faces distractions from a hostile opposition political party and its Progressive allies, particularly in the liberal media, as well as opposition from establishment Republicans in his own party.

Business executives are well suited to positions of leadership. They have more high-pressure decision-making experience than, for instance, a community organizer. However, they also face different challenges. Here are four challenges that Trump must overcome to accomplish his agenda and be the transformational president the country so desperately needs.

1. Thin Majority in the Senate

President Trump will get no help from Democrats in the House or the Senate; their Progressive base will not permit it. Republicans who believe otherwise are deceiving themselves. That means that any legislation must pass almost entirely with Republican votes. The president's party has fifty-one votes in the Senate. This means that even for legislation that doesn't require a filibuster proof majority, without Democratic support, the Republicans must achieve not just consensus but virtual unanimity to pass key parts of the administration's agenda. It's hard to get 97 percent of any group to agree to anything (let alone a group of politicians), but that is what Senate Republicans must achieve to pass almost any meaningful bill.

Yet, this small Senate majority does not excuse Congressional Republicans' biggest failure to date: failing to pass a simple repeal of Obamacare.

In every election since 2010, Republicans have run on a promise to end Obamacare. This promise was a significant factor in voters giving Republicans control of the House, the Senate, and the presidency. It was certainly reasonable for the American people to assume Republicans would deliver on their promise upon taking office. We have a president sitting in the White House willing, if not anxious, to sign a repeal-and-replace bill into law. Republicans in the House and the Senate had one job: to get it there.

Their first attempt was a resounding failure.

The House would have passed, and the president would have signed the Senate bill to repeal and replace Obamacare. The House had already passed a similar bill. The Senate's version was a very good bill.

It would have ended the employer and individual mandates, eliminating the government compulsion that drove up the cost of health insurance. This alone would have effectively repealed Obamacare.

In place of these mandates, the Senate bill would have inserted competition. Through refundable tax credits, the bill would have given people the economic resources to make their own decisions about what health insurance best suited their needs while incentivizing insurance companies to compete for their business. Competition would have replaced mandates; a free-market solution would have replaced a big-government solution that had clearly failed.

While Progressives disingenuously claimed otherwise, the Senate bill provided access to insurance for people with preexisting conditions by creating a fund to keep costs down and requiring that insurers offer them policies. It would have increased Medicaid spending by half a trillion dollars over ten years. It also would have addressed Obamacare's primary fault: the failure to incentivize young healthy people to purchase insurance.

Yes, it was always going to be hard to pass a bill in the Senate. Yes, the vast majority of Senate Republicans were willing to vote for the bill. But trying hard, on a measure of such importance to the lives, health, and pocketbooks of Americans, wasn't good enough.

The fact that Senate Republicans couldn't pass a bill after seven years of promises is indicative of a failure on the part of some Republicans to understand that politics is a team sport and they're on a team.

Perhaps there was a silver lining. When tax reform came up in the Senate, Republicans seemed to realize that they could not fail to come together yet again. If they failed on tax reform, their future as a party was dim. Their ability to win elections individually would also have been dim. So, after much negotiating and posturing, the historic tax reform, which is already accelerating economic growth and benefitting all Americans, passed. And, as part of that historic tax reform, they managed to repeal the individual mandate.

There also may be additional good news on the horizon.

First, the Republicans have a chance to increase their numbers in the Senate in the 2018 elections. There is an enormous difference between a majority of fifty-one and a majority of fifty-seven in the Senate; five extra votes would have meant that the Senate's Obamacare repeal-and-replace bill would have passed.

Senate Republicans also are becoming more of a team. Some of the strongest anti-Trump Republicans are leaving, and the crop of candidates in Senate races across the country includes many antiestablishment candidates.

The White House and Congressional Republicans are also working better together. The president is developing an effective rhythm for managing the congressional leadership, alternating between criticism and praise, using the carrot and stick effectively.

Unfortunately, the Progressive Left is much better at this. It's how they move initiatives forward over time.

Does anyone believe that Bernie Sanders actually liked Obamacare when he voted for it? He didn't. He's a socialist who has always wanted a single-payer, government-run system. In fact, does anyone actually believe that every Democrat who voted for Obamacare supported it personally or thought it was the best solution? The answer is they did not, but they all voted for it, 100 percent.

Generally speaking, Democrats understand power. Republicans do not.

Republicans had better figure it out in a hurry, particularly if they expect to retain and increase their congressional majorities in the coming years.

2. Gridlock: A Strategic Imperative for Progressives

Apart from the problems he faces in his own party, President Trump faces an even greater obstacle from the Left.

The Founders intentionally created a system of checks and balances between the branches of government, so change needs to happen incrementally and requires extensive negotiation and compromise. This system has advantages. It makes it difficult for politicians to enact poorly thought-out policies or legislate based on emotional reactions to major news events. It's the system to which President Wilson so objected.

These checks and balances prevented Barack Obama from continuing his Progressive legislative onslaught after his first two years. Many of Obama's antibusiness campaign promises never became law, including cap-and-trade, a program to prevent home foreclosures, a "green jobs" program, the repeal of the Bush tax cuts, or universal, socialist health care.[36] The legislative sessions from 2010 to 2014, when Republicans controlled the House of Representatives, were thankfully among the least productive in modern history.[37]

Trump is more eager to work with his political opponents, and his reputation as a tough negotiator who is also a deal maker is well deserved. Despite having a Republican majority in Congress, Trump reached out to Democrats early on to gauge their interest in working with him.[38] In his first year, he negotiated a bipartisan fiscal deal, discussed an immigration compromise with Democratic Party leaders, indicated a willingness to work with Democrats on health-care reform, and traveled with moderate Democratic senators to tout his tax reform plan.[39–41]

But Republicans who believe that the Democrats, particularly the increasingly influential Progressive Democrats, will work with President Trump are simply delusional. From a historical perspective, the Trump presidency poses an existential threat to Progressives, and they know it. Whether it's Progressive candidates or their allies in the media, the unions, the education establishment, or the entertainment industry, you can hear it in their voices. They are profane, demeaning, shrill, and often unbalanced. If Republicans are going to achieve anything of import legislatively, they will need unity. They will also need a way around the Senate filibuster.

Under the filibuster rule, a vote of three-fifths of the Senate (sixty senators) is required to end debate on a bill and get it to a vote. Most legislation is subject to filibuster in the Senate, and filibustering is very easy. Senators don't have to speak, or even be present on the Senate floor, to filibuster. They simply have to notify their party leadership that they object to voting on a bill. Given that the use of the filibuster has become routine, Republicans are, as a practical matter, nine votes short of a working majority, especially on regulatory legislation, which, generally speaking, cannot be passed through reconciliation or most of the other workarounds to the sixty-vote rule.

There is one avenue for passing regulatory relief that cannot be filibustered: The Congressional Review Act (CRA), which permits Congress to overturn a new administrative rule within sixty legislative days after an agency formally promulgates it. Bills which fall within the scope of the CRA are not subject to the filibuster.

It is noteworthy that in the first six months of the Trump administration, congressional Republicans passed and the president was able to sign fourteen regulatory repeal bills passed under the CRA.[42] The Senate can act, and Republicans can reduce the size of the regulatory apparatus, when they can avoid the filibuster.

Going forward, Republicans must eliminate or at least restrict use of the filibuster. On regulatory issues, it inherently favors the Progressives. When they control the presidency, they can enact much of their agenda administratively; only the power of Congress to pass statutes can effectively and permanently rein in government overreach.

There is precedent for restricting the filibuster. Under Harry Reid's leadership, the Senate Democrats eliminated the sixty-vote requirement for presidential appointments so as to get Senate approval for Obama's proposed appointments. Under Mitch McConnell's leadership, Republicans continued this trend by eliminating the sixty-vote requirement to confirm Supreme Court Justice Gorsuch.

Even seemingly routine matters in the best interests of both parties, such as passing a budget so the federal government can function, require sixty votes, which is why passage of a budget is so often used as a negotiating chip for other policy goals. The only way to overcome resistance from the Progressive Left is for Republicans to unify and either eliminate or restrict the sixty-vote requirement in the Senate.

Like it or not, there is no other way to turn back the clock on the Progressive power grab of the last hundred years.

3. The Media

Another challenge Trump has already faced (head on, I might add) is a very hostile, if not inflamed, press. Most journalists lack business experience, as you can easily discern from their reporting. In addition, most of the mainstream media outlets have become little more than propaganda arms of the Democratic Party and the Progressives and even more unabashedly so since President Trump's election.

The coverage of the Republican tax plan is a case in point. It was obvious from the start that mainstream media journalists and Progressive think tanks would decry *any* tax plan the Republicans released as "tax cuts for the rich."

It didn't take long to happen. Before Republicans even released details on tax brackets or deductions in their proposed tax plan, the *New York Times* was running an editorial titled "Tax Cuts for the Rich by Another Name."[43] Within days, they ran an article titled "Republican Tax Cut Would Benefit Wealthy and Corporations Most, Report Finds," citing a strongly left-wing think tank.[44] They even made an issue of Trump's wealth, blaring the headline "Trump Tax Plan Benefits Wealthy, Including Trump," as if billionaire Trump and his Republican allies are part of an elaborate plot to help Trump get four more billion dollars.[45]

The press has also panned Trump's regulatory accomplishments. The *Washington Post* described his reforms as "steps to erase the Obama administration's environmental record," noting that the "move risks running afoul of public opinion."[46] The *New York Times* attacked the very notion of deregulation and published articles with titles like "The Deep Industry Ties of Trump's Deregulation Teams" and "Secrecy and Suspicion Surround Trump's Deregulation Teams."[47–48] The left-wingers at Salon.com sounded the alarm, publishing an article titled "The Wall Street presidency: Donald Trump's deregulation scheme is yuge for big banks."[49] They even described his efforts to eliminate red tape as a "deregulatory fetish."[50]

When they cover deregulation, the mainstream media outlets inevitably make it seem like Trump is against the *goals* of the regulations he's eliminating rather than the impact of overregulation. When Trump promises to boost business and manufacturing, they accuse him of being their crony. When the economy prospers, they claim that the president doesn't control the economy or that any economic growth under President Trump was due to President Obama's economic policies. This, after eight years of taking Obama's anemic growth and making it sound like the substantial economic success of the Reagan or Clinton years, crediting Obama's supposed financial genius. Should the economy grow, the press will attempt to credit Obama. Should it falter, the press will blame Trump no matter the cause.

To overcome such bias, Trump must use his platform and media presence to get his message out. He has a huge advantage on social media and can continue discrediting fake news reports on Twitter. He has already had meaningful success in discrediting the biased coverage. Trump is the first president who can communicate with the American people directly and at any time he chooses over social media, principally Twitter. The media is then forced to react to the issues he raises. It infuriates them, it diminishes their importance, and it empowers the president to challenge as "fake news" what he considers biased coverage. While there are tweets he certainly could have better worded, this is actually working very well for him.

According to a May 2017 report from a Harvard-Harris poll, about two-thirds of Americans believe the mainstream press is full of fake news. According to the poll, 65 percent of voters hold this view, including 80 percent of Republicans, 60 percent of independents, and 53 percent of Democrats.[51] Harvard-Harris cofounder Mark Penn stated, "Much of the media is now just another part of the partisan divide in the country with Republicans not trusting the 'mainstream' media and Democrats seeing them as reflecting their beliefs."[52] They're both right.

Trump regularly and masterfully baits cable news channels into discussing his issues, even if they don't cover them his way. He should continue doing so while touting his economic message.

But the most powerful way to appeal to voters is by actually boosting the economy. More jobs, higher salaries, and more opportunity are a potent message that speaks for itself. As President Reagan proved, there's nothing the media can do if most Americans are better off in four years than they were in 2016.

4. Antibusiness Culture

President Trump will also have to defeat the Progressives' cultural war on capitalism.

As anyone who watches movies or has kids in school knows, cultural elites are constantly impugning their own economic system. Hollywood big shots have always hated capitalism (while immensely benefitting from it) and often devote movies and TV shows to attacking success and wealth, both subtly and not so subtly. Meanwhile, our schools and universities, even the most elite, have turned into incubators for Marxist and socialist thought. Liberals have dominated Hollywood and academia for a long time. But, emboldened by having a president with a "you didn't build that" attitude, it got a lot worse (with a lot more fawning) during the Obama years.

No one has ever had as much power to combat those forces as President Trump does now.

The president must remain a forceful advocate for capitalism to counterbalance the prevailing liberal cultural attitudes. Ronald Reagan is a good model for this—something President Trump clearly understands. Trump has referenced Reagan on Twitter hundreds of times and even tweeted out many of Reagan's best lines.[53]

In 2013, Trump tweeted, "The most terrifying words in the English language are: I'm from the government and I'm here to help," one of Reagan's most famous quotations.[54] In 2015, Trump tweeted another famous Reagan quote: "Government's first duty is to protect the people, not run their lives."[55] Trump channeled Reagan on welfare not once, but twice, in 2011 and 2013: "Welfare's purpose should be to eliminate, as far as possible, the need for its own existence."[56–57]

In a way, no one's ever been better positioned to be such a

forceful advocate for free-market capitalism than Trump. In his professional life, Trump both personified business success and promoted it in a way that appealed to the average American. The opening credits to *The Apprentice* featured Trump in his personal helicopter flying over Manhattan set to the song "For the Love of Money" by the O'Jays.[58]

In the "boardroom," where Trump determined which contestants to fire on the show, he'd often give business advice. In the introduction to season one, Trump talks about how "if you work hard, you can really hit it big."[59–60] He's written best-selling business books such as *The Art of the Deal, Think Big, How to Get Rich, Think like a Champion,* and *Surviving at the Top.* If anyone knows the language of business and how to make it appeal to a large audience, it's Donald Trump.

The question now is, will President Trump imitate Reagan and be a forceful rhetorical proponent of capitalism? Early indicators are that he will. In his first speech to the United Nations, that's exactly what he did, and with Reaganesque eloquence.

As he stared down delegations from socialist regimes around the world, Trump spoke in detail about the horrors that Venezuela's socialist government has inflicted on its people: "The socialist dictatorship of Nicolás Maduro has inflicted terrible pain and suffering on the good people of that country. This corrupt regime destroyed a prosperous nation by imposing a failed ideology that has produced poverty and misery everywhere it has been tried," Trump said. "The Venezuelan people are starving, and their country is collapsing."[61]

Then, with a single sentence, Trump delivered a devastating blow: "The problem in Venezuela is not that socialism has been poorly implemented, but that socialism has been faithfully implemented."[62]

Like Reagan before him, Trump made it clear that socialism

is a system destined to fail everywhere; "from the Soviet Union to Cuba to Venezuela, wherever true socialism or Communism has been adopted it has delivered anguish and devastation and failure. Those who preach the tenants of these discredited ideologies only contribute to the continued suffering of the people living under these cruel systems."[63]

The clarity of this message was exceeded only by its truthfulness.

Within eight years, America went from having a president who apologized for America to the world's dictators, demagogues, and socialists at the United Nations to a president ready, willing, and very able to reclaim American leadership on capitalism and democracy. If President Trump continues to advocate for the system that made this nation's people the most prosperous in all of human history, he will inspire untold numbers of Americans to return to the economic system that made this country great in the first place.

If President Trump is somehow able to match his rhetoric with pro-market policies, if he can garner the support of Republicans in the House and Senate, he may even bring about a national return to free-market capitalism, ushering in a new age of American prosperity and reaffirming the promise of American exceptionalism.

The Tide Is Turning

The fact is, the tide is already turning. Even though the Great Recession ended in June 2009, a dark cloud hung over America for nearly seven and a half more years. The United States was on the brink of introducing a new era of big government, with health-care mandates, destructive financial regulation, stifling emissions controls, higher taxes, and a federal government whose intrusiveness was increasing with every executive order and every new regulation.

In 2016, Donald Trump's election reversed all of that. Business was back in a big way. On January 30, 2018, Trump gave his first State of the Union address. He reviewed his administration's first year accomplishments in deregulating our economy and cutting taxes. He shared good news—that businesses were giving Americans much needed raises and bonuses, companies were bringing jobs back to America, black unemployment was at an historic low, and economic growth was returning. He reached out to Democrats asking that they join him in making America great again. They reacted as you would expect Progressives to react. They sat on their hands smirking or playing with their iPhones for all the world to see. The Progressives left little doubt that they simply want America to fail on President Trump's watch. But the American people got the message. A CBS News poll found that 75 percent of viewers approved of the president's speech, including 43 percent of Democrats, while 80 percent believed he was trying to unify the country.[64]

The Progressives' fears are justified. If President Trump can implement his pro-growth agenda, then he has the potential to be as transformative a president as Barack Obama hoped to be. Pro-business reforms at home, paired with pride in America's capitalist leadership on the world stage, will usher in an age of prosperity and economic growth that will be here to stay. The Progressives' era of big government will be over for good, returning our nation to a land of opportunity, limited government, and individual liberty—the capitalist comeback.

Acknowledgments

First and foremost, I want to thank my wife of thirty years. An attorney in her own right, Dee made the decision to raise our three boys as her full-time job. She's been a hugely supportive stepmom to my three older children and a stepgrandma to our six grandkids. She now spends her time working as an in-court children's advocate, doing horse therapy for children and spending the occasional night at the local hospital holding babies who need it. In her spare time, she takes care of me. She has supported me through the best of times and the worst of times. Without her, there would be no book.

There also would have been no book but for my friend, the former chief speechwriter for Ronald Reagan, Tony Dolan. Tony looked over a speech I was to give at Chapman University School of Law in 2014 and commented: "This should be a book." He set up a dinner at the longtime DC favorite Martin's Tavern in Georgetown, where he introduced me to Matt Latimer and Keith Urbahn of Javelin, a literary and creative agency. Matt, Keith, and a very talented young man named Dylan Colligan were instrumental in promoting the idea for this book, finding a publisher, and editing and guiding me through the process. I am more than happy to acknowledge that, without them, there would have been no book.

My very heartfelt thanks go out to my friend of nearly forty years and former Missouri senator Jim Talent for his review and comments. Jim's reasoned and politically astute contributions and edits made this book much better than it would otherwise have been. It's hard for me to overstate how much I appreciate his friendship and his contribution to the final product. My son Matt, wise beyond his twenty-five years, also took the time to review each chapter and provide his thoughts, notwithstanding his demanding work schedule. He made this a better book and one I hope is more accessible to his generation.

I also want to thank the entrepreneurs in my life who were my mentors, employers, clients, and friends: my father, Dick Lurie, Morris Shenker, Charles Seigel, Carl Karcher (to whom this book is dedicated), Bill Foley, Peter Copses, and Neal Aronson. Thank you for your inspiration and guidance.

Finally, I want to thank President Trump—despite the powerful forces aligned against him—for not only having the confidence to nominate me as his Secretary of Labor but, more importantly, for having the courage to stand up for our exceptional nation and the free enterprise system that drives it. I look forward to what his presidency will mean for generations yet to come.

Endnotes

Chapter One

1 Congressional Budget Office, "The Effects of a Minimum-Wage Increase on Employment and Family Income," February 18, 2014, https://www.cbo.gov/publication/44995.

2 Noam Scheiber, "Democrats and Allies Wage Fight to Derail Labor Secretary Pick," *New York Times,* January 12, 2017, https://www.nytimes.com/2017/01/12/business/andrew-puzder-labor-senate.html.

3 Sean Higgins, "Puzder's ex-wife disavows prior claims of domestic violence," *Washington Examiner,* February 3, 2017, http://www.washingtonexaminer.com/puzders-ex-wife-disavows-prior-claims-of-domestic-violence/article/2613890.

4 Diana Furchtgott-Roth, "Big Labor's Misleading Attacks On Andy Puzder," *Investor's Business Daily,* http://www.investors.com/politics/commentary/big-labors-misleading-attacks-on-andy-puzder/.

5 National Federation of Independent Businesses, *December 2017 Report: Small Business Optimism Index,* https://www.nfib.com/surveys/small-business-economic-trends.

6 NFIB, *December 2017 Report.*

7 The Conference Board, *Consumer Confidence Survey*, December 27, 2017, https://www.conference-board.org/data/consumerconfidence.cfm.

8 Lori Ann LaRocco, "Manufacturing CEO survey shows record high optimism on prospect of tax reform," CNBC, December 11, 2017, https://www.cnbc.com/2017/12/11/manufacturing-ceo-record-high-optimism-on-prospect-of-tax-reform.html.

9 Blake Neff, "Paul Krugman Says Markets Will 'Never' Recover from Trump; Dow Hits Record High," *The Daily Caller*, November 9, 2016, http://dailycaller.com/2016/11/09/paul-krugman-says-markets-will-never-recover-from-trump-dow-hits-record-high.

10 Fred Imbert and Evelyn Cheng, "Dow closes up 250 points; financials surge after Trump election upset," CNBC, November 10, 2016, https://www.cnbc.com/2016/11/09/us-markets.html.

11 Ryan Vlastelica, "The Dow just set a record for setting records," *MarketWatch*, December 19, 2017, https://www.marketwatch.com/story/the-dow-is-about-to-set-a-record-for-setting-records-2017-12-18.

12 Imbert and Cheng, "Dow."

13 Jeff Cox, "Stock market optimism from pros reaches highest level in nearly 32 years," CNBC, January 17, 2018, https://www.cnbc.com/2018/01/17/stock-market-optimism-from-pros-reaches-highest-level-since-1986.html.

14 Steve Liesman, "Economic optimism soars, boosting Trump's approval rating: CNBC survey," CNBC, December 18, 2017.

15 Clyde Wayne Crews, "Red Tape Rollback: Trump Least-Regulatory President Since Reagan," Competitive Enterprise Institute, October 1, 2017, https://cei.org/blog/red-tape-rollback-report-trump-ends-fiscal-year-americas-least-regulatory-president-reagan.

16 "FULL SPEECH: Donald Trump in Tampa, Florida," *The Hill*, August 24, 2016, http://thehill.com/blogs/pundits-blog/presidential-campaign/292520-full-speech-donald-trump-in-tampa-florida.

17 Donald J. Trump Contract with the American Voter, signed by Donald J. Trump, https://assets.donaldjtrump.com/CONTRACT_FOR_THE_VOTER.pdf.

18 "Full text: Donald Trump's Detroit speech on his economic plan," *Politico*, August 8, 2016, https://www.politico.com/story/2016/08/full-text-donald-trumps-detroit-speech-on-the-ecnomic-plan-226793.

19 Exec. Order No. 13777, 82 FR 12285.

20 Reince Priebus, "Memorandum for the Heads of Executive Departments and Agencies, Subject: Regulatory Freeze Pending Review," January 20, 2017, https://www.whitehouse.gov/the-press-office/2017/01/20/memorandum-heads-executive-departments-and-agencies.

21 The White House, Office of the Press Secretary, *Reducing Regulation and Controlling Regulatory Costs*, January 30, 2017, http://www.politico.com/f/?id=00000159-f049-d7d2-a97f-fcd922750000.

22 Office of Information and Regulatory Affairs, Office of Management and Budget, *Current Regulatory Plan and the Unified Agenda of*

Regulatory and Deregulatory Actions, https://www.reginfo.gov/public/do/eAgendaMain.

23 David Shepardson and Valerie Volcovici, "White House deregulation push clears hundreds of proposed rules," Reuters, July 20, 2017, https://www.reuters.com/article/us-usa-trump-regulation/white-house-deregulation-push-clears-out-hundreds-of-proposed-rules-idUSKBN1A51O1.

24 Melanie Arter, "Trump Touts Efforts to Level Playing Field for Manufacturing Industry," CNS News, September 29, 2017, https://www.cnsnews.com/news/article/melanie-arter/trump-touts-efforts-level-playing-field-us-workers-companies.

25 Neomi Rao, "Press Briefing by Office of Information and Regulatory Affairs Administrator Neomi Rao on the Unified Agenda of Regulatory and Deregulatory Actions," The White House, December 14, 2017, https://www.whitehouse.gov/briefings-statements/press-briefing-office-information-regulatory-affairs-administrator-neomi-rao-unified-agenda-regulatory-deregulatory-actions.

26 Jeffrey Bartash, "U.S. economy running at half speed, GDP shows," *MarketWatch*, July 29, 2016, https://www.marketwatch.com/story/second-quarter-gdp-rises-just-12-well-below-forecast-2016-07-29.

27 Kevin Hoffman, "Roskam says Obama admin the first to never top 3% in annual GDP growth," *Politifact Illinois*, March 16, 2017, http://www.politifact.com/illinois/statements/2017/mar/16/peter-roskam/rep-roskam-gdp-growth-obama.

28 Bureau of Economic Analysis, U.S. Department of Commerce, "National Economic Accounts, Gross Domestic Product (GDP)," https://bea.gov/national/index.htm.

29 Jeffrey M. Stupak, "Economic Growth Slower Than Previous 10 Expansions," CRS Insight, June 30, 2016, https://fas.org/sgp/crs/misc/IN10520.pdf.

30 Jason Furman, "Why US Growth of 2 Percent Is Plausible—And Unlikely to Get Much Higher," Peterson Institute for International Economics, March 21, 2017, https://piie.com/blogs/realtime-economic-issues-watch/why-us-growth-2-percent-plausible-and-unlikely-get-much-higher.

31 Lawrence H. Summers, "Larry Summers: Trump's budget is simply ludicrous," *Washington Post,* May 23, 2017, https://www.washingtonpost.com/news/wonk/wp/2017/05/23/larry-summers-trumps-budget-is-simply-ludicrous/?utm_term=.52721dc789d4.

32 Sho Chandra, "U.S. Third-Quarter Growth Revised to Three-Year High of 3.3%," *Bloomberg,* November 29, 2017, https://www.bloomberg.com/news/articles/2017-11-29/u-s-third-quarter-growth-revised-up-to-3-3-three-year-high.

33 Bureau of Economic Analysis, U.S. Department of Commerce, *National Income and Product Accounts Gross Domestic Product: Third Quarter 2017 (Third Estimate) Corporate Profits: Third Quarter 2017 (Revised Estimate),* December 21, 2017, https://bea.gov/newsreleases/national/gdp/gdpnewsrelease.htm.

34 Josh Mitchell, "GDP Grew 2.6% at Year End, Extending Strong Stretch," *Wall Street Journal,* January 26, 2018, https://www.wsj.com/articles/u-s-economy-grew-at-2-6-rate-in-fourth-quarter-1516973505.

35 Jeffry Bartash, "Third-quarter GDP raised to 3.3% to mark fastest U.S. economic growth in three years," *MarketWatch*, November 29, 2017, https://www.marketwatch.com/story/us-third-quarter-gdp-raised-to-33-fastest-economic-growth-in-three-years-2017-11-29.

36 Patrick Gillespie, "U.S. economy added 2 million jobs in 2017," CNN Money, video, January 5, 2018, http://money.cnn.com/2018/01/05/news/economy/december-2017-jobs-report/index.html?iid=EL.

37 Bureau of Labor Statistics, "Employment Situation Summary," January 5, 2018, https://www.bls.gov/news.release/empsit.nr0.htm.

38 Patrick Gillespie, "Black unemployment hits all-time low," CNN Money, video, January 5, 2018, http://money.cnn.com/2018/01/05/news/economy/black-unemployment/index.html.

39 Megan Brenan, "Americans' Optimism About Job Market Hit Record High in 2017," *Gallup News,* January 9, 2018, http://news.gallup.com/poll/225071/americans-optimism-job-market-hit-record-high-2017.aspx.

40 Sho Chandra, "U.S. Job Openings Hit Record High in April, Topping 6 Million," *Bloomberg,* June 6, 2017, https://www.bloomberg.com/news/articles/2017-06-06/job-openings-in-u-s-rise-to-record-in-april-topping-6-million.

41 John Kartch, "List of Tax Reform Good News," Americans for Tax Reform, January 24, 2018, https://www.atr.org/list.

42 AT&T, *With Tax Reform, AT&T Plans to Increase U.S. Capital Spending $1 Billion and Provide $1,000 Special Bonus to more than 200,000 U.S. Employees,* December 20, 2017, http://about.att.com/story/att_tax_reform.html.

43 Liz Moyer, "JP Morgan Chase to build 400 new branches, raise wages because of the tax cut," CNBC, January 23, 2018, https://www.cnbc

.com/2018/01/23/j-p-morgan-to-spend-20-billion-after-tax-cuts-on-jobs-branches.html.

44 Comcast, "Comcast Announces Special Holiday Bonus and Capital Investments," December 20, 2017, https://www.businesswire.com/news/home/20171220006153/en/Comcast-Announces-Special-Holiday-Bonus-Capital-Investments.

45 Apple, "Apple accelerates U.S. investment and job creation," January 17, 2018, https://www.apple.com/newsroom/2018/01/apple-accelerates-us-investment-and-job-creation.

46 "Cramer calls Apple's $350 billion investment in the U.S. economy a...," CNBC video, January 17, 2018, https://www.cnbc.com/video/2018/01/17/cramer-apples-tim-cook-credits-most-of-350b-plan-to-repatriation.html.

47 "Marshall Plan, 1948," Office of the Historian, https://history.state.gov/milestones/1945-1952/marshall-plan.

48 "John F. Kennedy on the Economy and Taxes," John F. Kennedy Presidential Library and Museum, https://www.jfklibrary.org/JFK/JFK-in-History/JFK-on-the-Economy-and-Taxes.aspx.

Chapter Two

1 Max Ehrenfreund, "A majority of millennials now reject capitalism, poll shows," *Washington Post*, April 26, 2016, https://www.washingtonpost.com/news/wonk/wp/2016/04/26/a-majority-of-millennials-now-reject-capitalism-poll-shows/?utm_term=.33652cdd4fc5.

2 Ralph Raico, "What is Classical Liberalism," Mises Institute, August 16, 2010, https://www.mises.org/library/what-classical-liberalism.

3 Adam Smith, *An Inquiry into the Nature and Causes of the Wealth of Nations,* Book I, Chapter I, Library of Economics and Liberty, http://www.econlib.org/library/Smith/smWN.html.

4 Adam Smith, *An Inquiry into the Nature and Causes of the Wealth of Nations,* Book I, Chapter 1, Library of Economics and Liberty, http://www.econlib.org/library/Smith/smWN.html.

5 Adam Smith, *An Inquiry into the Nature and Causes of the Wealth of Nations,* Book I, Chapter 2, Library of Economics and Liberty, http://www.econlib.org/library/Smith/smWN.html.

6 Adam Smith, *An Inquiry into the Nature and Causes of the Wealth of Nations,* Book IV, Chapter 2, Library of Economics and Liberty, http://www.econlib.org/library/Smith/smWN.html.

7 Robert L. Hazel, *The Relevance of Adam Smith* (Richmond, VA: Federal Reserve Bank of Richmond), http://ecedweb.unomaha.edu/roas.pdf.

8 Henry Louis Gates, Jr., *Finding Your Roots, Season 2: The Official Companion to the PBS Series* (Chapel Hill: UNC Press, 2016), 106.

9 "Cornelius Vanderbilt: Industrial/Commerce Leader," New Netherland Institute, https://www.newnetherlandinstitute.org/history-and-heritage/dutch_americans/cornelius-vanderbilt/.

10 "Cornelius Vanderbilt: Industrial/Commerce Leader," New Netherland Institute.

11 "Cornelius Vanderbilt: Industrial/Commerce Leader," New Netherland Institute.

12 Mike Wallace and Edwin Burrows, quoted in T. J. Styles, *The First Tycoon: The Epic Life of Cornelius Vanderbilt* (New York: Knopf, 2009).

13 Quoted in Styles, *The First Tycoon: The Epic Life of Cornelius Vanderbilt.*

14 Quoted in Styles, *The First Tycoon: The Epic Life of Cornelius Vanderbilt.*

15 Quoted in Styles, *The First Tycoon: The Epic Life of Cornelius Vanderbilt.*

16 Gates, *Finding Your Roots*, 106.

17 Margo Jefferson, "Worth More Than It Costs: The life story of the washerwoman who turned a hair tonic into an economic revolution for African-Americans," *New York Times,* April 1, 2001, http://www.nytimes.com/books/01/04/01/reviews/010401.01jeffert.html.

18 Gentry Menzel, "Madam C.J. Walker: Hair Care Millionaire," PBS, http://www.pbs.org/wgbh/roadshow/stories/articles/2014/4/7/madam-cj-walker-hair-care-millionaire.

19 Henry Louis Gates, Jr., "Madam Walker, the First Black American Woman to Be a Self-Made Millionaire," PBS, http://www.pbs.org/wnet/african-americans-many-rivers-to-cross/history/100-amazing-facts/madam-walker-the-first-black-american-woman-to-be-a-self-made-millionaire.

20 Jefferson, "Worth More."

21 Jennifer Latson, "How America's First Self-Made Female Millionaire Built Her Fortune," *Time,* December 23, 2014, http://time.com/3641122/sarah-breedlove-walker.

22 Tim Evans, " 'Madam C.J.' Walker still inspires beauty entrepreneurs," *USA Today,* February 12, 2015, https://www.usatoday.com/story/money/2015/02/12/black-history-beauty-entrepreneurs/23316523.

23 "The Philosophies of Madam Walker and J.C. Penney," *Determining the Facts,* National Park Service, https://www.nps.gov/nr/twhp/wwwlps/lessons/walker/WAfacts3.htm.

24 "The Philosophies of Madam Walker and J.C. Penney," *Determining the Facts,* National Park Service.

25 "Wealthiest Negress Dead," obituary, *New York Times*, May 26, 1919, http://www.nytimes.com/learning/general/onthisday/bday/1223.html.

26 Latson, "How America's First Self-Made Female Millionaire Built Her Fortune."

27 Jefferson, "Worth More."

28 Daniel Feller, "Andrew Jackson: Life Before the Presidency," University of Virginia, Miller Center, https://millercenter.org/president/jackson/life-before-the-presidency.

29 Michael Burlingame, "Abraham Lincoln: Life Before the Presidency," University of Virginia, Miller Center, https://millercenter.org/president/lincoln/life-before-the-presidency.

30 Jeffrey H. Anderson, "Obama's Historically Bad Economy," *The Weekly Standard,* August 8, 2016, http://www.weeklystandard.com/obamas-historically-bad-economy/article/2003730.

31 Gwenda Blair, "The Man Who Made Trump Who He Is," *Politico Magazine*, August 24, 2015, http://www.politico.com/magazine/story/2015/08/the-man-who-made-trump-who-he-is-121647.

32 Danny Collins, "Don's Own Migrant History: How Donald Trump's German immigrant grandfather Friedrick found his fortune running brothel hotels for miners on America's brutal gold rush frontier," *The Sun*, January 30, 2017, https://www.thesun.co.uk/news/2739172/how-donald-trumps-immigrant-grandfather-friedrich-found-his-fortune-as-a-bar-owner-on-americas-brutal-gold-rush-frontier.

Chapter Three

1 Brian Domitrovic, "US Economic History—Economic Growth in the Gilded Age," Learn Liberty, May 4, 2017, video, http://www.learnliberty.org/videos/us-economic-history-5-economic-growth-in-the-gilded-age.

2 Bradley Thompson, "On Defending the Indefensible, Part One," Ashbrook, Ashland University, April 1994, http://ashbrook.org/publications/onprin-v2n2-thompson.

3 Thompson, "On Defending the Indefensible, Part One."

4 Homestead Act of 1862 (12 Stat. 392).

5 Pacific Railway Act of 1862 (12 Stat. 489).

6 "Rise of Industrial America, 1876–1900," Library of Congress, http://loc.gov/teachers/classroommaterials/presentationsandactivities/presentations/timeline/riseind/railroad/

7 Lawrence C. Kingsland, "The United States Patent Office," 13 *Law and Contemporary Problems* 354-354 (Spring 1948), https://scholarship.law.duke.edu/lcp/vol13/iss2/8.

8 US Patent and Trade Office, "U.S. Patent Activity Calendar Years 1790 to the Present," https://www.uspto.gov/web/offices/ac/ido/oeip/taf/h_counts.htm.

9 "Historical Timeline—Farm and Machinery & Technology," Growing a Nation: The Story of American Agriculture, https://www.agclassroom.org/gan/timeline/farm_tech.htm.

10 US Census Bureau, "Measuring America: The Decennial Censuses from 1790 to 2000," https://www.census.gov/history/pdf/measuringamerica.pdf.

11 Thompson, "On Defending the Indefensible, Part One."

12 Brian Domitrovic, "US Economy History 5—Economic Growth in the Gilded Age," video, Learn Liberty, May 4, 2017, http://www.learnliberty.org/videos/us-economic-history-5-economic-growth-in-the-gilded-age.

13 Domitrovic, "US Economy History 5—Economic Growth in the Gilded Age."

14 Domitrovic, "US Economy History 5—Economic Growth in the Gilded Age."

15 Domitrovic, "US Economy History 5—Economic Growth in the Gilded Age."

16 Domitrovic, "US Economy History 5—Economic Growth in the Gilded Age."

17 Ronald J. Pestritto and William J. Atto, *American Progressivism: A Reader* (Lanham, MD: Lexington Books, 2008), 2.

18 Pestritto and Atto, *American Progressivism,* 3.

19 Pestritto and Atto, *American Progressivism,* 2.

20 Karl Marx and Friedrich Engels, "Manifesto of the Communist Party," Chapter 1, Marxist Internet Archive, https://www.marxists.org/archive/marx/works/1848/communist-manifesto/ch01.htm

21 Marx and Engels, Chapter 1, Note 1.

22 Marx and Engels, Chapter 2.

23 Woodrow Wilson, "Socialism and Democracy," https://online.hillsdale.edu/document.doc?id=278.

24 Wilson, "Socialism and Democracy."

25 Wilson, "Socialism and Democracy."

26 James Madison, *The Federalist*, no. 51.

27 Woodrow Wilson, "The New Freedom," in *Woodrow Wilson: The Essential Political Writings,* ed. R. J. Pestritto (Lanham, MD: Lexington Books, 2005), 122.

28 Woodrow Wilson, *Constitutional Government in the United States* (New York: Columbia University Press, 1911), 16.

29 Paul Moreno, "A Concise History of the American Constitution," 619 https://online.hillsdale.edu/document.doc?id=475.

30 Woodrow Wilson, "The New Freedom," https://online.hillsdale.edu/document.doc?id=475.

31 Woodrow Wilson, *Congressional Government in the United States* (Boston: Houghton Mifflin, 1901), 5.

32 Wilson, *Congressional Government*, 333.

33 Woodrow Wilson, "The Study of Administration," *Political Science Quarterly* 2, no. 2 (1887): 197–222.

34 Wilson, "The Study of Administration."

35 Wilson, "The Study of Administration."

36 James Madison, "The Particular Structure of the New Government and the Distribution of Power Among Its Different Parts," *New York Packet*, February 1, 1788, https://www.congress.gov/resources/display/content/The+Federalist+Papers#TheFederalistPapers-47.

37 Wilson, *Constitutional Government,* 56–57.

38 Ronald J. Pestritto, "Woodrow Wilson and the Rejection of the Founders' Constitution," Hillsdale College, https://online.hillsdale.edu/document.doc?id=318.

39 Rebecca Kaplan, "Obama: I will use my pen and phone to take on Congress," CBS, video, January 14, 2014, http://www.cbsnews.com/news/obama-i-will-use-my-pen-and-phone-to-take-on-congress.

40 *The Founders Constitution,* Volume 1, Chapter 8, Document 41, The University of Chicago Press, http://press-pubs.uchicago.edu/founders/documents/v1ch8s41.html.

41 Louise Carroll Wade, "The Problem with Classroom Use of Upton Sinclair's The Jungle," *American Studies* 32, no. 2 (Fall 1991): 82.

42 Wade, "The Problem with Classroom Use of Upton Sinclair's The Jungle," 82.

43 Wade, "The Problem with Classroom Use of Upton Sinclair's The Jungle," 82.

44 Upton Sinclair, *The Jungle* (Chicago, 1906), 328

45 Upton Sinclair, *The Jungle* (Chicago, 1906), 376–377

46 Quoted in Wade, "The Problem with Classroom Use of Upton Sinclair's The Jungle," 84.

47 Quoted in Wade, "The Problem with Classroom Use of Upton Sinclair's The Jungle," 83.

48 Wade, "The Problem with Classroom Use of Upton Sinclair's The Jungle," 82–83.

49 Wade, "The Problem with Classroom Use of Upton Sinclair's The Jungle," 97.

50 Quoted in Wade, "The Problem with Classroom Use of Upton Sinclair's The Jungle," 80.

51 Quoted in Wade, "The Problem with Classroom Use of Upton Sinclair's The Jungle," 97.

52 Quoted in Wade, "The Problem with Classroom Use of Upton Sinclair's The Jungle," 84.

53 Quoted in Wade, "The Problem with Classroom Use of Upton Sinclair's The Jungle," 85.

54 Wade, "The Problem with Classroom Use of Upton Sinclair's The Jungle," 85.

55 Theodore Roosevelt, "First Annual Message," December 3, 1901, The American Presidency Project, http://www.presidency.ucsb.edu/ws/?pid=29542.

56 Wade, "The Problem with Classroom Use of Upton Sinclair's The Jungle," 87.

57 Wade, "The Problem with Classroom Use of Upton Sinclair's The Jungle," 88.

58 Quoted in Wade, "The Problem with Classroom Use of Upton Sinclair's The Jungle," 80.

59 Wade, "The Problem with Classroom Use of Upton Sinclair's The Jungle," 90.

60 Wade, "The Problem with Classroom Use of Upton Sinclair's The Jungle," 90.

61 Quoted in Wade, "The Problem with Classroom Use of Upton Sinclair's The Jungle," 91.

62 "Rahm Emanuel: You never want a serious crisis to go to waste," YouTube video, February 9, 2009, https://www.youtube.com/watch?v=1yeA_kHHLow.

63 George Selgin, "New York's Bank: The National Monetary Commission and the Founding of the Fed," Cato Institute Center for Monetary and Financial Alternatives, June 21, 2016, https://object.cato.org/sites/cato.org/files/pubs/pdf/pa-793.pdf.

64 Joint Economic Committee, *An Economic History of Federal Spending and Debt: Economic Growth and Federal Budgeting Trends with Insights for the Future,* September 10, 2015, https://www.jec.senate.gov/public/_cache/files/aeeff50d-dc8e-4e0b-ab9f-def32f184179/20150910-jec-spendingstudy.pdf.

65 Pestritto and Atto, *American Progressivism,* 27.

66 Calvin Coolidge, "Address at the Celebration of the 150th Anniversary of the Declaration of Independence," July 5, 1926, The American Presidency Project, http://www.presidency.ucsb.edu/ws/?pid=408.

67 Franklin D. Roosevelt, "Commonwealth Club Address," September 23, 1932, American Rhetoric Online Speech Bank, http://www.americanrhetoric.com/speeches/fdrcommonwealth.htm.

68 Roosevelt, "Commonwealth Club Address."

69 Amity Shlaes, *The Forgotten Man* (New York: HarperCollins, 2007), 8.

70 Shlaes, *Forgotten Man,* 8.

71 Dr. Troy L. Kickler, "The Conservative Manifesto," North Carolina History Project, http://northcarolinahistory.org/encyclopedia/the-conservative-manifesto.

72 Shlaes, *Forgotten Man,* 9.

73 George F. Will, "Trifle with government? Just ask Jacob Maged," *Washington Post,* September 16, 2010, http://www.washingtonpost.com/wp-dyn/content/article/2010/09/15/AR2010091505090.html.

74 "Democrats lost over 1,000 seats under Obama," FOX News, video, December 27, 2016, http://www.foxnews.com/politics/2016/12/27/democrats-lost-over-1000-seats-under-obama.html.

75 Melanie Arter, "Trump Touts Efforts to Level Playing Field for Manufacturing Industry," CNS News, September 29, 2017, https://www.cnsnews.com/news/article/melanie-arter/trump-touts-efforts-level-playing-field-us-workers-companies.

Chapter Four

1 Philip Taft and Philip Ross, "American Labor Violence: Its Causes, Character, and Outcome," in *The History of Violence in America: A Report to the National Commission on the Causes and Prevention of Violence*, ed. Hugh Davis Graham and Ted Robert Gurr, 1969.

2 Henry George, "The Condition of Labor: An Open Letter to Pope Leo XIII" (London, Swan Sonnenschein & Company, 1898), 117.

3 George, "The Condition of Labor," 117.

4 George, "The Condition of Labor," 117.

5 John McClain, "Coal Miners' President Says Violence Possible," Associated Press, September 3, 1993.

6 "Verdict in Strike Slaying," *New York Times*, June 27, 1994, http://www.nytimes.com/1994/06/27/us/verdict-in-strike-slaying.html.

7 Carl Horowitz, "UAW Organizers Step up Use of 'Scab Lists,'" National Legal and Policy Center, December 9, 2014, http://nlpc.org/2014/12/09/uaw-organizers-step-use-scab-lists.

8 Horowitz, "UAW Organizers."

9 Horowitz, "UAW Organizers."

10 Bill Roberts, "Eugene V. Debs and the U.S. socialist tradition," *Socialist Worker,* July 20, 2007, http://socialistworker.org/2007-2/638/638_12_Debs.shtml.

11 "RADICALS: Eugene V. Debs," *Time*, November 1, 1926, http://content.time.com/time/magazine/article/0,9171,722648,00.html.

12 Roberts, "Eugene V. Debs."

13 *The Debs Foundation Newsletter*, Spring 2008, p. 2, http://debsfoundation.org/pdf/newsletters/spring2008.pdf.

14 "Political Activist," Eugene V. Debs Foundation, http://debsfoundation.org/index.php/landing/debs-biography/political-activist/.

15 "Eugene V. Debs Award," Eugene V. Debs Foundation, http://debsfoundation.org/index.php/landing/eugene-v-debs-award.

16 "Trumka to Receive 1994 Debs Award," *The Debs Foundation Newsletter,* Fall 1994, p. 1, http://debsfoundation.org/pdf/newsletters/fall1994.pdf.

17 "Union leader makes stunning admission," Glenn Beck, January 6, 2011, http://www.glennbeck.com/2011/01/06/union-leader-makes-stunning-admission.

18 Bret Jacobson, "AFL-CIO: Yeah, You Can Call That Socialist," Breitbart, June 2, 2011, http://www.breitbart.com/big-government/2011/06/02/afl-cio-yeah-you-can-call-that-socialist.

19 Lawrence H. Summers, "Unemployment," *The Concise Encyclopedia of Economics,* Library of Economics and Liberty, http://www.econlib.org/library/Enc/Unemployment.html.

20 Lauren Carroll, "Trump: Since China joined WTO, U.S. has lost 60,000 factories," Politifact, March 24, 2017, http://www.politifact.com/truth-o-meter/statements/2017/mar/24/donald-trump/trump-china-joined-wto-us-has-lost-60000-factories.

21 Nick Salvatore, "Gompers, Samuel," American National Biography, http://www.anb.org/articles/15/15-00278.html.

22 "A News Account of an Address in Louisville," May 2, 1890, in Stuart B. Kaufman, ed., *The Samuel Gompers Papers: The Early Years of the American Federation of Labor, 1887–90* (University of Illinois Press, 1986), 313.

23 "Fair Labor Standards Act of 1938: Maximum Struggle for a Minimum Wage," United States Department of Labor, https://www.dol.gov/oasam/programs/history/flsa1938.htm.

24 "Labor and Capital," *The Gompers Papers,* http://www.gompers.umd.edu/quotes.htm#LABOR.

25 United States Department of Labor, Bureau of Labor Statistics, "Fastest growing jobs, 2000-2010," https://www.bls.gov/opub/ted/2001/dec/wk1/art02.htm.

26 United States Department of Labor, Bureau of Labor Statistics, "Fastest Growing Occupations," https://www.bls.gov/ooh/fastest-growing.htm.

27 "Most Say Union Leaders Out of Touch with Members," Rasmussen Reports, August 10, 2016. http://www.rasmussenreports.com/public_content/politics/general_politics/august_2016/most_say_union_leaders_out_of_touch_with_members.

28 Brody Mullins, Rebecca Ballhaus, and Michelle Hackman, "Labor Unions Step Up Presidential-Election Spending," *Wall Street Journal*, October 18, 2016. https://www.wsj.com/articles/big-labor-unions-step-up-presidential-election-spending-1476783002.

29 Mullins, Ballhaus, and Hackerman, "Labor Unions Step Up Presidential-Election Spending."

30 CNN Politics, *Exit Polls*, last updated November 23, 2017, 11:58 a.m., http://www.cnn.com/election/results/exit-polls.

31 Seamus Daniels, "Government Executive 2016 Presidential Poll: Post-Election," *Government Executive,* January 18, 2017, http://www.govexec.com/insights/reports/government-executive-2016-presidential-poll-post-election/134667/?oref=insights-top-story.

32 Steven Greenhouse, "Share of the Work Force in a Union Falls to a 97-Year Low, 11.3%," *New York Times*, January 23, 2013, http://www.nytimes.com/2013/01/24/business/union-membership-drops-despite-job-growth.html.

33 Neal E. Boudette, "Union Suffers Big Loss at Tennessee VW Plant," *Wall Street Journal*, February 15, 2014, https://www.wsj.com/articles/union-vote-at-volkswagen-tennessee-plant-heading-to-close-1392379887?mod=WSJ_hp_LEFTTopStories&tesla=y.

34 Chris Isidore, "Volkswagen employees say 'no' to United Auto Workers in Tennessee," CNN, February 15, 2014, http://www.cnn.com/2014/02/14/us/tennessee-vw-union-vote.

35 Boudette, "Union Suffers Big Loss."

36 Noam Sheiber and Bill Vlasic, "U.A.W. Says Nissan Workers Seek a Union Vote in Mississippi," *New York Times*, July 11, 2017, https://www.nytimes.com/2017/07/11/business/nissan-uaw-mississippi-union.html.

37 Bernie Sanders, "Nissan dispute could go down as most vicious anti-union crusade in decades," *Guardian*, August 3, 2017, https://www.theguardian.com/us-news/2017/aug/03/nissan-workers-union-bernie-sanders.

38 "Nissan workers reject UAW in Mississippi," KPC News, August 5, 2017, http://kpcnews.com/business/latest/kpcnews/article_89be2afc-5af8-5893-b1c5-bb212ffbc036.html.

39 Terry Bowman, "The UAW is helping itself at US workers' expense," *Washington Examiner,* October 16, 2017, http://www.washingtonexaminer.com/the-uaw-is-helping-itself-at-us-workers-expense/article/2637505.

40 Chris Isidore, "Boeing workers in South Carolina overwhelmingly reject union," CNN Money, February 15, 2017, http://money.cnn.com/2017/02/15/news/companies/boeing-union-vote/index.html.

41 Meg Kinnard, "Union voted down at Boeing's South Carolina plant," *Press Herald,* February 16, 2017, http://www.pressherald.com/2017/02/16/union-voted-down-at-boeings-south-carolina-plant.

42 Ken Thomas, "Bob King: If UAW can't organize foreign plants, 'I don't think there's a long-term future' for union," Crain's Detroit Business, January 18, 2011, http://www.crainsdetroit.com/article/20110118/FREE/110119848/bob-king-if-uaw-cant-organize-foreign-plants-i-dont-think-theres-a.

43 Joe Davidson, "50 years ago, Kennedy's order empowered federal unions," *Washington Post*, January 19, 2012, https://www.washingtonpost.com/politics/50-years-ago-kennedys-order-empowered-federal-unions/2012/01/19/gIQA3g82BQ_story.html?utm_term=.2f1473e42ba3.

44 United States Department of Labor, Bureau of Labor Statistics, "Union Membership (Annual) News Release" January 19, 2018, https://www.bls.gov/news.release/union2.htm.

45 Franklin D. Roosevelt, "Letter on the Resolution of Federation of Federal Employees Against Strikes in Federal Service," August 16, 1937, The American Presidency Project, http://www.presidency.ucsb.edu/ws/?pid=15445.

46 "Right to Work States," National Right to Work Legal Defense Foundation, http://nrtw.org/right-to-work-states.

47 Jason Hart, "State, local laws force public employees to pay labor unions," Watchdog, September 24, 2014, https://www.watchdog.org/kentucky/state-local-laws-force-public-employees-to-pay-labor-unions/article_502aecf1-141a-58f2-b83c-6ee2d94599f4.html.

48 *Janus v. American Federation of State, County, and Municipal Employees, Council 31*, Oyez, accessed January 26, 2018, https://www.oyez.org/cases/2017/16-1466.

49 "Supreme Court to Take Up Anti-Union Janus Case This Term," AFSCME Now, September 28, 2017, https://www.afscme.org/now/supreme-court-to-take-up-anti-union-janus-case-this-term.

50 Stephanie Simon, "For unions, not a fatal verdict," *Politico*, June 30, 2014, https://www.politico.com/story/2014/06/supreme-court-harris-v-quinn-ruling-108428.

51 Steve Eiken, Kate Sredl, Rebecca Woodward, and Paul Saucier, "Medicaid Expenditures for Section 1915(c) Waivers in FY 2015," July 10, 2017, https://www.medicaid.gov/medicaid/ltss/downloads/reports-and-evaluations/1915c-expenditures-fy2015.pdf.

52 Steve Eiken, "Medicaid Section 1915(c) Waiver Data based on the CMS 372 Report, 2013–2014," Truven Health Analytics, September 6, 2017, https://www.medicaid.gov/medicaid/ltss/downloads/reports-and-evaluations/cms-372-report-2014.pdf.

53 Simon, "For unions, not a fatal verdict."

54 Simon, "For unions, not a fatal verdict."

55 United States Department of Labor, Bureau of Labor Statistics, "Union Members Summary," January 19, 2018, https://www.bls.gov/news.release/union2.nr0.htm.

56 Greenhouse, "Share of the Work Force."

57 Greenhouse, "Share of the Work Force."

58 United States Department of Labor, Bureau of Labor Statistics, *Union Members Summary*.

59 "Labor and Capital," *The Gompers Papers*.

60 Senator Sanders (VT). "Remarks on the Border Security, Economic Opportunity, and Immigration Modernization Act," *Congressional Record* 159:87, June 18, 2013, S4557, https://www.congress.gov/crec/2013/06/18/CREC-2013-06-18-senate.pdf.

61 Congressional Budget Office, "The Effects of a Minimum-Wage Increase on Employment and Family Income," February 18, 2014, https://www.cbo.gov/publication/44995.

62 David Neumark, "The Effects of Minimum Wages on Employment," Federal Reserve Bank of San Francisco, FRBSF Economic Letter, December 21, 2015, http://www.frbsf.org/economic-research/publications/economic-letter/2015/december/effects-of-minimum-wage-on-employment.

63 Dara Lee Luca and Michael Luca, "Survival of the Fittest: The Impact of the Minimum Wage on Firm Exit (April 2017)," Harvard Business School NOM Unit Working Paper No. 17-088, https://ssrn.com/abstract=2951110 or http://dx.doi.org/10.2139/ssrn.2951110.

64 Ekaterina Jardim, Mark C. Long, Robert Plotnick, Emma van Inwegen, Jacob Vigdor, and Hilary Wething, "Minimum Wage Increases, Wages, and Low-Wage Employment: Evidence from Seattle," National Bureau of Economic Research, June 2017, http://www.nber.org/papers/w23532.

65 Grace Lordan and David Neumark, "People Versus Machines: The Impact of Minimum Wages on Automatable Jobs," National Bureau of Economic Research, August 2017, http://www.nber.org/papers/w23667?utm_campaign=ntw&utm_medium=email&utm_source=ntw.

66 Lordan and Neumark, "People Versus Machines: The Impact of Minimum Wages on Automatable Jobs."

67 "The Right to Minimum Wage: $0.00," *New York Times*, January 14, 1987, http://www.nytimes.com/1987/01/14/opinion/the-right-minimum-wage-0.00.html.

68 Justin Caruso, "Nancy Pelosi: GOP Tax Plan is an 'Armageddon,'" video, *Daily Caller,* October 22, 2017, http://dailycaller.com/2017/10/22/nancy-pelosi-trump-cutting-taxes-is-armageddon-video.

69 Jason Kurtz, "Sen Sanders: New tax bill 'a disaster for the American people,'" CNN, December 26, 2017, http://www.cnn.com/2017/12/20/politics/bernie-sanders-wolf-blitzer-tax-bill-cnntv/index.html.

70 Tom Rogan, "Elizabeth Warren just gave Trump a 2020 campaign ad," *Washington Examiner,* December 20, 2017, http://www.washingtonexaminer.com/elizabeth-warren-just-gave-trump-a-2020-campaign-ad/article/2644026.

71 AT&T, "With Tax Reform, AT&T Plans to Increase U.S. Capital Spending $1 Billion and Provide $1,000 Special Bonus to more than 200,000 U.S. Employees," http://about.att.com/story/att_tax_reform.html.

72 Rachel Louise Ensign, "Bank of America to Give Bonuses to About 145,000 Employees Following Tax Overhaul," *Wall Street Journal*, December 22, 2017, https://www.wsj.com/articles/bank-of-america-to-give-employee-bonuses-following-tax-overhaul-1513959707.

73 Boeing, "Boeing CEO Muilenburg Applauds Tax Law, Announces $300 Million in Employee-Related and Charitable Investments to Spur Innovation and Growth," December 20, 2017, http://boeing.mediaroom.com/2017-12-20-Boeing-CEO-Muilenburg-Applauds-Tax-Law-Announces-300-Million-in-Employee-Related-and-Charitable-Investments-to-Spur-Innovation-and-Growth.

74 Wells Fargo, "Wells Fargo to Raise Minimum Hourly Pay Rate to $15, Target $400 Million in 2018 Philanthropic Contributions, Including Expanded Support for Small Businesses and Homeownership," December 20, 2017, https://newsroom.wf.com/press-release/corporate-and-financial/wells-fargo-raise-minimum-hourly-pay-rate-15-target-400.

75 Fifth Third Bancorp, "Fifth Third Bancorp Invests in Employees," December 20, 2017, https://www.businesswire.com/news/home/20171220006042/en/Bancorp-Invests-Employees?cid=soc:tw:small-play:PR:wage-increase.

76 Comcast, "Comcast Announces Special Holiday Bonus and Capital Investments," December 20, 2017, https://www.businesswire.com/news/home/20171220006153/en/Comcast-Announces-Special-Holiday-Bonus-Capital-Investments.

77 "Sinclair Broadcast Group announces bonuses as a result of tax reform passage," KATU, December 22, 2017, http://katu.com/news/nation-world/sinclair-broadcast-group-announces-bonuses-as-a-result-of-tax-reform-passage.

78 Eric Levitz, "Corporate PR Stunts Won't Save the Working Class," *New York Magazine,* December 21, 2017, http://nymag.com/daily/intelligencer/2017/12/corporate-pr-stunts-wont-save-the-working-class.html.

79 Paul Gores, "Associated Bank to boost minimum wage to $15, pay one-time bonuses when tax reform is signed," *Post-Crescent,* December 21, 2017, http://www.postcrescent.com/story/money/business/2017/12/21/associated-bank-boost-minimum-wage-15-pay-one-time-bonuses-when-tax-reform-signed/975154001.

80 "BB&T Corp. (BBT) Raises Minimum Wage to $15/Hr, Announces $1,200 Bonus," Street Insider, December 22, 2017, https://www.streetinsider.com/Corporate+News/BB%26T+Corp.+%28BBT%29+Raises+Minimum+Wage+to+%2415Hr%2C+Announces+%241%2C200+Bonus/13628004.html.

81 "PNC Financial Services (PNC) Announces $1k Bonus, Raises Minimum Wage to $15/hr, to Contribute Additional $1.5k to Pension Accounts," Street Insider, December 22, 2017, https://www.streetinsider.com/Corporate+News/PNC+Financial+Services+%28PNC%29+Announces+%241K+Bonus%2C+Raises+Minimum+Wage+to+%2415hr%2C+to+Contribute+Additional+%241.5K+to+Pension+Accounts/13627843.html.

82 GlobeNewswire, "OceanFirst Financial Corp. Announaces Commitment to Increase the Minimum Hourly Wage to $15," Nasdaq, December 22, 2017, http://www.nasdaq.com/press-release/oceanfirst-financial-corp-announces-commitment-to-increase--the-minimum-hourly-wage-to-15-20171222-00490.

83 Phil W. Hudson, "SunTrust CEO: Tax reform will improve competitiveness of American business, promote economic growth," *Atlanta Business Chronicle,* December 28, 2017, https://www.bizjournals.com/atlanta/news/2017/12/28/suntrust-ceo-tax-reform-will-improve-the.html.

84 U.S. Bank, "U.S. Bank to invest in employees, community and customers as a result of tax reform package," January 2, 2018, https://www.usbank.com/newsroom/news/us-bank-to-invest-in-employees-community-and-customers-as-a-result-of-tax-reform-package.html.

85 Anna Hrushka, "Bank of Hawaii increases minimum wage, awards cash bonuses," *Pacific Business News,* December 22, 2017, https://www.bizjournals.com/pacific/news/2017/12/22/bank-of-hawaii-increases-minimum-wage-awards-cash.html.

86 Jamie Lovegrove, "Republican tax cut leads Nephron Pharmaceuticals in S.C. to give raises to its employees," *Post and Courier,* December 27, 2017, https://www.postandcourier.com/politics/republican-tax-cut-leads-nephron-pharmaceuticals-in-s-c-to/article_10a61438-eb19-11e7-a7a3-bbc228135bd8.html.

87 Walmart, "Walmart to Raise U.S. Wages, Provide One-Time Bonus and Expand Hourly Maternity and Parental Leave," January 11, 2018, https://news.walmart.com/2018/01/11/walmart-to-raise-us-wages-provide-one-time-bonus-and-expand-hourly-maternity-and-parental-leave.

88 John Kartch, "List of Tax Reform Good News," Americans for Tax Reform," January 26, 2018, https://www.atr.org/list.

89 Richard Trumka, "Working people are watching, Mr. President," *The Hill,* January 1, 2018, http://thehill.com/opinion/immigration/369338-working-people-are-watching-mr-president.

90 Trumka, "Working people are watching, Mr. President."

91 Apple, "Apple accelerates U.S. investment and job creation," January 17, 2018, https://www.apple.com/newsroom/2018/01/apple-accelerates-us-investment-and-job-creation.

92 Chaim Gartenberg, "Apple is giving employees $2,500 bonuses in restricted stock units after new tax law," *The Verge,* January 17, 2018, https://www.theverge.com/2018/1/17/16902812/apple-2500-bonus-restricted-stock-units-tax-code-employees.

93 Brittany De Lea, "Fight for 15 strikes dramatically decline in 2017, new research shows," FOX Business, August 11, 2017, http://www.foxbusiness.com/politics/2017/08/11/fight-for-15-strikes-dramatically-decline-in-2017-new-research-shows.amp.html.

94 U.S. Department of Labor, Office of Labor-Management Standards, *Form LM-2 Labor Organization Annual Report,* http://laborpains.org/wp-content/uploads/2017/04/SEIU-2011-LM2.pdf.

95 Ginger Adams Otis, "Fight for $15 movement to protest nationwide against Labor Secretary pick Andy Puzder, a wage raise foe," *Daily News,* January 11, 2017, http://www.nydailynews.com/news/politics/fight-15-movement-protest-andy-puzder-nationwide-article-1.2944171.

96 Stacey Barchenger, "Protesters ask labor nominee Puzder to stay home in Franklin," *Tennessean,* February 11, 2017, http://www.tennessean.com/story/news/2017/02/11/protesters-ask-andrew-puzder-stay-home-franklin/97788404.

97 Jobs With Justice, "Middle Tennessee Jobs With Justice," http://www.jwj.org/about-us/our-network/middle-tennessee-jobs-with-justice.

98 Jobs With Justice, "About Us," http://www.jwj.org/about-us.

99 Eugene V. Debs Foundation, http://debsfoundation.org/index.php/category/history.

100 Bill McMorris, "Puzder: Opponents Sent White Powder to My Wife," *Washington Free Beacon,* February 27, 2017, http://freebeacon.com/issues/puzder-opponents-sent-white-powder-wife.

Chapter Five

1 "Towards the end of poverty," *Economist*, June 1, 2013, https://www.economist.com/news/leaders/21578665-nearly-1-billion-people-have-been-taken-out-extreme-poverty-20-years-world-should-aim.

2 "Remarkable Declines in Global Poverty, But Major Challenges Remain," The World Bank, April 17, 2013, http://www.worldbank.org/en/news/press-release/2013/04/17/remarkable-declines-in-global-poverty-but-major-challenges-remain.

3 Anthony B. Kim and Patrick Tyrell, "Economic Freedom Enables Great Escape From Poverty," The Heritage Foundation, February 13, 2018, https://www.heritage.org/poverty-and-inequality/commentary/economic-freedom-enables-great-escape-poverty.

4 "Societies Thrive as Economic Freedom Grows," *2018 Index of Economic Freedom*, The Heritage Foundation, https://www.heritage.org/index/book/chapter-2.

5 "About The Index," *2018 Index of Economic Freedom*, The Heritage Foundation, https://www.heritage.org/index/about.

6 Kim, "Economic Freedom."

7 Perry Chiaramonte, "Millennials think socialism would create a great safe space, study finds," Fox News, November 3, 2017, http://www.foxnews.com/us/2017/11/03/millennials-think-socialism-would-create-great-safe-space-study-finds.html.

8 Alex Thompson and Diamond Naga Siu, "Socialism is surging on college campuses," Vice News, October 27, 2017, https://news.vice.com/en_us/article/mb9p44/socialism-is-surging-on-college-campuses-this-fall.

9 Cabot Phillips, "Students love socialism!... whatever that is...," Campus Reform, July 15, 2017, https://www.campusreform.org/?ID=9443.

10 "2018 Index of Economic Freedom," The Heritage Foundation, http://www.heritage.org/index/about.

11 Kyle Feldscher, "Trump: Venezuela in crisis because 'socialism has been faithfully implemented,'" *Washington Examiner*, September 19, 2017, http://www.washingtonexaminer.com/trump-venezuelan-in-crisis-because-socialism-has-been-faithfully-implemented/article/2634867.

12 Felicity Barringer, "The Mainstreaming of Marxism in U.S. Colleges," *New York Times,* October 25, 1989, http://www.nytimes.com/1989/10/25/us/education-the-mainstreaming-of-marxism-in-us-colleges.html?mcubz=0.

13 Barringer, "Mainstreaming."

14 Eric Owens, "Fancypants College Professors Favor Democrats Over Republicans By Mind-Blowing 11.5-to-1 Ratio," *The Daily Caller*, October 4, 2016, http://dailycaller.com/2016/10/04/fancypants-college-professors-favor-democrats-over-republicans-11-5-to-1/.

15 Mitchell Langbert, Anthony J. Quain, and Daniel B. Klein, "Faculty Voter Registration in Economics, History, Journalism, Law, and Psychology," *Econ Journal Watch* 13, no. 3 (2016): 424, https://econjwatch.org/file_download/944/LangbertQuainKleinSept2016.pdf?mimetype=pdf.

16 Langbert, Quain, and Klein, "Faculty Voter Registration," 424.

17 Samuel Goldman, "Why Isn't My Professor Conservative?" *American Conservative,* January 7, 2016, http://www.theamericanconservative.com/articles/why-isnt-my-professor-conservative/.

18 "Welcome," Heterodox Academy, https://heterodoxacademy.org/.

19 Neil Gross and Solon Simmons, "The Social and Political Views of American Professors," September 24, 2007, http://citeseerx.ist.psu.edu/viewdoc/download?doi=10.1.1.147.6141&rep=rep1&type=pdf.

20 Bryan Caplan, "The Prevalence of Marxism in Academia," Library of Economics and Liberty, March 31, 2015, http://econlog.econlib.org/archives/2015/03/the_prevalence_1.html.

21 Michael Burawoy, "103rd ASA President Erik Olin Wright: Reinventing Sociology," American Sociological Association, http://www.asanet.org/about-asa/asa-story/asa-history/past-asa-officers/past-asa-presidents/erik-olin-wright.

22 Erik Olin Wright, "Chapter 1: Why Be an Anti-Capitalist?" in *How to be an Anticapitalist for the 21st Century*, https://www.ssc.wisc.edu/~wright/Sydney%20seminar%202016/Chapter%201%20%20-%20Why%20be%20an%20anticapitalist%20-%20draft%202.0.pdf.

23 Erik Olin Wright, "Chapter 1: Why Be an Anti-Capitalist?" in *How to be an Anticapitalist for the 21st Century,* 1.

24 Erik Olin Wright, "How to Be an Anticapitalist Today," *Jacobin,* December 2, 2015, https://www.jacobinmag.com/2015/12/erik-olin-wright-real-utopias-anticapitalism-democracy/.

25 "An open letter to Scott Walker from UW-Madison faculty," *Badger Herald,* February 21, 2011, https://badgerherald.com/opinion/2011/02/21/an-open-letter-to-sco/.

26 Eric Owens, "Capitalism-Hating Marxist Professor Rakes In $170,000 Per Year At U. Wisconsin," *The Daily Caller,* August 21, 2015, http://dailycaller.com/2015/08/21/marxist-professor-rakes-in-170000-per-year-at-u-wisconsin/.

27 Erik Olin Wright, "Singing Solidarity Forever in the Wisconsin State Capitol," YouTube video, March 15, 2011, https://www.youtube.com/watch?v=Kz1bMOH2en8.

28 Burawoy, "Erik Olin Wright."

29 Burawoy, "Erik Olin Wright."

30 Owens, "Marxist Professor."

31 "People," Department of Anthropology, London School of Economics, http://www.lse.ac.uk/anthropology/people/departmentalstaff.aspx.

32 Jeff Sharlet, "Inside Occupy Wall Street," *Rolling Stone,* November 10, 2011, http://www.rollingstone.com/politics/news/occupy-wall-street-welcome-to-the-occupation-20111110.

33 Mark F. Bernstein, "Margaret Mead meets Morgan Stanley," *Princeton Alumni Weekly,* September 23, 2009, https://paw.princeton.edu/article/margaret-mead-meets-morgan-stanley.

34 "Kshama Iyengar Sawant," Seattle City Council, http://www.seattle.gov/council/sawant.

35 "Economics (High School Version), 2nd Edition" Amazon.com, https://www.amazon.com/Economics-High-School-Version-Krugman/dp/1429218266.

36 "The Sveriges Riksbank Prize in Economic Sciences in Memory of Alfred Nobel 2008, Paul Krugman," The Royal Swedish Academy of Sciences, October 13, 2008, https://www.nobelprize.org/nobel_prizes/economic-sciences/laureates/2008/press.html.

37 Paul Krugman, "Hearts and Heads," *New York Times,* April 22, 2001, http://www.nytimes.com/2001/04/22/opinion/reckonings-hearts-and-heads.html?mcubz=0.

38 Krugman, "Hearts and Heads."

39 Paul Krugman, "Health Care Horror Hooey," *New York Times,* February 23, 2014, https://www.nytimes.com/2014/02/24/opinion/krugman-health-care-horror-hooey.html?ref=paulkrugman&_r=1.

40 Paul Krugman, "Notes on Brexit," *New York Times,* June 12, 2016, https://krugman.blogs.nytimes.com/2016/06/12/notes-on-brexit/?mcubz=0.

41 Paul Krugman, "The Axis of Climate Evil," *New York Times,* August 11, 2017, https://www.nytimes.com/2017/08/11/opinion/climate-science-denial.html.

42 Paul Krugman, Twitter, July 10, 2017, https://twitter.com/paulkrugman/status/884403567049625601.

43 Paul Krugman, "Understanding Republican Cruelty," *New York Times,* June 30, 2017, https://www.nytimes.com/2017/06/30/opinion/understanding-republican-cruelty.html?mcubz=0&_r=0.

44 Paul Krugman, "The Tainted Election," *New York Times,* December 12, 2016, https://www.nytimes.com/2016/12/12/opinion/the-tainted-election.html.

45 Deirdre Fernandes, "Socialists, look to economists at UMass Amherst for support," *Boston Globe,* March 1, 2016, https://www.bostonglobe.com/business/2016/02/29/umass-economists-find-place-during-year-outsider/BoYaoXTDa2cIYJGLglCnKJ/story.html.

46 "Department of Economics, Graduate Courses," University of Massachusetts Amherst, https://www.umass.edu/economics/graduate/courses.

47 "Department of Economics, Graduate Courses," University of Massachusetts Amherst.

48 Fernandes, "Socialists."

49 Paul Krugman, "What Has the Wonks Worried," *New York Times,* February 17, 2016, https://krugman.blogs.nytimes.com/2016/02/17/what-has-the-wonks-worried/.

50 Timothy Dionisopoulos, "Upcoming workshop at Brown Univ. set to help queer minorities overcome attraction to queer whites," Campus Reform, March 19, 2013, https://www.campusreform.org/?ID=4672.

51 Maggie Lit, "Cornell students blame 'rape culture' on capitalism and 'cisheteropatriarchy,'" Campus Reform, October 29, 2014, https://www.campusreform.org/?ID=5961.

52 Lit, "Cornell students."

53 "Dr Russell Rickford speaks @ Black Lives Matter Ithaca, NY June 8 2016," YouTube video, July 8, 2016, https://www.youtube.com/watch?v=63J7oUdTQOE.

54 "Dr Russell Rickford speaks."

55 Christopher Ingraham, "What Ivy League students are reading that you aren't," *Washington Post,* February 3, 2016, https://www.washingtonpost.com/news/wonk/wp/2016/02/03/what-ivy-league-students-are-reading-that-you-arent/?utm_term=.aaa1c26cdedb.

56 Jose A. Delreal, "Students Walk Out of Ec 10 in Solidarity with 'Occupy,'" *Harvard Crimson,* November 2, 2011, http://www.thecrimson.com/article/2011/11/2/mankiw-walkout-economics-10/.

57 Delreal, "Students Walk Out."

58 N. Gregory Mankiw, "Know What You're Protesting," *New York Times,* December 3, 2011, http://www.nytimes.com/2011/12/04/business/know-what-youre-protesting-economic-view.html.

59 John Dewey, *My Pedagogic Creed* (New York: E.L. Kellog & Co., 1897), 16.

60 Dewey, *My Pedagogic Creed,* 16.

61 Dewey, *My Pedagogic Creed,* 16.

62 "Teachers Unions," Center for Responsive Politics, https://www.opensecrets.org/industries/contrib.php?cycle=2016&ind=L1300.

63 "Privatization," National Education Association, http://www.nea.org/home/16355.htm.

64 "Affordable Health Care for America," National Education Association, http://www.nea.org/home/16326.htm.

65 "NEA on Health Care," National Education Association, http://www.nea.org/home/19380.htm.

66 "Teachers Unions," Center for Responsive Politics.

67 "Divestment from Fossil Fuel Industries," American Federation of Teachers, https://www.aft.org/resolution/divestment-fossil-fuel-industries.

68 "Take On Wall Street," American Federation of Teachers, https://www.aft.org/resolution/take-wall-street.

69 "Take On Wall Street," American Federation of Teachers.

70 "Take On Wall Street," American Federation of Teachers.

71 Lois Weiner, "The CTU's Strike for Democracy," *Jacobin,* April 1, 2016, https://www.jacobinmag.com/2016/04/chicago-teachers-union-strike-karen-lewis/.

72 Amy Korte, "Chicago Teachers Highest Paid Among Nation's 50 Largest School Districts," Illinois Policy, Feburary 5, 2016, https://www.illinoispolicy.org/cps-pays-the-highest-salaries-of-any-of-the-50-largest-school-districts/.

73 Micah Uetricht, "The Next Great Chicago Strike, an Interview with Sarah Chambers," *Jacobin,* March 31, 2016, https://www.jacobinmag.com/2016/03/chicago-teachers-union-strike-core-karen-lewis/.

74 Kari Lydersen & Emma Brown, "Chicago teachers go on strike, shutting down nation's third-largest school system," *Washington Post,* April 1, 2016, https://www.washingtonpost.com/news/education/wp/2016/04/01/chicago-teachers-to-strike-friday-shutting-down-nations-third-largest-school-system/?utm_term=.56d8abe4f0eb.

75 Fight for 15 Chicago, Twitter, March 24, 2016, https://twitter.com/chifightfor15/status/713030169150300160.

76 Micah Uetricht, "The Chicago Teachers' Strike Is Unlike Any Other in Recent Memory," Vice News, April 1, 2016, https://news.vice.com/article/the-chicago-teachers-strike-is-unlike-any-other-in-recent-memory.

77 Uetricht, "The Chicago Teachers' Strike."

78 Lydersen and Brown, "Chicago teachers."

79 "What is WWP?" Workers World Party, http://www.workers.org/wwp/what-is-wwp/.

80 "WWP salutes Chicago teachers strike," Workers World Party, April 1, 2016, http://www.workers.org/2016/04/05/wwp-salutes-chicago-teachers-strike/.

81 Micah Uetricht, "Uncommon CORE," *Jacobin,* March 6, 2014, https://www.jacobinmag.com/2014/03/uncommon-core-chicago-teachers-union/.

82 Uetricht, "Uncommon CORE."

83 Uetricht, "Uncommon CORE."

84 Lee Sustar, "Chicago Teachers Draw a Line," *Indypendent,* August 31, 2012, https://indypendent.org/2012/08/chicago-teachers-draw-a-line/.

85 Lauren FitzPatrick, "CPS reading scores dip; barely 1 in 4 read at grade level," *Chicago Sun-Times,* October 31, 2016, http://chicago.suntimes.com/news/cps-reading-scores-dip-barely-1-in-4-read-at-grade-level/.

86 "2015 Reading Trial Urban District Snapshot Report: Chicago, Grade 4, Public Schools," National Center for Education Statistics, https://nces.ed.gov/nationsreportcard/subject/publications/dst2015/pdf/2016048XC4.pdf.

87 "CPS Students Outpace Growth of National Urban, State Peers in Reading, Math," Chicago Public Schools, October 28, 2015, http://cps.edu/News/Press_releases/Pages/PR1_10_28_2015.aspx.

88 Juan Perez Jr. and Kyle Bentle, "Chicago Public Schools touts improved graduation rate," *Chicago Tribune,* September 5, 2016, http://www.chicagotribune.com/news/ct-chicago-schools-graduation-rates-20160905-htmlstory.html.

89 Jodi S. Cohen and Juan Perez Jr., "Study: More CPS graduates completing college, but rate still troubling," *Chicago Tribune,* December 8, 2014, http://www.chicagotribune.com/news/ct-cps-college-story-20141208-story.html.

90 "5 things to know about the Chicago teachers strike," *Chicago Tribune,* March 31, 2016, http://www.chicagotribune.com/news/local/breaking/ct-chicago-teachers-walkout-5-things-to-know-met-0401-20160331-story.html.

91 "Our Story," Association of Raza Educators, http://aresandiego.weebly.com/our-story.html.

92 "Education for Liberation Network," http://www.edliberation.org/.

93 "Teachers 4 Social Justice," https://t4sj.org/.

94 "Teachers for Social Justice," http://www.teachersforjustice.org/.

95 "Longevity Salary Increases," United Federation of Teachers, http://www.uft.org/our-rights/longevity-increases.

96 "Salary Schedules for 2009-2018 Contract," United Federation of Teachers, http://www.uft.org/files/attachments/secure/teacher-schedule-2009-2018.pdf.

97 "CTU Quest Center Reports on the Truth about Merit Pay," Chicago Teachers Union, https://www.ctunet.com/research/merit-pay-position-paper.

98 Kristen Butler, "Disabled teacher fired for urinating in classroom," UPI, April 25, 2013, https://www.upi.com/blog/2013/04/25/Disabled-teacher-fired-for-urinating-in-classroom/7721366910901/.

99 Kristen Butler, "Disabled teacher."

100 Danielle Arndt, "Teacher firing upheld: Former Huron orchestra teacher Chris Mark's appeal denied," *Ann Arbor News*, March 28, 2013, http://www.annarbor.com/news/education/teacher-firing-upheld-former-huron-high-school-orchestra-teacher-chris-marks-appeal-denied/.

101 Jeanette Rundquist, "States increasingly take aim at teachers' tenure as legal fees mount to fire some," NJ.com, March 21, 2010, http://www.nj.com/news/index.ssf/2010/03/states_increasingly_take_aim_a.html.

102 Madhu Krishnamurthy, "State's attorney investigates Dist. 207's handling of ex-teacher's case," *Daily Herald,* September 16, 2013, http://www.dailyherald.com/article/20130916/news/709169929/.

103 Susan Edelman, "City pays exiled teachers to snooze as 'rubber rooms' return," *New York Post,* January 17, 2016, http://nypost.com/2016/01/17/city-pays-exiled-teachers-to-snooze-as-rubber-rooms-return/.

104 Selim Algar, "City spent $25M on teachers removed from permanent gigs," *New York Post,* August 18, 2017, http://nypost.com/2017/08/18/city-spent-25m-on-teachers-banned-from-permanent-gigs/.

105 "Court decision in Vergara v. California," *Washington Post,* https://apps.washingtonpost.com/g/documents/local/court-decision-in-vergara-v-california/1031/.

106 Kyle Stokes, "Vergara v California: Ruling that would have ended state's teacher tenure rejected on appeal," KPCC, April 14, 2016, http://www.scpr.org/news/2016/04/14/59624/appeals-court-overturns-lower-court-s-ruling-on-ca/.

107 Charlie Kirk, "Liberal Bias Starts in High School Economics Textbooks," Breitbart, April 26, 2012, http://www.breitbart.com/big-government/2012/04/26/liberal-bias-starts-in-high-school-economics/.

108 Martin Duberman, *Howard Zinn: A Life on the Left* (New York: The New Press, 2012), 199.

109 "A People's History of the United States," Amazon.com, https://www.amazon.com/Peoples-History-United-States/dp/0060838655.

110 Howard Zinn, *A People's History of the United States, Abridged Teaching Edition* (New York: The New Press, 2003), 477.

111 Zinn, *A People's History,* 477.

112 Zinn, *A People's History,* 477.

113 David J. Bobb, "Howard Zinn and the Art of Anti-Americanism," *Wall Street Journal,* August 12, 2013, https://www.wsj.com/articles/david-j-bobb-howard-zinn-and-the-art-of-antiamericanism-1376348093.

114 "A People's History of the United States," Amazon.com, https://www.amazon.com/Peoples-History-United-States/dp/0060838655.

115 "Rethinking Mathematics: Teaching Social Justice by the Numbers," The Zinn Education Project, https://zinnedproject.org/materials/rethinking-mathematics-teaching-social-justice-by-the-numbers/.

116 David J. Bobb, "Howard Zinn and the Art of Anti-Americanism," *Wall Street Journal,* August 12, 2013, https://www.wsj.com/articles/david-j-bobb-howard-zinn-and-the-art-of-antiamericanism-1376348093.

117 Palash Ghosh, "How Many People Did Joseph Stalin Kill?," *International Business Times*, March 5, 2013, http://www.ibtimes.com/how-many-people-did-joseph-stalin-kill-1111789.

118 Lee Edwards, "The Legacy of Mao Zedong is Mass Murder," The Heritage Foundation, February 2, 2010, https://www.heritage.org/asia/commentary/the-legacy-mao-zedong-mass-murder.

119 Madeline Farber, "Nearly Two-Thirds of Americans Can't Pass a Basic Test of Financial Literacy," *Fortune,* July 12, 2016, http://fortune.com/2016/07/12/financial-literacy/.

120 Justin McCarthy and Anita Pugliese, "Two in Three Adults Worldwide Are Financially Illiterate," Gallup, November 18, 2015, http://www.gallup.com/poll/186680/two-three-adults-worldwide-financially-illiterate.aspx.

121 Terry M. Moe, "The End of Teachers Unions," Hoover Institution, July 18, 2012, http://www.hoover.org/research/end-teachers-unions.

122 Richard D. Kahlenberg, "Can Vouchers Save Failing Schools?" *Atlantic,* January 31, 2017, https://www.theatlantic.com/education/archive/2017/01/can-vouchers-save-failing-schools/515061/.

123 Steve Birr, "DC Mayor Breaks With Obama To Support GOP-Backed School Choice Bill," *The Daily Caller,* April 27, 2016, http://dailycaller.com/2016/04/27/dc-mayor-breaks-with-obama-to-support-gop-backed-school-choice-bill/.

124 Kate Zernike, "Betsy DeVos, Trump's Education Pick, Has Steered Money From Public Schools," *New York Times,* November 23, 2016, https://www.nytimes.com/2016/11/23/us/politics/betsy-devos-trumps-education-pick-has-steered-money-from-public-schools.html?_r=0.

125 Foundation for Teaching Economics, https://www.fte.org/.

126 Kevin Roose, "Why Are College Students Flocking to Economics?" *New York Magazine*, May 29, 2013, http://nymag.com/daily/intelligencer/2013/05/why-are-college-students-flocking-to-economics.html.

Chapter Six

1 Quoted in Fred Hiatt, "Letter from Moscow," *Washington Post,* December 4, 1993, https://www.washingtonpost.com/archive/lifestyle/1993/12/04/letter-from-moscow/80641c14-0d2c-4264-853b-b4f512d6945e/?utm_term=.8c9e648a3a5c.

2 Peter Schweizer, "One Man Battalion" in *Reagan's War: The Epic Story of His Forty-Year Struggle and Final Triumph Over Communism* (New York: Doubleday, 2002).

3 Matt Chaban, "Susan Sarandon Gets the House (Well, Technically, It's a Chelsea Loft)," *Observer,* June 15, 2011, http://observer.com/2011/06/susan-sarandon-gets-the-house-well-technically-its-a-chelsea-loft.

4 Elise Knutsen, "Suddenly Susan Sarandon Has Three NYC Apartments: Actress Buys in Brooklyn," *Observer,* January 30, 2012, http://observer.com/2012/01/suddenly-susan-sarandon-has-three-nyc-apartments-actress-buys-in-brooklyn.

5 "Susan Sarandon Gets Emotional About Bernie Sanders Movement," YouTube video, January, 28, 2016, https://www.youtube.com/watch?v=1tFR2MIOgUY.

6 "Susan Sarandon Gets Emotional About Bernie Sanders Movement."

7 Stein/Baraka Headquarters, "Personal Letter of Endorsement from Susan Sarandon," http://www.jill2016.com/sarandon.

8 "The Green New Deal," Jill2016, http://www.jill2016.com/greennewdeal.

9 "The Green New Deal," Jill2016.

10 The Artists and Cultural Leaders for Bernie Sanders, "Endorsement Letter," https://berniesanders.com/artists.

11 Candace Taylor, "Danny DeVito and Rhea Perlman Sell Beverly Hills Home for $28 Million," *Wall Street Journal*, April 30, 2015, https://www.wsj.com/articles/danny-devito-and-rhea-perlman-sell-beverly-hills-home-for-28-million-1430424434?mg=prod/accounts-wsj.

12 Mark David, "Mark Ruffalo Takes a Loss on Brooklyn Brownstone," *Variety,* May 9, 2017, http://variety.com/2017/dirt/real-estalker/mark-ruffalo-brooklyn-house-1202419187.

13 Julie Kelly, "And the Academy Award for Hollywood Hypocrisy Goes to: Mark Ruffalo," *National Review,* February 20, 2016, http://www.nationalreview.com/article/431636/mark-ruffalo-environmental-hypocrite-academy-award-nominee.

14 The Artists and Cultural Leaders for Bernie Sanders, "Endorsement Letter."

15 "That's Rich! Daniel Craig Set to Score Whopping $150 Million As James Bond," Radar Online, September 3, 2016, http://radaronline.com/celebrity-news/sony-offers-daniel-craig-millions-two-more-james-bond-films.

16 Bradford Richardson, "Bond actor donates $47,000 to Sanders PAC," *The Hill,* September 10, 2015, http://thehill.com/blogs/ballot-box/fundraising/253305-bond-actor-donates-50000-to-sanders-pac.

17 Seth MacFarlane, Twitter, October 13, 2015, https://twitter.com/SethMacFarlane/status/653971463960031232.

18 Josh Dean, "Seth MacFarlane's $2 Billion Family Guy Empire," *Fast Company,* November 1, 2008, https://www.fastcompany.com/1042476/seth-macfarlanes-2-billion-family-guy-empire.

19 American Jobs Creation Act (118 Stat. 1418-1660).

20 Gavrielle Gemma, "Venezuelan president meets with New York unionists," Workers World, October 10, 2009, http://www.workers.org/2009/us/venezuelan_president_1015.

21 Gemma, "Venezuelan president."

22 Juliet Litman, "Divorce Court: Who Won Sean Penn and Robin Wright's Breakup?" *Grantland,* February 14, 2014, http://grantland.com/hollywood-prospectus/divorce-court-who-won-sean-penn-and-robin-wrights-split.

23 Rebecca Ford, "Sean Penn on Hugo Chavez's Death: 'I Lost a Friend,'" *Hollywood Reporter,* March 5, 2013, http://www.hollywoodreporter.com/news/hugo-chavez-dead-sean-penn-426205.

24 "Venezuela: Chavez's Authoritarian Legacy," Human Rights Watch, March 5, 2013, https://www.hrw.org/news/2013/03/05/venezuela-chavezs-authoritarian-legacy.

25 "Venezuela: Chavez's Authoritarian Legacy," Human Rights Watch.

26 "Esta noche se estrenara documental Mi Amigo Hugo, de Oliver Stone," Agencia Venezolana de Noticias, April 3, 2014, http://www.avn.info.ve/contenido/pel%C3%ADcula-mi-amigo-hugo-oliver-stone-se-estrenar%C3%A1-este-mi%C3%A9rcoles-telesur.

27 Roy Carroll, "Venezuela giving Danny Glover $18m to direct film on epic slave revolt," *Guardian,* May 20, 2007, https://www.theguardian.com/world/2007/may/21/film.venezuela.

28 Carroll, "Venezuela."

29 "Hugo Chavez: Danny Glover praises 'social champion,'" *The Telegraph,* March 6, 2013, http://www.telegraph.co.uk/news/worldnews/southamerica/venezuela/9914179/Hugo-Chavez-Danny-Glover-praises-social-champion.html.

30 "Actor Danny Glover voices support for Venezuelan president during visit to honour Hugo Chavez as anti-government protests continue," *National Post,*

March 7, 2014, http://nationalpost.com/g00/scene/actor-danny-glover-supports-venezuelan-government-during-visit-to-honour-hugo-chavez/wcm/61f2aee8-2499-4916-a5c6-15e51d77ed7e?i10c.referrer=.

31 Michael Moore, Twitter, March 5, 2013, https://twitter.com/mmflint/status/309124649244057600?lang=en.

32 "Venezuela's Maduro says 2013 annual inflation was 56.2 pct," Reuters, December 30, 2013, https://www.reuters.com/article/venezuela-inflation-annual-idUSL2N0K90V020131230.

33 "Venezuela's president blames soaring inflation on 'parasitic bourgeoisie,' deploys army to force stores to slash prices," *National Post,* November 12, 2013, http://nationalpost.com/news/world/venezuelas-president-blames-soaring-inflation-on-parasitic-bourgeoisie-deploys-army-to-force-retailers-to-slash-prices.

34 Emily Diaz-Struck and Juan Forero, "Venezuelan president's backers laud war on 'capitalist parasites,' but others see difficulties," *Washington Post,* November 20, 2013, https://www.washingtonpost.com/world/venezuelan-presidents-backers-laud-war-on-capitalist-parasites-but-others-see-difficulties/2013/11/20/20526d9e-5213-11e3-9ee6-2580086d8254_story.html?utm_term=.86b2f7fd7bf0.

35 Kenzi Abou-Sabe, "Photos: Venezuelans contend with food, medicine shortages, as low oil prices cripple economy," PBS, August 22, 2015, http://www.pbs.org/newshour/rundown/venezuelans-battle-chronic-shortages-low-oil-prices-leave-economy-crippled.

36 Diego Ore and Andrew Cawthorne, "Venezuela's Maduro decried as 'dictator' after Congress annulled," Reuters, March 30, 2017, http://www.reuters.com/article/us-venezuela-politics-idUSKBN17122M.

37 Stephen Gutowski, "Socialist Venezuelan Leader Steps Up Arming of Supporters After Outlawing, Confiscating Civilian Guns," *Washington Free Beacon,* April 19, 2017, http://freebeacon.com/issues/socialist-venezuelan-leader-steps-arming-supporters-outlawing-confiscating-civilian-guns.

38 Frances Martel, "Venezuela: Regime Claims 'Complete Normalcy' as 'Sham' Election Leaves Over Dozen Dead," Breitbart, July 30, 2017, http://www.breitbart.com/national-security/2017/07/30/venezuela-sham-election-leaves-15-dead-consolidates-power-socialists.

39 Corina Pons, "Venezuela 2016 inflation hits 800 percent, GDP shrinks 19 percent: document," Reuters, January 20, 2017, https://www.reuters.com/article/us-venezuela-economy/venezuela-2016-inflation-hits-800-percent-gdp-shrinks-19-percent-document-idUSKBN154244.

40 Paul P. Murphy, "Daughter, father, future doctor: Victims of unrest in Venezuela," CNN, May 11, 2017, http://www.cnn.com/2017/05/10/world/venezuela-victims/index.html.

41 Meridith Kohut and Isayen Herrera, "As Venezuela Collapses, Children Are Dying of Hunger," *New York Times,* December 17, 2017, https://www.nytimes.com/interactive/2017/12/17/world/americas/venezuela-children-starving.html.

42 Alexandra Ulmer, "Venezuela supermarkets besieged after government forces price cuts," Reuters, January 6, 2018, https://www.yahoo.com/news/venezuela-supermarkets-besieged-government-forces-price-cuts-164822021.html.

43 Jonathan Hoenig, "Hugo Chavez's Control: Property Rights in Venezuela," Fox News, May 3, 2007, http://www.foxnews.com/story/2007/05/03/hugo-chavez-control-property-rights-in-venezuela.html.

44 William T. Walker, *McCarthyism and the Red Scare: A Reference Guide* (ABC-CLIO, 2013), 136.

45 Andrew Breitbart and David Ehrenstein, "Holly-cons: in the closet?," *Los Angeles Times,* September 27, 2007, http://www.latimes.com/la-op-dustup27sep27-story.html.

46 Donald Lambro, "Breitbart: Blacklist then and now," *Washington Times,* July 28, 2008, https://www.washingtontimes.com/news/2008/jul/28/bean-there-done-that-blacklist-then-and-now.

47 Jerome Hudson, "James Woods: I've 'Accepted The Fact That I'm Blacklisted' In Hollywood," Breitbart, August 22, 2017, http://www.breitbart.com/big-hollywood/2017/08/22/james-woods-republicans-in-hollywood-terrified-over-being-blacklisted.

48 Brad Slager, "Robert Davi Shares Proof of Hollywood's Bias Against Conservatives," PopZette, August 5, 2017, http://www.lifezette.com/popzette/robert-davi-proof-of-hollywoods-bias-against-conservatives.

49 Michelle Pollino, "Conservative in Hollywood? Be a 'Democrat publicly,' industry vet says," Fox News, video, June 19, 2017, http://www.foxnews.com/entertainment/2017/06/19/conservative-in-hollywood-be-democrat-publicly-industry-vet-says.html.

50 Paulina Firozi, "Tim Allen: Being a conservative in Hollywood 'is like '30s Germany,'" *The Hill,* March 19, 2017, http://thehill.com/blogs/in-the-know/in-the-know/324719-tim-allen-on-being-a-conservative-in-hollywood-this-is-like-30s.

51 Nelli Andreeva, "Tim Allen Comedy 'Last Man Standing' Canceled by ABC After 6 Seasons," Deadline, May 10, 2017, https://deadline.com/2017/05/last-man-standing-canceled-by-abc-after-6-seasons-1202089263.

52 Tim Allen, Twitter, May 16, 2017, https://twitter.com/ofctimallen/status/864514490804523009?lang=en.

53 Dan Evon, "Tim Allen Show 'Last Man Standing' Cancelled For Political Reasons?," Snopes, May 18, 2017, http://www.snopes.com/tim-allen-cancelled-political-views.

54 Lesley Goldberg, "The Many Reasons Behind ABC's 'Last Man Standing' Cancellation," *Hollywood Reporter,* May 16, 2017, http://www.hollywoodreporter.com/live-feed/why-last-man-standing-was-canceled-tim-allen-responds-1004414.

55 *Goldfinger,* directed by Guy Hamilton, Eon Productions, 1964.

56 *Glengarry Glen Ross,* directed by James Foley, New Line Cinema, 1992.

57 *The Social Network,* directed by David Fencher, Columbia Pictures, 2010.

58 David Batty and Chris Johnston, "Social Network 'made up stuff that was hurtful,' says Mark Zuckerberg," *Guardian,* November 14, 2014, https://www.theguardian.com/technology/2014/nov/08/mark-zuckerberg-social-network-made-stuff-up-hurtful.

59 *Jobs,* directed by Joshua Michael Stern, Open Road Films, 2013.

60 Susan Wloszczyna, review of *Jobs*, RobertEbert.com, August 15, 2013, http://www.rogerebert.com/reviews/jobs-2013.

61 *Wolf of Wall Street,* directed by Martin Scorsese, Paramount, 2013.

62 *Wall Street,* directed by Oliver Stone, 20th Century Fox, 1987.

63 "Money Never Sleeps," *Wall Street,* directed by Oliver Stone, 20th Century Fox, 1987.

64 "Gordon Gekko Address to Teldar Paper Stockholders," *Wall Street,* directed by Oliver Stone, 20th Century Fox, 1987.

65 Oliver Stone, "Oliver Stone on Wall Street, Gordon Gekko, and Hugo Chavez," *The Christian Science Monitor,* August 3, 2010, https://www.csmonitor.com/Commentary/Global-Viewpoint/2010/0803/Oliver-Stone-on-Wall-Street-Gordon-Gekko-and-Hugo-Chavez.

66 David M. Ewalt, "No. 12 Burns, C. Montgomery," *Forbes*, Games, April 14, 2010, https://www.forbes.com/2010/04/13/montgomery-burns-bio-opinions-fictional-15-10-simpsons.html.

67 Laura Schreffler, "The Simpsons creator Matt Groening splashes out on $11.7m mansion," *Daily Mail,* November 11, 2011, http://www.dailymail.co.uk/tvshowbiz/article-2058820/The-Simpsons-creator-Matt-Groening-splashes-11-7-million-mansion.html.

68 *The Lego Movie,* directed by Phil Lord and Christopher Miller, Warner Bros., 2014.

69 *Dallas,* aired 1978–1991 on CBS, https://www.amazon.com/dp/B006I0GG86.

70 *Dynasty*, aired 1981–1989 on CBS, https://www.amazon.com/Dynasty-Season-1/dp/B0093SKX8O.

71 Jeremy W. Peters and Brian Stelter, "Trump for President in 2012? Maybe. Trump for Trump? Without Question," *New York Times,* April 2, 2011, http://www.nytimes.com/2011/04/03/business/media/03trump.html.

72 Julia La Roche, "Goldman Sachs' newly minted CEO Lloyd Blankfein grew up in the projects of Brooklyn," Business Insider, July 17, 2015, http://www.businessinsider.com/lloyd-blankfein-rags-to-riches-story-2015-7.

73 Michael Lambert, "Donald Trump Waves LGBT Rainbow Flag at Colorado Rally," *Advocate,* October 31, 2016, https://www.advocate.com/2016/10/31/donald-trump-waves-lgbt-rainbow-flag-colorado-rally.

74 Chris Harris, "Barack Obama Answers Your Questions About Gay Marriage, Paying for College, and More," MTV News, November 1, 2008, http://www.mtv.com/news/1598407/barack-obama-answers-your-questions-about-gay-marriage-paying-for-college-more.

75 Deena Zaru, "Caitlyn Jenner takes Trump up on bathroom offer," CNN Politics, August 16, 2017, http://www.cnn.com/2016/04/28/politics/caitlyn-jenner-bathroom-trump-tower-donald-trump/index.html.

76 Susan Milligan, "Donald Trump's Good Call on the Transgender Miss Universe Contestant," *U.S. News and World Report,* April 4, 2012, https://www.usnews.com/opinion/blogs/susan-milligan/2012/04/04/donald-trumps-good-call-on-the-transgender-miss-universe-contestant.

77 Maggie Haberman, "Mar-a-Lago, the Future Winter White House and Home of the Calmer Trump," *New York Times,* January 1, 2017, https://www.nytimes.com/2017/01/01/us/trump-mar-a-lago-future-winter-white-house.html?_r=0.

78 Alexandra Berzon and Richard Rubin, "Trump's Father Helped GOP Candidate With Numerous Loans," *Wall Street Journal,* September 23, 2016, https://www.wsj.com/articles/trumps-father-helped-gop-candidate-with-numerous-loans-1474656573?mod=e2tw.

79 Jennifer Harper, "Trump's high-flying jet: 24 karat gold-plated seat belts, 57-inch TV, 2 bedrooms," *Washington Times,* September 7, 2015, http://www.washingtontimes.com/news/2015/sep/7/donald-trumps-high-flying-jet-24-karat-gold-plated.

80 Michele Corriston and Gabrielle Olya, "Jon Stewart Will Leave Earth in a Rocket if Donald Trump is Elected President: 'Clearly this Planet's Gone Bonkers,'" *People,* September 21, 2015, http://people.com/awards/emmys-2015-jon-stewart-will-leave-earth-if-donald-trump-is-elected-president.

81 Ned Ehrbar, "Cher says if Trump wins she's going 'to have to leave the planet,'" CBS, November 7, 2016, http://www.cbsnews.com/news/cher-says-if-trump-wins-shes-going-to-have-to-leave-the-planet.

82 Society of Professional Journalists, *Code of Ethics*, https://www.spj.org/pdf/ethicscode.pdf.

83 Fred Barnes, "Liberal Media Evidence," *Weekly Standard,* May 27, 2004, http://www.weeklystandard.com/liberal-media-evidence/article/5369.

84 Thomas E. Patterson, "News Coverage of Donald Trump's First 100 Days," Harvard Kennedy School Shorenstein Center on Media, Politics and Public Policy, May 18, 2017, https://shorensteincenter.org/news-coverage-donald-trumps-first-100-days.

85 Patterson, "News Coverage of Donald Trump's First 100 Days."

86 Patterson, "News Coverage of Donald Trump's First 100 Days."

87 Patterson, "News Coverage of Donald Trump's First 100 Days."

88 Patterson, "News Coverage of Donald Trump's First 100 Days."

89 Amy Nitchell, Jeffrey Gottried, Galen Stocking, Katerina Eva Matsa, and Elizabeth Grieco, "Covering President Trump in a Polarized Media Environment," Pew Research Center, October 2, 2017, http://www.journalism.org/2017/10/02/covering-president-trump-in-a-polarized-media-environment.

Chapter Seven

1 John F. Kennedy, "Remarks of Senator John F. Kennedy, Allentown, PA," October 28, 1960, The American Presidency Project, http://www.presidency.ucsb.edu/ws/?pid=74265.

2 Theodore Sorensen, *Kennedy* (New York: Harper and Row, 1965), 394.

3 Sorensen, *Kennedy,* 394.

4 Sorensen, *Kennedy,* 394.

5 John F. Kennedy, "Remarks of Senator John F. Kennedy, Chamber of Commerce Dinner, Lynchburg, Virginia," April 4, 1957, John F. Kennedy Presidential Library and Museum, https://www.jfklibrary.org/Research/Research-Aids/JFK-Speeches/Lynchburg-VA_19570404.aspx.

6 Sorensen, *Kennedy,* 394.

7 Sorensen, *Kennedy,* 394.

8 Ira Stroll, "JFK Was a Political Conservative," *Time,* October 14, 2013, http://ideas.time.com/2013/10/14/jfk-was-a-political-conservative.

9 Lawrence Kudlow and Brian Domitrovic, "John F. Kennedy and Ronald Reagan Proved Tax Cuts Work," *Time*, September 29, 2016, http://time.com/4511870/john-f-kennedy-and-ronald-reagan-tax-policy.

10 Kudlow and Domitrovic, "John F. Kennedy and Ronald Reagan Proved Tax Cuts Work."

11 Kudlow and Domitrovic, "John F. Kennedy and Ronald Reagan Proved Tax Cuts Work."

12 "John F. Kennedy on the Economy and Taxes," John F. Kennedy Presidential Library and Museum, https://www.jfklibrary.org/JFK/JFK-in-History/JFK-on-the-Economy-and-Taxes.aspx.

13 "John F. Kennedy on the Economy and Taxes," John F. Kennedy Presidential Library and Museum.

14 Kudlow and Domitrovic, "John F. Kennedy and Ronald Reagan Proved Tax Cuts Work."

15 John F. Kennedy, "Address and Question and Answer Period at the Economic Club of New York," December 14, 1962, The American Presidency Project, http://www.presidency.ucsb.edu/ws/?pid=9057.

16 John F. Kennedy, "Income Tax Cut, Kennedy Hopes to Spur Econony," August 13, 1962, https://www.youtube.com/watch?v=0QU3SG1bbRQ.

17 Kennedy, "Income Tax Cut, Kennedy Hopes to Spur Economy."

18 "John F. Kennedy on the Economy and Taxes," John F. Kennedy Presidential Library and Museum.

19 Amity Shales, "Kennedy Strikes Back," *Forbes,* November 13, 2013, https://www.forbes.com/sites/currentevents/2013/11/13/kennedy-strikes-back/#e42b43120115.

20 Stroll, "JFK Was a Political Conservative."

21 Kyle Longley, *Albert Gore Sr.: Tennessee Maverick* (Baton Rouge: LSU Press, 2004), 171.

22 John Fitzgerald Kennedy, "JFK's never-delivered speech from Dallas," November 22, 1963, *Pittsburgh Post-Gazette,* http://www.post-gazette.com/news/nation/2013/11/22/Full-text-JFK-s-never-delivered-speech-from-Dallas/stories/201311210356.

23 Elizabeth MacDonald, "Bring Back the Kennedy Democrats," Fox Business, December 11, 2014, http://www.foxbusiness.com/features/2014/12/11/bring-back-kennedy-democrats.html.

24 Jonathan Colman, *Foreign Policy of Lyndon B. Johnson: The United States and the World, 1963–1969*, 189.

25 Brian Domitrovic, "Trashing JFK's Tax Cuts, One of the Greatest Policy Successes of All Time," *Forbes,* March 12, 2013, https://www.forbes.com/sites/briandomitrovic/2013/03/12/trashing-jfks-tax-cuts-one-of-the-greatest-policy-successes-of-all-time/#6b25d4a3e2f8.

26 Andy Romey, "Clinton sends video address to Boys Nation," The American Legion, July 20, 2013, https://www.legion.org/boysnation/216613/clinton-sends-video-address-boys-nation.

27 "The Day Bill Clinton Met JFK," ABC News, video, http://abcnews.go.com/US/video/day-bill-clinton-met-jfk-23387874.

28 "Bill Clinton in 1992 ad: 'A plan to end welfare as we know it,'" *Washington Post,* video, August 30, 2016, https://www.washingtonpost.com/video/politics/bill-clinton-in-1992-ad-a-plan-to-end-welfare-as-we-know-it/2016/08/30/9e6350f8-6ee0-11e6-993f-73c693a89820_video.html.

29 Louis Jacobson, "Bill Clinton takes credit for 'flowering' of economy in the 1990s," Politifact, April 19, 2010, http://www.politifact.com/truth-o-meter/statements/2010/apr/19/bill-clinton/bill-clinton-takes-credit-flowering-economy-1990s.

30 Todd S. Purdum, "Clinton Angers Friend and Foe in Tax Market," *New York Times,* October 18, 1995, http://www.nytimes.com/1995/10/19/us/clinton-angers-friend-and-foe-in-tax-remark.html.

31 Purdum, "Clinton Angers Friend and Foe in Tax Remark."

32 William J. Clinton, "Address Before a Joint Session of Congress on the State of the Union," January 23, 1996, The American Presidency Project, http://www.presidency.ucsb.edu/ws/?pid=53091.

33 Jamie Fuller, "The third most memorable State of the Union address: Bye Bye, Big Government," *Washington Post,* January 26, 2014, https://www

.washingtonpost.com/news/the-fix/wp/2014/01/26/the-3rd-most-memorable-state-of-the-union-address-bye-bye-big-government/?utm_term=.ca85d042d1ab.

34 Ron Haskins and Peter H. Schuck, "Op-Ed: Welfare Reform Worked," Brookings Institute, February 28, 2012, https://www.brookings.edu/opinions/welfare-reform-worked.

35 Haskins and Schuck, "Op-Ed: Welfare Reform Worked."

36 Joe Klein, "What Today's Democrats Can Learn from Bill Clinton's Crime and Welfare-Reform Bills," *Time,* April 14, 2016, http://time.com/4293546/what-todays-democrats-can-learn-from-bill-clintons-crime-and-welfare-reform-bills.

37 Haskins and Schuck, "Op-Ed: Welfare Reform Worked."

38 J.D. Foster, "Tax Cuts, Not the Clinton Tax Hike, Produced the 1990s Boom," The Heritage Foundation, March 4, 2008, http://www.heritage.org/taxes/report/tax-cuts-not-the-clinton-tax-hike-produced-the-1990s-boom.

39 Jim Dexter, "CNN Fact Check: The last president to balance the budget," CNN, February 3, 2010, http://politicalticker.blogs.cnn.com/2010/02/03/cnn-fact-check-the-last-president-to-balance-the-budget/

40 Tyler Cowen, "Did the Gramm-Leach-Bliley Act cause the housing bubble?," Marginal Revolution, September 19, 2008, http://marginalrevolution.com/marginalrevolution/2008/09/did-the-gramm-l.html.

41 Maria Bartiromo, "Bill Clinton on the Banking Crisis, McCain, and Hillary," *Bloomberg Businessweek,* September 24, 2008, https://www.bloomberg.com/news/articles/2008-09-23/bill-clinton-on-the-banking-crisis-mccain-and-hillary.

42 Randy Yeip and Tynan DeBold, "Obama's 2016 Budget: Behind the Numbers," *Wall Street Journal,* February 2, 2015, http://graphics.wsj.com/obamas-2016-budget-behind-the-numbers.

43 Katie McKenna, "Obama's Final Economic Record Not Great," Fox Business, March 30, 2017, http://www.foxbusiness.com/markets/2017/03/30/obamas-final-economic-record-not-great.html.

44 "Obama Fires a 'Robin Hood' Warning Shot," *New York Post,* October 15, 2008, http://nypost.com/2008/10/15/obama-fires-a-robin-hood-warning-shot.

45 Conn Carroll, "Day 8: Obama edict repealed 1996 welfare reform's work requirement," *Washington Examiner,* September 25, 2013, http://www.washingtonexaminer.com/day-8-obama-edict-repealed-1996-welfare-reforms-work-requirement/article/2536341.

46 "Supplemental Nutrition Assistance Program Participation and Costs," data as of January 5, 2018, https://fns-prod.azureedge.net/sites/default/files/pd/SNAPsummary.pdf.

47 Tim Hains, "Obama: Forget The Difference Between Capitalism And Communism, "Just Decide What Works," *Real Clear Politics,* March 25, 2016, https://www.realclearpolitics.com/video/2016/03/25/obama_forget_the_difference_between_capitalism_and_communism_just_decide_what_works.html.

48 Will Cabaniss, "George Will describes Bernie Sanders' Soviet Union honeymoon," Punditfact, August 12, 2015, http://www.politifact.com/punditfact/statements/2015/aug/12/george-will/george-will-reminds-readers-about-bernie-sanders-u.

49 Paul Sperry, "Don't be fooled by Bernie Sanders—He's a diehard communist," *New York Post,* January 16, 2016, http://nypost.com/2016/01/16/dont-be-fooled-by-bernie-sanders-hes-a-diehard-communist.

50 James Hohmann, "The Daily 202: Bernie Sanders has a Eugene V. Debs problem," *Washington Post,* January 22, 2016, https://www.washingtonpost.com/news/powerpost/wp/2016/01/22/the-daily-202-bernie-sanders-has-a-eugene-v-debs-problem/?utm_term=.31444ee82ee2.

51 Hohmann, "The Daily 202: Bernie Sanderes has a Eugene V. Debs problem."

52 Bernie Sanders, "Close The Gaps: Disparities That Threaten America," *Valley News*, August 5, 2011, https://www.sanders.senate.gov/newsroom/must-read/close-the-gaps-disparities-that-threaten-america.

53 Philip Klein, "Here's a list of Bernie Sanders' $19.6 trillion in tax hikes," *Washington Examiner,* January 19, 2016, http://www.washingtonexaminer.com/heres-a-list-of-bernie-sanders-19.6-trillion-in-tax-hikes/article/2580846.

54 Dylan Stableford, " 'It hurt': Clinton says Sanders dragged out nomination fight," Yahoo!, September 12, 2017, https://www.yahoo.com/news/hurt-clinton-says-sanders-dragged-nomination-fight-135139249.html.

55 Angie Drobnic Holan and Nai Issa, "In Context: Hillary Clinton and Don't let anybody tell you that corporations create jobs," Politifact, October 30, 2014, http://www.politifact.com/truth-o-meter/article/2014/oct/30/context-hillary-clinton-and-dont-let-anybody-tell-/.

56 Maggie Haberman, "Hillary Clinton clarifies jobs comment," *Politico,* October 27, 2014, http://www.politico.com/story/2014/10/hillary-clinton-jobs-comment-112225.

57 Catherine Garcia, "Clinton: Republicans 'don't mind having big government interfere with a woman's right to choose,'" *The Week,* October 13, 2015, http://theweek.com/speedreads/583151/clinton-republicans-dont-mind-having-big-government-interfere-womans-right-choose.

58 Scott Greenberg, "Summary of the Latest Federal Income Tax Data, 2016 Update," Tax Foundation, February 1, 2017, https://taxfoundation.org/summary-latest-federal-income-tax-data-2016-update.

59 Daniel Marans and Jonathan Cohn, "Bernie Sanders Announces Single-Payer Bill With Major Support In Senate," Huffington Post, September 13, 2017, http://www.huffingtonpost.com/entry/bernie-sanders-single-payer-bill-major-support-senate_us_59b87dc1e4b02da0e13d465f.

60 Marans and Cohn, "Bernie Sanders Announces."

61 Elizabeth Warren: 'There is nobody in this country who got rich on his own,'" CBS, September 22, 2011, https://www.cbsnews.com/news/elizabeth-warren-there-is-nobody-in-this-country-who-got-rich-on-his-own.

62 Heather Long, "Elizabeth Warren: The market is broken," CNN Money, video, September 5, 2014, http://money.cnn.com/2014/09/05/news/economy/elizabeth-warren-market-broken/index.html.

63 Benjamin Brown, "Democrat Warren confronted over her 'One Percent' status," Fox News, video, September 22, 2017, http://www.foxnews.com/politics/2017/09/22/democrat-warren-confronted-over-her-one-percent-status.html.

Chapter Eight

1 "President Obama on inequality (transcript)," *Politico,* December 4, 2013, https://www.politico.com/story/2013/12/obama-income-inequality-100662.

2 Bernie Sanders, "Income and Wealth Inequality," https://berniesanders.com/issues/income-and-wealth-inequality/.

3 "Americans' Views on Income Inequality and Workers' Rights," *New York Times,* June 3, 2015, https://www.nytimes.com/interactive/2015/06/03/business/income-inequality-workers-rights-international-trade-poll.html?_r=0.

4 David Satter, "100 Years of Communism—and 100 Million Dead," *Wall Street Journal,* November 6, 2017, https://www.wsj.com/article_email/100-years-of-communismand-100-million-dead-1510011810-lMyQjAxMTI3NDA0NzgwNTc5Wj/.

5 Satter, "100 Years."

6 Mary Anastasia O'Grady, "Venezuela is Starving Its People," *Wall Street Journal,* November 19, 2017, https://www.wsj.com/article_email/maduro-is-starving-his-own-people-1511071600-lMyQjAxMTA3NTI4MDkyODA0Wj/.

7 Meridith Kohut and Isayen Herrera, "As Venezuela Collapses, Children Are Dying of Hunger," *New York Times,* December 17, 2017, https://www.nytimes.com/interactive/2017/12/17/world/americas/venezuela-children-starving.html.

8 "Venezuela Goes Bust," *Wall Street Journal,* November 15, 2017, https://www.wsj.com/articles/venezuela-goes-bust-1510703305.

9 Margaret Thatcher, "TV Interview for Thames TV This Week," February 5, 1976, http://www.margaretthatcher.org/document/102953.

10 "Fall of the Soviet Union," The Cold War Museum, http://www.coldwar.org/articles/90s/fall_of_the_soviet_union.asp.

11 "The deal's off," *Economist,* March 24, 2012, http://www.economist.com/node/21550421.

12 Ronald Coase and Ning Wang, "How China Became Capitalist," *Cato Policy Report,* The Cato Institute, January/February 2013, https://www.cato.org/policy-report/januaryfebruary-2013/how-china-became-capitalist.

13 Coase and Wang, "How China."

14 Bernie Sanders, "Senator Bernie Sanders on Democratic Socialism in the United States," November 19, 2015, https://berniesanders.com/democratic-socialism-in-the-united-states/.

15 Sam Frizell, "Here's How Bernie Sanders Explained Democratic Socialism," *Time,* November 19, 2015, http://time.com/4121126/bernie-sanders-democratic-socialism/.

16 Ezra Klein, "Bernie Sanders, The Vox conversation," Vox, July 28, 2015, https://www.vox.com/2015/7/28/9014491/bernie-sanders-vox-conversation.

17 Ryan Teague Beckwith, "Transcript: Read the Full Text of the Primetime Democratic Debate," *Time,* October 26, 2015, http://time.com/4072553/democratic-debate-transcript-primetime-cnn/.

18 Frizell, "Here's How."

19 Bernie Sanders, "Making the Wealthy, Wall Street, and Large Corporations Pay their Fair Share," https://berniesanders.com/issues/making-the-wealthy-pay-fair-share/.

20 Dan Mangan, "Bernie Sanders' budget would add $21 trillion to debt: Analysis," CNBC, May 10, 2016, https://www.cnbc.com/2016/05/09/bernie-sanders-budget-would-add-21-trillion-to-debt-analysis.html.

21 David Weigel, "Sanders introduces universal health care, backed by 15 Democrats," *Washington Post,* September 13, 2017, https://www.washingtonpost.com/powerpost/sanders-will-introduce-universal-health-care-backed-by-15-democrats/2017/09/12/d590ef26-97b7-11e7-87fc-c3f7ee4035c9_story.html?utm_term=.175f5544a776.

22 Office of Management and Budget, "A New Foundation for American Greatness: Budget of the United States Government, Fiscal Year 2018" (Washington: US Government Printing Office, 2017), 25, https://www.whitehouse.gov/sites/whitehouse.gov/files/omb/budget/fy2018/budget.pdf.

23 Weigel, "Sanders introduces."

24 Ricardo Alonso-Zaldivar and Emily Swanson, "AP-GfK Poll: Downsides cut into support for Sanders' health plan," Associated Press, February 25, 2016, https://www.usnews.com/news/business/articles/2016-02-25/ap-gfk-poll-support-shaky-for-sanders-medicare-for-all.

25 Austin Smith, "Bernie Sanders' income tax brackets: How much would you owe?" The Motley Fool, *USA Today,* May 12, 2016, https://www.usatoday.com/story/sponsor-story/motley-fool/2016/05/12/motley-fool-bernie-sanders-income-tax-brackets/32607881/.

26 Ian Schwartz, "Scandinavian To Sanders: You Want To Spend Like A Scandinavian, But Not Tax Like One," RealClearPolitics, October 19, 2017, https://www.realclearpolitics.com/video/2017/10/19/scandinavian_to_sanders_you_want_to_spend_like_a_scandinavian_but_not_tax_like_one.html.

27 Schwartz, "Scandinavian to Sanders."

28 Schwartz, "Scandinavian to Sanders."

29 Alan Coe and Scott Greenberg, "Details and Analysis of Senator Bernie Sanders's Tax Plan," Tax Foundation, January 28, 2016, https://taxfoundation.org/details-and-analysis-senator-bernie-sanders-s-tax-plan/.

30 Coe and Greenberg, "Details and Analysis."

31 Ilan Ben-Meir, "Bernie Sanders Despised Democrats In 1980s, Said A JFK Speech Once Made Him Sick," BuzzFeed, July 16, 2015, https://www.buzzfeed.com/ilanbenmeir/bernie-sanders-despised-democrats-in-1980s-said-a-jfk-speech?utm_term=.wwwq2RJK3q#.lr5yeJDQly.

32 Sanders, "Democratic Socialism."

33 Jeff Jacoby, "No, Bernie Sanders, Scandinavia is not a socialist utopia," *Boston Globe,* October 15, 2015, https://www.bostonglobe.com/opinion/2015/10/15/bernie-sanders-scandinavia-not-socialist-utopia/lUk9N7dZotJRbvn8PosoIN/story.html.

34 Ezra Klein, "Bernie Sanders and Hillary Clinton's debate over capitalism, explained," Vox, October 14, 2015, https://www.vox.com/2015/10/14/9528873/bernie-sander-hillary-clinton-socialist-debate.

35 Matthew Yglesias, "Denmark's prime minister says Bernie Sanders is wrong to call his country socialist," Vox, October 31, 2015, https://www.vox.com/2015/10/31/9650030/denmark-prime-minister-bernie-sanders.

36 Terry Jones, "Bernie Sanders Is Right: The U.S. Should Copy Denmark," *Investor's Business Daily,* August 30, 2017, http://www.investors.com/politics/commentary/bernie-sanders-is-right-the-u-s-should-copy-denmark/.

37 2018 Index of Economic Freedom, *The Heritage Foundation,* https://www.heritage.org/index/

38 "Executive Summary," *2008 Index of Economic Freedom,* The Heritage Foundation, http://thf_media.s3.amazonaws.com/index/pdf/2008/Index2008_ExecutiveSummary.pdf.

39 "Welfare," *Denmark.dk, The Official Website of Denmark,* Ministry of Foreign Affairs of Denmark, http://denmark.dk/en/society/welfare/.

40 "What can the U.S. learn from Denmark?," Associated Press, October 15, 2015, https://www.pbs.org/newshour/world/can-u-s-learn-denmark.

41 Peter Levring, "Denmark Decides to Make It 'More Attractive to Work,'" *Bloomberg,* August 29, 2017, https://www.bloomberg.com/news/articles/2017-08-29/denmark-targets-deep-cuts-to-reduce-world-s-biggest-tax-burden.

42 "Denmark Personal Income Tax Rate," Trading Economics, https://tradingeconomics.com/denmark/personal-income-tax-rate.

43 Jeanne Sahadi, "Top income tax rate: How U.S. really compares," CNN Money, April 1, 2013, http://money.cnn.com/2013/04/01/pf/taxes/top-income-tax/index.html.

44 Sahadi, "Top income tax rate."

45 "Working and Living in Denmark, Tax 2017," Deloitte, https://www2.deloitte.com/content/dam/Deloitte/dk/Documents/tax/Deloitte-Working-living-in-Denmark.pdf.

46 Michael Barrett, "Explained: Denmark's crazy car registration tax," *The Local,* November 20, 2015, https://www.thelocal.dk/20151120/whats-the-deal-with-denmarks-car-registration-tax.

47 "Human Development Index 1975–2005," United Nations Development Programme, 2008, https://photius.com/rankings/human_developement_index_1975-2005.html.

48 "Australia Could Become Regional Talent Hub: Mercer's 2016 Cost of Living Survey," Mercer, June 22, 2016, https://www.mercer.com.au/newsroom/australia-could-become-regional-talent-hub.html.

49 Suzanne Daley, "Danes Rethink a Welfare State Ample to a Fault," *New York Times,* April 20, 2013, http://www.nytimes.com/2013/04/21/world/europe/danes-rethink-a-welfare-state-ample-to-a-fault.html?_r=0.

50 Daley, "Danes Rethink."

51 Daley, "Danes Rethink."

52 Daley, "Danes Rethink."

53 Daley, "Danes Rethink."

54 "Real GDP forecast," Organization for Economic Cooperation and Development, https://data.oecd.org/gdp/real-gdp-forecast.htm.

55 Levring, "Denmark Decides."

56 Levring, "Denmark Decides."

57 Levring, "Denmark Decides."

58 Peter Levring, "Welfare Icon Now Wants People to Take Care of Themselves," *Bloomberg,* March 1, 2017, https://www.bloomberg.com/news/articles/2017-03-01/welfare-icon-now-wants-people-to-take-care-of-themselves.

59 Edward Cody, "Socialists cut Spain's welfare state, riling Spaniards," *Washington Post,* March 21, 2011, https://www.washingtonpost.com/world/europe/socialists-cut-spains-welfare-state-riling-spaniards/2011/05/19/AFr6go7G_story.html?utm_term=.0defd2701c76.

60 Cody, "Socialists cut."

61 Cody, "Socialists cut."

62 Cody, "Socialists cut."

63 "Greek pensions, Why they are a flashpoint," *Economist,* June 18, 2015, https://www.economist.com/blogs/freeexchange/2015/06/greek-pensions.

64 "Greek pensions," *Economist.*

65 "Greece Youth Unemployment Rate," Trading Economics, https://tradingeconomics.com/greece/youth-unemployment-rate.

66 "Acropolis Now," *Economist,* April 29, 2010, http://www.economist.com/node/16009099.

67 Marcus Walker, "Greek Court Finds Former Statistics Chief Guilty of Breaching Duties," *Wall Street Journal,* August 1, 2017, https://www.wsj.com/articles/greek-court-finds-former-statistics-chief-guilty-of-breaching-duties-1501592204.

68 "Acropolis Now," *Economist.*

69 Aaron Smith, "Greek crisis fears deepen," CNN Money, April 28, 2010, http://money.cnn.com/2010/04/28/news/international/greek_bonds/.

70 Helena Smith, "Tax hikes threaten to brew up a storm for Greece's coffee drinkers," *Guardian,* May 16, 2016, https://www.theguardian.com/world/2016/may/16/tax-hikes-greece-coffee-austerity-economy-bailout.

71 Smith, "Tax hikes threaten."

72 Nektaria Stamouli, "Last Lifelines Crumble for Many Greek Families as New Conflict With Creditors Looms," *Wall Street Journal,* January 13, 2017, https://www.wsj.com/articles/last-lifelines-crumble-for-many-greek-families-as-new-conflict-with-creditors-looms-1484303414.

73 Smith, "Tax hikes threaten."

74 Smith, "Tax hikes threaten."

75 Stamouli, "Last Lifelines Crumble."

76 "GDP growth (annual %)," The World Bank, https://data.worldbank.org/indicator/NY.GDP.MKTP.KD.ZG?locations=GR.

77 "Greece Youth Unemployment Rate," Trading Economics.

78 Stamouli, "Last Lifelines Crumble."

79 Stamouli, "Last Lifelines Crumble."

80 "Full transcript: President Obama's remarks on the economy at Knox College," *Washington Post,* July 24, 2013, https://www.washingtonpost.com/politics/full-text-of-president-obamas-remarks-on-the-economy-at-knox-college-as-prepared-for-delivery/2013/07/24/fd580f6a-f47f-11e2-a2f1-a7acf9bd5d3a_story.html?utm_term=.bdd17c1d8488.

81 "Income Inequality," *New York Times,* https://www.nytimes.com/topic/subject/income-inequality.

82 Sanders, "Income and Wealth Inequality."

83 "The Distribution of Household Income and Federal Taxes, 2013," Congressional Budget Office, June 2016, 22, https://www.cbo.gov/sites/default/files/114th-congress-2015-2016/reports/51361-householdincomefedtaxesone col.pdf.

84 "The Distribution of Household Income and Federal Taxes, 2013," Congressional Budget Office, June 2016, 22, https://www.cbo.gov/sites/default/files/114th-congress-2015-2016/reports/51361-householdincomefedtaxesone col.pdf.

85 Demian Brady, "Who Pays Taxes 2015," National Taxpayers Union Foundation, October 11, 2017, https://www.ntu.org/foundation/blog/who-pays-taxes-2015.

86 Sanders, "Income and Wealth Inequality."

87 Emmanuel Saez, "Striking it Richer: The Evolution of Top Incomes in the United States," University of California, Berkeley, June 30, 2016, https://eml.berkeley.edu/~saez/saez-UStopincomes-2015.pdf.

88 "The Distribution of Household Income and Federal Taxes, 2013," Congressional Budget Office, 44.

89 "The Distribution of Household Income and Federal Taxes, 2013," Congressional Budget Office, 31.

90 "The Distribution of Household Income and Federal Taxes, 2013," Congressional Budget Office, 31.

91 Gerald Auten and David Splinter, "Income Inequality in the United States: Using Tax Data to Measure Long-term Trends," November 12, 2017, 20, http://davidsplinter.com/AutenSplinter-Tax_Data_and_Inequality.pdf.

92 Auten and Splinter, "Income Inequality," 20.

93 Auten and Splinter, "Income Inequality," 20.

94 Auten and Splinter, "Income Inequality," 20.

95 Auten and Splinter, "Income Inequality," 20.

96 Michael D. Tanner, "Five Myths about Economic Inequality in America," Cato Institute, September 7, 2016, https://www.cato.org/publications/policy-analysis/five-myths-about-economic-inequality-america.

97 "Trends in Family Wealth, 1989 to 2013," Congressional Budget Office, August 2016, 1, https://www.cbo.gov/sites/default/files/114th-congress-2015-2016/reports/51846-Family_Wealth.pdf.

98 Rich Smith, "7 Years After Crisis, Americans Still Spooked Over Stocks," AOL, June 17, 2015, https://www.aol.com/article/finance/2015/06/17/americans-still-spooked-over-stocks-financial-crisis/21197325/.

99 Nathan Vardi, "Inside The Obama Stock Market's 235% Return," *Forbes,* January 17, 2017, https://www.forbes.com/sites/nathanvardi/2017/01/17/inside-the-obama-stock-markets-235-rise/#5eb280cb16d1.

100 "Financial Accounts of the United States, Second Quarter 2017," Federal Reserve Statistical Release, September 21, 2017, https://www.federalreserve.gov/releases/z1/20170921/z1.pdf.

101 "Financial Accounts of the United States, Third Quarter 2017," Federal Reserve Statistical Release, December 7, 2017, https://www.federalreserve.gov/releases/z1/Current/z1.pdf.

102 "Financial Accounts of the United States, Third Quarter 2017," Federal Reserve Statistical Release.

103 "Historical Poverty Tables: People and Families—1959 to 2016," United States Census Bureau, https://www.census.gov/data/tables/time-series/demo/income-poverty/historical-poverty-people.html.

104 Missy Sullivan, "Lost Inheritance," *Wall Street Journal,* March 8, 2013, https://www.wsj.com/articles/SB10001424127887324662404578334663271139552.

105 Tanner, "Five Myths."

106 Ron Haskins, "Three Simple Rules Poor Teens Should Follow to Join the Middle Class," The Brookings Institution, March 13, 2013, https://www.brookings.edu/opinions/three-simple-rules-poor-teens-should-follow-to-join-the-middle-class/.

107 Tanner, "Five Myths."

108 "Forbes 400," *Forbes,* https://www.forbes.com/forbes-400/list/#version:static.

109 "Forbes 400," *Forbes.*

110 Erin Carlyle, "How America's Wealthiest Get Rich," *Forbes,* March 13, 2012, https://www.forbes.com/sites/erincarlyle/2012/03/13/how-americas-wealthiest-get-rich/#6cdc5023506e.

111 Rakesh Kochhar, "How Americans compare with the global middle class," Pew Research Center, July 9, 2015, http://www.pewresearch.org/fact-tank/2015/07/09/how-americans-compare-with-the-global-middle-class/.

112 Drew Desilver, "For most workers, real wages have barely budged for decades," Pew Research Center, October 9, 2014, http://www.pewresearch.org/facttank/2014/10/09/for-most-workers-real-wages-have-barely-budged-for-decades/.

113 "The Distribution of Household Income and Federal Taxes, 2013," Congressional Budget Office, 33.

114 Edward Conard, *The Upside of Inequality: How Good Intentions Undermine the Middle Class* (New York: Penguin, 2016), 39.

115 Conard, *Upside of Inequality,* 14.

116 Conard, *Upside of Inequality,* 50.

117 Victor Tan Chen, "Manufacturing Employment (United States)," April 25, 2016, https://victortanchen.com/manufacturing-employment-united-states/.

118 "Gross Domestic Product Per Capita for Hong Kong," Economic Research, Federal Reserve Bank of St. Louis, https://fred.stlouisfed.org/series/PCAGDPHKA646NWDB.

119 Pak Yiu and Stefanie McIntyre, "Hong Kong wealth gap at its widest in decades as handover anniversary nears," Reuters, June 27, 2017, https://www.reuters.com/article/us-hongkong-anniversary-wealth-gap/hong-kong-wealth-gap-at-its-widest-in-decades-as-handover-anniversary-nears-idUSKBN19I1E2.

120 Yiu and McIntyre, "Hong Kong wealth gap."

121 "Angus Maddison 1926–2010," Groningen Growth and Development Centre, University of Groningen, https://www.rug.nl/ggdc/historical development/maddison/original-maddison.

122 Derek Thompson, "The Economic History of the Last 2000 Years: Part II," *Atlantic,* June 20, 2012, https://www.theatlantic.com/business/archive/2012/06/the-economic-history-of-the-last-2000-years-part-ii/258762/.

123 Jonathan Haidt, "How Capitalism Changes Conscience," Center for Humans & Nature, https://www.humansandnature.org/culture-how-capitalism-changes-conscience.

124 Haidt, "How Capitalism Changes Conscience."

125 Ian Vasquez, "The Dramatic Decline in World Poverty," *Cato at Liberty,* Cato Institute, October 7, 2015, https://www.cato.org/blog/dramatic-decline-world-poverty.

126 "Millions of Poor vs. Poverty Headcount, 1990–2015," The World Bank, http://databank.worldbank.org/data/views/reports/ReportWidgetCustom.aspx?Report_Name=pov_cou_1_2017&Id=c028ff64&tb=y&dd=n&pr=n&export=y&xlbl=y&ylbl=y&legend=y&isportal=y&inf=n&exptypes=Excel&country=CHN&series=SI.POV.NOP1,SI.POV.DDAY&zm=n.

Chapter Nine

1 "Mid-Session Review, Budget of the U.S. Government, Fiscal Year 2010," Office of Management and Budget, https://www.gpo.gov/fdsys/pkg/BUDGET-2010-MSR/pdf/10msr.pdf.

2 John Mackey, "The Whole Foods Alternative to ObamaCare," *Wall Street Journal,* August 11, 2009, http://www.wsj.com/articles/SB10001424052970204251404574342170072865070.

3 Lila Shapiro, "Whole Foods CEO: 'The Whole Foods Alternative To ObamaCare'—Just Eat Whole Foods!" Huffington Post, September 13, 2009, http://www.huffingtonpost.com/2009/08/13/whole-foods-ceo-the-whole_n_259020.html.

4 Brian Beutler, "Whole Foods Exec Slams Health Care Reform, Says People Should Just Eat Whole Foods," Talking Points Memo, August 13, 2009, http://talkingpointsmemo.com/dc/whole-foods-exec-slams-health-care-reform-says-people-should-just-eat-whole-foods.

5 Tiffany O'Callaghan, "Whole Foods C.E.O. infuriates liberal customers by condemning universal health care," *Time,* August 14, 2009, http://healthland.time.com/2009/08/14/whole-foods-c-e-o-infuriates-liberal-customers-by-condemning-universal-health-care/.

6 Byron Tau, "Papa John's: 'Obamacare' will raise pizza prices," *Politico,* August 7, 2012, http://www.politico.com/blogs/politico44/2012/08/papa-johns-obamacare-will-raise-pizza-prices-131331.

7 Harry Bradford, "Papa John's CEO John Schnatter Says Company Will Reduce Workers' Hours In Response To Obamacare," Huffington Post, November 9, 2012, http://www.huffingtonpost.com/2012/11/09/papa-johns-obamacare-john-schnatter_n_2104202.html.

8 Bradford, "Papa John's."

9 John Schnatter, "The Real Scoop on Papa John's and Obamacare," Huffington Post, November 20, 2012, http://www.huffingtonpost.com/john-h-schnatter/papa-johns-obamacare_b_2166209.html.

10 Megan Carpentier, "Colbert: 'Obamacare' isn't worth higher prices for Papa John's 'hot turd pizza,'" Raw Story, August 9, 2012, http://www.rawstory.com/2012/08/colbert-obamacare-isnt-worth-higher-prices-for-papa-johns-hot-turd-pizza/.

11 John Warner, "Papa John's CEO John Schnatter is a Moral Monster," *Inside Higher Ed,* November 18, 2012, https://www.insidehighered.com/blogs/just-visiting/papa-johns-ceo-john-schnatter-moral-monster.

12 Tommy Christopher, "Papa John's Pizza CEO John Schnatter Owes President Obama Two Words: Thank You," Mediaite, November 13, 2012, http://www.mediaite.com/tv/papa-johns-pizza-ceo-john-schnatter-owes-president-obama-two-words-thank-you/.

13 Sarah Firshein, "Here Now, the Utterly Bonkers Manse That Papa John's Built," Curbed, August 10, 2012, https://www.curbed.com/2012/8/10/10341516/here-now-the-utterly-bonkers-manse-that-papa-johns-built.

14 Jenn Taylor, "Libs call for boycott of Papa John's as CEO anticipates cut in workers' hours," Twitchy, November 10, 2012, http://twitchy.com/2012/11/10/libs-call-for-boycott-of-papa-johns-as-ceo-anticipates-cut-in-workers-hours/.

15 Christopher, "Papa John's Pizza CEO."

16 Naomi Lim, "Bill Clinton calls Obamacare 'the craziest thing in the world,' later tries to walk it back," CNN, October 5, 2016, http://www.cnn.com/2016/10/04/politics/bill-clinton-obamacare-craziest-thing/index.html.

17 Kate Taylor, "Carl's Jr.'s CEO says he dreams of a day when human workers are obsolete," Business Insider, March 17, 2016, http://www.businessinsider.in/Carls-Jr-s-CEO-says-he-dreams-of-a-day-when-human-workers-are-obsolete/articleshow/51434324.cms.

18 Whitney Filloon, "Carl's Jr. CEO Wants to Open an Automated Restaurant Free of Human Workers," Eater, March 17, 2016, https://www.eater.com/2016/3/17/11254072/carls-jr-robot-restaurant.

19 "Order up: Robots may take over Carl's Jr.," RT, March 17, 2016, https://www.rt.com/usa/335889-carls-jr-hardees-fully-automated/.

20 Michael Addady, "This Fast Food CEO Wants to Replace Workers With Robots," *Fortune,* March 17, 2016, http://fortune.com/2016/03/17/automate-fast-food/.

21 Kate Taylor, "Fast-food CEO says 'it just makes sense' to consider replacing cashiers with machines as minimum wages rise," Business Insider, January 9, 2018, http://www.businessinsider.com/jack-in-the-box-ceo-reconsiders-automation-kiosks-2018-1.

22 Etan Vlessing, "Disney CEO Bob Iger Addresses Participation in Trump Task Force," *The Hollywood Reporter,* March 8, 2017, http://www.hollywoodreporter.com/news/disney-ceo-bob-iger-asked-participation-trump-task-force-984398.

23 Daniel Nussbaum, "Disney CEO Bob Iger Quits Trump Advisory Council Over U.S. Withdrawal from Paris Agreement," Breitbart, June 2, 2017, http://

www.breitbart.com/big-hollywood/2017/06/02/disney-ceo-bob-iger-quits-trump-advisory-council-paris-agreement-withdrawal/.

24 Robert Ferris, "Tesla fans say they are canceling Model 3 orders over Musk's Trump connection," CNBC, January 31, 2017, https://www.cnbc.com/2017/01/31/tesla-fans-say-they-are-cancelling-model-3-orders-over-musks-trump-connection.html.

25 Julia Horowitz, "Elon Musk to Trump: Ditch Paris deal and I'll quit as your adviser," CNN Money, May 31, 2017, http://money.cnn.com/2017/05/31/news/elon-musk-paris-climate-deal-trump/.

26 President Donald Trump, Twitter, August 16, 2017, https://twitter.com/realDonaldTrump/status/897869174323728385.

27 Julia Horowitz, "Blackstone and JPMorgan CEOs still under pressure over Trump," CNN Money, August 16, 2017, http://money.cnn.com/2017/08/16/news/blackstone-jpmorgan-trump-business-council/index.html.

28 "Distributional Analysis of the Conference Agreement for the Tax Cuts and Jobs Act," Tax Policy Center, December 18, 2017, http://www.taxpolicycenter.org/publications/distributional-analysis-conference-agreement-tax-cuts-and-jobs-act/full.

Chapter Ten

1 Christina Romer and Jared Bernstein, "The Job Impact of the American Recovery and Reinvestment Plan," January 9, 2009, 4, http://www.economy.com/mark-zandi/documents/The_Job_Impact_of_the_American_Recovery_and_Reinvestment_Plan.pdf.

2 Barack Obama, "The President-Elect's Radio Address," January 10, 2009, The American Presidency Project, http://www.presidency.ucsb.edu/ws/?pid=85391.

3 Senate Republican Conference, "'Shovel-Ready Was Not as Shovel-Ready as We Expected': The Obama Stimulus Record," YouTube video, June 14, 2012, https://www.youtube.com/watch?v=skAOLejB4BA.

4 Rep. Darrell Issa, "$825 billion earmark," *Washington Times,* January 28, 2009, https://www.washingtontimes.com/news/2009/jan/28/825-billion-earmark/.

5 Marshall Lux and Robert Greene, "Dodd-Frank is Hurting Community Banks," *New York Times,* April 14, 2016, https://www.nytimes.com/roomfordebate/2016/04/14/has-dodd-frank-eliminated-the-dangers-in-the-banking-system/dodd-frank-is-hurting-community-banks.

6 Clyde Wayne Crews, Jr., "Obama's Legacy: 2016 Ends With A Record-Shattering Regulatory Rulebook," *Forbes,* December 30, 2016, https://www.forbes.com/sites/waynecrews/2016/12/30/obamas-legacy-2016-ends-with-a-record-shattering-regulatory-rulebook/#297dfe441398.

7 W. Mark Crain and Nicole V. Crain, "The Cost of Federal Regulation to the U.S. Economy, Manufacturing and Small Business," National Association of Manufacturers, September 10, 2014, 1, http://www.nam.org/Data-and-Reports/Cost-of-Federal-Regulations/Federal-Regulation-Full-Study.pdf.

8 James Gattuso and Diane Katz, "Red Tape Rising 2016: Obama Regs Top $100 Billion Annually," The Heritage Foundation, May 23, 2016, http://www.heritage.org/government-regulation/report/red-tape-rising-2016-obama-regs-top-100-billion-annually.

9 Gattuso and Katz, "Red Tape."

10 Katie McKenna, "Obama's Final Economic Record Not Great," Fox News, March 30, 2017, http://www.foxbusiness.com/markets/2017/03/30/obamas-final-economic-record-not-great.html.

11 Aaron Sorkin, "Read the Letter Aaron Sorkin Wrote His Daughter After Donald Trump Was Elected President," *Vanity Fair,* November 9, 2016, https://www.vanityfair.com/hollywood/2016/11/aaron-sorkin-donald-trump-president-letter-daughter.

12 Heather Long, "A Trump win would sink stocks. What about Clinton?" CNN Money, October 24, 2016, http://money.cnn.com/2016/10/24/investing/stocks-donald-trump-hillary-clinton/index.html.

13 "The economic consequences of Donald Trump," *Economist,* November 9, 2016, https://www.economist.com/blogs/freeexchange/2016/11/global-economy.

14 Kurt Eichenwald, Twitter, November 8, 2016, https://twitter.com/kurteichenwald/status/796211475270471680?lang=en.

15 Jon Ronson, "Who Lives Up There?" *New York Times,* June 5, 2016, https://www.nytimes.com/interactive/2016/06/05/magazine/new-york-life.html?_r=0#/who-lives-up-there-living-at-high-altitude.

16 Tom Huddleston, Jr., "Now Carl Icahn is endorsing Donald Trump," *Fortune,* September 28, 2015, http://fortune.com/2015/09/28/carl-ichan-endorse-trump/.

17 "Here's Donald Trump's Presidential Announcement Speech," *Time,* June 16, 2015, http://time.com/3923128/donald-trump-announcement-speech/.

18 Ana Swanson, "The myth and the reality of Donald Trump's business empire," *Washington Post,* February 29, 2016, https://www.washingtonpost.com/news/wonk/wp/2016/02/29/the-myth-and-the-reality-of-donald-trumps-business-empire/?utm_term=.a2cb76ff886c.

19 "Real Estate Portfolio, New York—The Grand Hyatt Hotel," The Trump Organization, https://www.trump.com/real-estate-portfolio/new-york-past/grand-hyatt-hotel/.

20 "This Is How Donald Trump Actually Got Rich," Investopedia, November 9, 2016, https://www.investopedia.com/updates/donald-trump-rich/#ixzz55JqYA8X0.

21 "This Is How Donald Trump Actually Got Rich," Investopedia.

22 "This Is How Donald Trump Actually Got Rich," Investopedia.

23 Karen S. Schneider, "The Donald Ducks Out," *People,* May 19, 1997, http://people.com/archive/cover-story-the-donald-ducks-out-vol-47-no-19/.

24 David S. Hilzenrath and Michelle Singletary, "Trump Went Broke, but Stayed on Top," *Washington Post,* November 29, 1992, https://www.washingtonpost.com/archive/politics/1992/11/29/trump-went-broke-but-stayed-on-top/e1685555-1de7-400c-99a8-9cd9c0bca9fe/?utm_term=.55f9ab330b33.

25 Heather Long, "Trump Organization is now America's 48th largest private company," CNN Money, December 15, 2016, http://money.cnn.com/2016/12/15/investing/trump-organization-48th-largest-private-company/.

26 Long, "Trump Organization."

27 "The Definitive Net Worth of Donald Trump," *Forbes,* September 2017, https://www.forbes.com/donald-trump/#6c47b66d2899.

28 Danielle Kurtzleben, "How The Donald Trump Cabinet Stacks Up, In 3 Charts," NPR, December 28, 2016, http://www.npr.org/2016/12/28/506299885/how-the-donald-trump-cabinet-stacks-up-in-3-charts.

29 Rupert Neate, "Donald Trump faces Senate backlash over 'cabinet of billionaires,'" *Guardian,* December 17, 2016, https://www.theguardian.com/us-news/2016/dec/18/donald-trump-senate-backlash-cabinet-of-billionaires.

30 Kurtzleben, "How The Donald Trump Cabinet."

31 Lauren Collins, "Team of Brainiacs," *New Yorker,* December 15, 2008, https://www.newyorker.com/magazine/2008/12/15/team-of-brainiacs.

32 Collins, "Team of Brainiacs."

33 Collins, "Team of Brainiacs."

34 David Paul Kuhn, "None of Your Business: On Obama's Public Sector Cabinet," RealClearPolitics, September 3, 2010, https://www.realclearpolitics.com/articles/2010/09/03/none_of_your_business_on_obamas_public_sector_cabinet_107001.html.

35 Kuhn, "None of Your Business."

36 Linda Qiu, "Barack Obama's top 25 campaign promises: How'd he do?" PolitiFact, January 5, 2017, http://www.politifact.com/truth-o-meter/article/2017/jan/05/tracking-obamas-top-25-campaign-promises/.

37 Qiu, "Barack Obama's top 25 campaign promises."

38 Peter Baker and Sheryl Gay Stolberg, "Energized Trump Sees Bipartisan Path, at Least for Now," *New York Times,* September 7, 2017, https://www.nytimes.com/2017/09/07/us/politics/trump-pelosi-daca.html?_r=0.

39 Philip Rucker and Jenna Johnson, "In North Dakota, Trump calls embattled Democratic Sen. Heidi Heitkamp a 'good woman,'" *Washington Post,* September 6, 2017, https://www.washingtonpost.com/news/post-politics/wp/2017/09/06/in-north-dakota-trump-calls-embattled-democratic-sen-heidi-heitkamp-a-good-woman/?utm_term=.fa0b6c0289e7.

40 Daniel Strauss and Matthew Nussbaum, "Democratic senator will accompany Trump to tax reform event," *Politico,* September 26, 2017, http://www.politico.com/story/2017/09/26/joe-donnelly-trump-tax-reform-243177.

41 Baker and Stolberg, "Energized Trump."

42 Danny Vinik, "After six months of Trump, Obama's legacy holds on," *Politico,* July 20, 2017, https://www.politico.com/agenda/story/2017/07/20/six-months-trump-obama-legacy-000477.

43 "Tax Cuts for the Rich by Another Name," *New York Times,* September 21, 2017, https://www.nytimes.com/2017/09/21/opinion/tax-cuts-for-the-rich-by-another-name.html.

44 Alan Rappeport, "Republican Tax Cut Would Benefit Wealthy and Corporations Most, Report Finds," *New York Times,* September 29, 2017, https://www.nytimes.com/2017/09/29/us/politics/republican-tax-cut-would-benefit-wealthy-and-corporations-most-report-finds.html.

45 Binyamin Appelbaum, "Trump Tax Plan Benefits Wealthy, Including Trump," *New York Times,* September 27, 2017, https://www.nytimes.com/2017/09/27/us/politics/trump-tax-plan-wealthy-middle-class-poor.html.

46 Emily Guskin, "By the numbers, Trump's big environmental regulation rollback is all kinds of unpopular," *Washington Post,* March 29, 2017, https://www.washingtonpost.com/news/the-fix/wp/2017/03/29/trumps-rollback-of-obamas-environmental-legacy-is-all-kinds-of-unpopular/?utm_term=.4ba0475eda75.

47 Danielle Ivory and Robert Faturechi, "Secrecy and Suspicion Surround Trump's Deregulation Teams," *New York Times,* August 7, 2017, https://www.nytimes.com/2017/08/07/business/trump-deregulation-teams-transportation-department.html.

48 Danielle Ivory and Robert Faturechi, "The Deep Industry Ties of Trump's Deregulation Teams," *New York Times,* July 11, 2017, https://www.nytimes.com/2017/07/11/business/the-deep-industry-ties-of-trumps-deregulation-teams.html.

49 Matthew Rozsa, "The Wall Street presidency: Donald Trump's deregulation scheme is yuge for big banks," Salon, April 21, 2017, https://www.salon.com/2017/04/21/the-wall-street-presidency-donald-trumps-deregulation-scheme-is-yuge-for-big-banks/.

50 Rozsa, "The Wall Street presidency."

51 Jonathan Easley, "Poll: Majority says mainstream media publishes fake news," *The Hill,* May 24, 2017, http://thehill.com/homenews/campaign/334897-poll-majority-says-mainstream-media-publishes-fake-news.

52 Easley, "Poll: Majority says."

53 "reagan from:realdonaldtrump," Twitter, https://twitter.com/search?l=&q=reagan%20from%3Arealdonaldtrump&src=typd&lang=en.

54 Donald Trump, Twitter, May 16, 2013, https://twitter.com/realdonaldtrump/status/335110438058610688?lang=en.

55 Donald Trump, Twitter, July 28, 2015, https://twitter.com/realDonaldTrump/status/626116620646264833.

56 Donald Trump, Twitter, October 15, 2013, https://twitter.com/realDonaldTrump/status/390213518290464768.

57 Donald Trump, Twitter, December 6, 2011, https://twitter.com/realDonaldTrump/status/144136183562252289.

58 "The Celebrity Apprentice 5 - Opening Credits," YouTube video, March 5, 2012, https://www.youtube.com/watch?v=crpIuhB2x2s.

59 "The Apprentice, Intro Season 1, Donald Trump," YouTube video, March 22, 2016, https://www.youtube.com/watch?v=5ZXgzxGyxWM.

60 "The Apprentice, Intro Season 1, Donald Trump," YouTube video.

61 "Full text: Trump's 2017 U.N. speech transcript," *Politico,* September 19, 2017, http://www.politico.com/story/2017/09/19/trump-un-speech-2017-full-text-transcript-242879.

62 "Full text: Trump's 2017 U.N. speech transcript," *Politico.*

63 "Full text: Trump's 2017 U.N. speech transcript," *Politico.*

64 Jonathan Easley, "Poll: 75 percent of voters approve of Trump's State of the Union," *The Hill,* January 31, 2018, http://thehill.com/homenews/administration/371597-poll-75-percent-of-voters-approve-of-trumps-state-of-the-union.

Index

About the Author

Andrew F. Puzder was chief executive officer of CKE Restaurants for more than sixteen years, following a career as an attorney. President Trump nominated him to serve as US Secretary of Labor. He lives with his family in Tennessee.